Economic History of India

Economic History of India

S. R. BAKSHI

Raj Publications
Delhi-110009

Published By :

Smt. Poonam Goel
For Raj Publications
R-115/2, Model Town - III
Delhi-110009
Phone : 7136455

ISBN-81-86208-04-6

1996

The responsibility for the facts or opinions expressed is entirly of the Author and not of the Publisher.

Laser Typesetting By :

Ajay Computer Centre
97/109, Sunder Palace,
Jwalaheri Market, Paschim Vihar,
New Delhi-110063

Printed at :

Contents

PREFACE

The economic policy of the British government in India was geared up in accordance with the dire necessity of the efficient working of the administrative machinery. Being a huge sub-continent, its multifarious problems could only be tackled on sound footing if the financial aspect was strengthened from time to time, the main source of income was the land revenue which was taken care of by several settlements. The other economic aspects which were mostly developmental in temperament were attended to by the bureaucracy, functioning at various levels.

The chapters deal with the revenue policy, ryotwari land tenure, the Meston Settlement, industrial development, the mineral resources, the Federal finance and the labour problem.

I have collected the material from Nehru Memorial Museum and Library, Sapru House Library and Indian Council of Historical Research Library and feel beholden to these institutions for their academic support to me during my researches.

S.R. BAKSHI

1

The Revenue Policy

During the developments of the eighteenth century the principle that the revenue was a fixed share of the gross produce of the soil had in practice become altogether obscured, and had been largely replaced by the rule of taking as much as could be got without checking cultivation. The early English officers had absolutely no information as to the amount of the produce, and could not have revived the original principle had they wished to do so; their object was to find the owners of the land, and to take from them as much revenue as could be got for immediate needs; and it was hoped that when experience of the capacities of this source of revenue had been gained, the assessment might be made permanent, and the revenue thus assimilated in its nature to the more familiar land tax of the English finance of the period.

The first settlements of the revenue were naturally very summary. From contemporary descriptions, it may be gathered that the ordinary procedure was somewhat as follows:- When the Collector sat to assess revenue, he was accompanied by the kanungo of the pargana, who was hereditary official (generally remunerated by a grant of land free of revenue), and whose duties were to register deeds and keep a record of revenue payments. The kanungo first furnished a statement of the revenue hitherto paid by the area under consideration, and gave the names of those persons whom he considered to be entitled to engage for its payment. The various claimants to this position were heard, and the collector usually made the settlement with the man who appeared to have the best claims to the zamindari, provided he was willing to pay a sum that seemed to be fair on the basis of the kanungo's figures, and also provided that no higher bid was made. The settlements thus combined as element of the auction-room with an attempt to decide on the validity of the various claims; and it will be readily understood that the latter object was very imperfectly realised.

The engagements taken in these early settlements were usually for five years at a time, and they were renewed or revised as they fell in. It soon became obvious that the methods adopted were inequitable; there was no adequate basis on which to calculate the revenue that could be paid, and there was no certainty that the men with the best claims were admitted to the engagement. Very many zamindars, too, were unable to pay the amount for which they had engaged, had in accordance with the practice of the country they were summarily dispossessed, and the right to engage sold to the highest bidder. It is of some interest to see why these early engagements so frequently resulted in default. The theory which the revenue officers had brought from Bengal was that the revenue should amount to the *net assets* less a reasonable allowance to the zamindar for the cost of collection; the *net assets* meant the amount which the zamindar could be expected to realise from the cultivators and from miscellaneous sources, and it was thought that about ten per cent of the net assets would be sufficient to remunerate the zamindar; in other words, the theory was that Government should take 90 per cent of what the zamindar could make from the land. Now there were no means of ascertaining the net assets, but the theory justified the collectors in taking the highest offer they could get. On the other side, there was no adequate realisation that the engagements would be strictly enforced. Recent experience suggested that all governments, were temporary affairs, and that engagements were made to be modified; a man would promise to pay a larger sum than the land could yield, in order to keep out other claimants, or to get footing on a desirable plot of land, and he had an expectation (justified by the history of the recent period) that once the engagement was made he would be able to work quietly for its modification in his favour. But the English principle was that revenue was assessed to be collected : an offer was not as a rule refused because of its excessive amount, and if the zamindar did not pay his dues he was promptly sold up. No doubt these early auction-sales displaced many speculators and left the way open for the ultimate recognition of claims of greater validity; but, on the other side, many rightful claimants had engaged for excessive amounts and their default in payment naturally oprated to extinguish their claims. As experience accumulated, it became clear that the whole system of revenue assessment must be based on an accurate knowledge of the assets; in other words, of the capacity of the land to yield a surplus after maintaining the cultivators; substantially the same lesson had been learned by Akbar and his administrators. The subsequent history of the administration consists largely of the successive approximations to a detailed and accurate knowlege of the assets.

The first step was taken in 1822, when it was decided to introduce a very elaborate scheme of surveys and detailed valuations, to be extended gradually over the whole area of the province as then constituted. It broke down hopelessly because of the enormous expense and the inherent difficulties in valuing the land on the lines adopted; after ten years' experience, it was found that something like half a century would be required for its completion, and it was replaced by the simpler system prescribed under Regulation IX of 1833, in accordance with which the first regular settlements were carried out in the bulk of what is now the Province of Agra.

These settlements were based on records (1) of rights, and (2) of assets, prepared through the agency of the patwaris, whose potential utility had been recognised. The combination of a record of *rights* with the record of *assets* should be regarded as fortuitous: Government wanted to know what rights existed at the same time as it required information as to the assets, and the records were prepared to answer both questions. But for many years the term "settlement" continued to denote both processes, and it is only in the Land Revenue Act of 1901 that the process of maintaining and revising the record of rights is formally separated from the operations for revising the assessment of the revenue. The record framed by the patwaris gave details of each field or plot in the mahal the area, class of land, nature of cultivation, name of cultivator, rent paid, and the like: and from these details it was possible to sum up the cultivated area and the rental demand of a mahal, and thus to frame the first rough draft of an assessment statement from which the net assets could be calculated. But the assessment of a mahal was not made directly on these data : a long process of elaborating methods to secure accuracy was required before this step became possible. Armed with statistics of the area tilled, the crops sown, and the rent demanded, the settlement officer estimated a fair revenue for a pargana as a whole, having special regard to what it had actually paid in the past, and to the formula now prescribed that the revenue should amount to from 65 to 70 per cent. of the net assets (instead of the original figure of 90 per cent). Calculations were then made of the rates to be charged on various classes of land to produce approximately this revenue, and these assessment rates were applied to the areas contained in individual mahals to give the revenue payable by each. The process therefore still depended largely on estimates, though a basis of fact had been introduced.

The records prepared for this settlement contained also a list of zamindars actually in possession of what had been recognised as proprietary right, and claims to be entered in this list were heard and determined by the settlement officer in accordance with the principle laid down in Regulation VII of 1822 that "It shall be the duty of collectors, on the occasion of making or revising settlements of the land revenue, to unite, with the adjustment of the assessment and the investigation of the extent and produce of the lands, the object of ascertaining and recording the fullest possible information in regard to landed tenures, the rights, interests and privileges of the various classes of the agricultural community." The Regulation (sec.9) goes on to prescribe "a specification of all persons enjoying the possession and property of the soil, or vested with any heritable or transferable interest in the land or rents of it."

At this point we may turn aside to notice briefly the controversy which was carried on with so much heat during the early years of the nineteenth century as to the seat of the right of ownership in the land of the country. The most prebable conclusion is that the conception of ownership of land in the English sense was unknown when the English came to India. The real question was, what persons were entitled to take a share of the cultivator's produce and the answer, roughly speaking, was that those persons were so entitled who were permitted to engage for the payment of the Government revenue. But the English administration inevitably looked for owners, and the question then arose : Is the ownership vested in the state, or in the zamindars, or in the cultivators? All these views found earnest advocates, and the discussion could not be confined to the question of legal rights, but necessarily involved reference to political considerations. On the one side were grouped the officers who maintained the ownership of the state or of the cultivators, and who could talk in enthusiastic terms of the great social and political advantages to be derived from a hardy yeomanry holding its land direct from Government and free from parasitic zamindars; while the other side was equally enthusiastic regarding the benefits the country would receive from an enlightened landed aristocracy, whose interests would necessarily keep them loyal to the existing Governemnt and who would develop their property to the advantage of the state, the cultivators and themselves. As is usual when a controversy is acute, there was much to be said for both views : and the early administrators-

-eachofwhomheldhisownvieusstronglyandwassubjecttocomparatively little control–seem to have been much influenced by these political considertions in deciding who should be permitted to engage for the revenue. With one school the presumption was that the settlement should bemadewiththecultivatingcommunity,andanyintermediarywhoclaimed to engage as zamindar was put to (relatively) strict proof; with the other school the presumption was in favour of the intermediary, and the settlement was made with the cultivators only when no intermediary appeared with a reasonably good case. It will be uderstood that in nearly all these cases direct and true evidence was hard to obtain, though it was not difficult to produce a plausible case, and the questions that came up had to be decided largely on the balance of probabilities, where the predilections of the deciding officer would naturally, though unconsciously, have great weight.

In this way the conflicting claims to zamindari rights and duties were gradually sorted out; hard cases were, as was inevitable, numerous; and claims that might have prevailed before one officer were rejected by another. In the province of Agra neither school won a decisive victory, and the existing diversity of position among the landholders is, in great part, the result of the conflict. In all districts there are both largeestatesandcultivatingcommunitiesholdingdirectfromGovernment, but the former predominate in some and the latter in others, the decisions of the early courts being stereotyped by the legislation.

But the adverse decisions were not in all cases absolute: in some cases the intermediary was recognised to have certain rights, which were satisfied by a decree of what is called *malikana*, that is, a right to receive a portion of the revenue paid into the treasury, and many of these rights still subsist. In other cases it was held that the proprietary right should be divided between the intermediaries and the cultivators; the former engaged to pay the revenue, but a sub-settlement was made on their behalf with the cultivators, who were allowed to hold pukhta, that is, were given a free hand in the management of the land so long as they paid to the intermediaries a fixed sum representing the Government revenue and the intermediaries' share of the produce. In this way arose the technical distinction between superior and inferior proprietors, cases of which were met with in many parts of the province of Agra, but which were most numerous in Oudh.

The controversy regarding rights of ownership thus gradually settled itself in the area which we are considering. It broke out again on the annexation of the Punjab, Where - under the more effective centraladministrationthathadcomeintoexistence - itwassettleddefinitely in favour of the'hardy yeomanry'; and the Punjab is consequently a province mainly of peasant proprietors. The annexation of Oudh revived the controversy in a still more acute form; at one time the 'hardy yeomanry' won, but the eventual decision was in favour of the 'enlightened; land--holders' (talukdars), and Oudh became pre-eminently a province of large land-holders, but with the subordinate rights more generously recognised then was the case in Arga, as is seen by the large area held in sub-settlement by the numerous cultivating communities (pukhtadars), the number of under-proprietors (matahatdars) holding specific areas on an extraordinary variety of tenures, the occupancy tenants holding, as defined in section 4 of Act XXII of 1886, and the variety of tenants possessing special rights which differ from case to case and are (or ought to be) defined in each case by the settlement decree, which is the sole title-deed of the tenant in possession.

In leaving this controversy, it is perhaps not unfair to say that, while on the legal aspect of the dispute both sides were probably mistaken in their fundamental assumption, on the political aspect both were too sanguine of the prospects of an early millennium. That condition has been attained neither by the Punjab nor by Oudh: the revenue administration of each province has problems of its own, and if the difficulties of both appear in Agra with its mixed tenures, this very mixture tends to mitigate their intensity.

The experience gained of the working of the settlement made under the Regulation of 1833 showed that the method of asessment were by no means perfect; and when the time came for revision of these settlement, changes were introduced which began with the rules issued for the Saharanpur Settlement of 1855. It must be remembered that the settlements of all districts do not fall in at once; they are made usually for a term of 30 years, and settlement operations are ordinarily in progress in some part of the province. The settlements which began in 1855 were interrupted by the Mutiny and were spread over a period of 20 years, while the first regular settlements of Oudh were made in the same period and generally on the same lines, Nor must it be thought that any one set of settlements is made throughout on uniform 'lines: almosteverysettlementofficerhitsonsomeimprovementinmethod, which is enjoined on his successors, and in this way the rules prescribing the procedure of settlement have grown up grodually as the result of accumulated experience. It is, however, possible to mark a few epochs in this process of growth where a distinct step forward was made.

The Saharanpur rules mark such an epoch. Under them records were prepared as before by the patwaris, but the rates to be used in valuing land were arrived at less on general grounds than from a study of the rents actually claimed by the landholders– a study rendered possible by the increased accuracy of the records. These rates were then applied to the land of each mahal, and the resulting valuation was compared with the actual rental of the mahal, and the revenue assessed after consideration of the two valuations. Thus these settlements were based more on facts, and less on conjecture, than those made under the Regulation of 1833, and in pariticular more attention was assured to the peculiarities of each individual mahal, since where the two valuations gave discordant results it was necessary to search for the reasons. This system of settlement was worked out by a series of officers of exceptional ability and devotion and was undoubtedly a great advance on its predecessor. Yet it did not give wholly satisfactory result, and in some cases it undoubtedly resulted in over-assessment, nainly because it gave too much scope for considerations of what the land might yield under efficient management, as opposed to its actual yield at the time of assessment. It will readily be understood that landholders appreciated the importance of the record of rents preceding a new assessment; careful men would keep the rents low till the assessment was made, while others would attempt (and sometimes with success) to falsify the record, just as generations of cultivators had learnt to conceal the amount of produce when the assessment was made on that basis. When therefore the rental of a mahal fell below the settlement officer's valuation, he at once became suspicious, and he was apt to attach more weight to his valuation than to the record, and to assume that once the assessment was made the latter would approximate to the former. He thus took into account in some cases, not only the actual income or assets of a mahal, but also what are known as prospective assets, that is to say, the income which a careful landholder might hope to secure; and where he was too sanguine in his estimates, overassessment naturally resulted. In some cases, too, there was a tendency to pitch rates for valuation on rather a higher scale than was warranted by all the circumstances, and then the discrepancies between the recorded and the estimated valuation naturally became more important.

Before the completion of this series of settlements, a beginning had been made with the maintenance of the annual land records, designed largely to facilitate the work of future settlement officers; and when the next set of settlements began (with Saharanpur in Agra and Unao in Oudh), the rules contemplated a much greater degree of reliance of the facts recorded for each mahal than had previously been possible. The settlement officer was dircted to accept as the basis of his valuation the recorded rents of each mahal in all cases where they could not be shown to be fraudulent or utterly inadequate : while he was expected ordinarily of value the unrented land (that is the land cultivated by the landholders, the rent free grants, and so forth), on a scale warranted by the recorded rents. He had now to frame standard rates for valuation and compare the result with the records, whereas he had previously to compare the records with his valuation ; and any assessment of prospective or speculative assets was prohibited.

These rules then were marked by a much greater degree of reliance on recorded facts than had hither to been possible; they were indeed parodied in the epigram that a settlement officers' business was to add up the rents and divide by two to get the revenue. Their strong point was their reliance on facts to the exclusion of estimates; their weakness lay in their failure to recognise explicitly that all facts are not of the same value. Assuming the record to be ture, as is now the case in the great majority of mahals, the recorded rents should show what the landholder hopes to get from the land, but they cannot show how far his hopes are reasonable, and thus they offer–as they stand--an imperfect basis for estimating his assured income. It is obvious that if they could be supplemented by a true statement of the rents actually collected year by year, the difficulty would disappear; but, as we shall see later on, it has not yet been found possible to secure anything like an accurate record of rent-collections, and in the meantime the most that can be done is to subject the recorded rents to careful scrutiny and criticism, and decide in each case whether they are substantially accurate indications of the landholder's income or whether they must be discarded in favour of other sources of information. This system of criticism forms the distinguishing feature of the assessment rules first issued in 1896, which will be found (with minor alterations) as Circular No. I-I issued by the Board of Revenue.

The procedure laid down by these rules falls into two main divisions, the preliminary study of the circumstances of the area to be assessed, and the assessment of the individual mahals. The first step is to frame assessment circles; that is, to group together those villages which are sufficiently alike in agricultural and economic conditions to be studied as a whole. Then the cultivated land has to be classified according to the productive value of the soil, and the settlement officer proceeds to ascertain the fair letting-value in the local conditions of the typical land of each class. This process of ascertaining rates (formerly spoken of as standard rates) is too complex to be described here: its basis is an analysis of the rents actually paid in the circle, putting aside all those that are in any way exceptional, and dividing the remainder so as to give the fair valuation-rate for each class of soil. The result is submitted for criticism in what is known as the Rent Rate Report, in which the settlement officer has to explain and justify his rates. when the circle rates have been approved, he proceeds to the second portion of operations, which consist of a criticism of the recorded rental of each mahal, a decision what rents are sufficiently "genuine" and "stable" to be accepted as the basis of valuation, and a valuation of the remaining land by the accepted rent rates, or by some other system, the use of which has to be justified. Here, too, the procedure is too technical and too difficult to be explained in a first sketch of the subject. Readers who wish to know more of it are advised first to make themselves absolutely sure of the definitions and instructions in the Circular which has been quoted, and then to study the Rent Rate and Assessment Reports, together with some of the assessment of statements, of a district that had come under settlement.

The practical effect of this procedure is to ascertain-in most cases with a high degree of precision-the income which each individual landholder can expect to secure from his estate *in the existing economic circumstances.* The state then takes approximately half of this income for the next thirty years, during which period the landholder has the full benefit of any favourable economic change. In theory he ought to take in like measure the full risk of any unfavourable change, but experience has shown that landholders as a body are not in a position (either financially or morally) to average their risks to this extent, and will not put aside income obtained in favourable years to meet prospective losses. In practice, therefore, the state has assumed the greater part of the responsibility for loss by future changes, and, on the occurrence of such loss, endeavours to adjust the burden of the revenue by methods which will be described in subsequent sections. Subject to this proviso, which is of much practical importance, it may be said that the state takes 50 per cent of the rent of land, and its demand is not limited to the unearned increment. Income derived from capital expenditure on improvements is exempted from assessment for the term of one settlement after that during which it was incurred (that is for from 30 to 60 years in all); after that period the full share of it is taken by the state. Taxation on this scale would undoubtedly be open to the charge of injustice if imposed for the first time on landowners who had hitherto enjoyed the entire income of their estates, and many of whom had purchased the land in expectation of doing so: but the foregoing historical sketch of the rise of landholders in the United Provinces will, it is hoped, have made it sufficiently clear that they obtained their titles to their estates subject to the payment of this revenue, the equivalent of which was realised from the land before their rights had come into existence.

There are two ways in which the state is financially interested in agricultural prosperity, apart from the general consideration that all prosperity is a source of increased revenue. In the first place, and obviously, the state is interested in seeing that the assured income of the landholders is as large as possible, for the simple reason that it has a roversionary interest in one-half of any increase in that income; and from this point of view it might be regarded as in a partnership with the landholders to get as much out of the cultivators as possible; while in the second place, it is less obviously but even more immediately concerned in seeing that the landholder's present income is assured; in other words, in seeing that the cultivators are protected so far as may be against all the dangers that threaten their industry, and are in a position to pay their rents even in unfavourable seasons. From this point of view the state is in partnership with both landholdrs and cultivators; its object must be to work for the prosperity of the cultivator, thereby ensuring the stability of the landholder's income and consequently of its own revenue.

These two conceptions of partnership may at first sight seem antagonistic; the state and the landholder are first opposed to and next joined with the cultivator: but a slight acquaintance with the conditions of agricultural success is sufficient to show that no such antagonism exists. The question is however of such fundamental importnace to the future of all classes in the province that it is worth while to follow it out carefully. Let us take the case of an individual landholder succeeding to a large estate, and anxious to increase his income from it. He has two courses open to him–to take a larger share of the present produce of the land, or to increase the produce and divide the increase with the cultivators. The first course may be justifiable on estates where the rents are very low, but if existing rents are fair it is almost certain to lead to ultimate loss. The landholder will pick out all the cultivators who are making a little money, and will proceed to raise their rents. He will thus have a larger rent-roll and will probably for the time being be able to collect more than hitherto: but in unfavourable seasons his collections (that is, his income) will probably be no better than before, and in order to secure this temporary increase in his income, he will have struck a blow at the most important asset of his estate, the self-interest which is the cultivator's motive for making the best use of the land. It has to be remembered that in the greater part of the province the competition for land to cultivate is sufficiently keen to enable a landholder, if not restrained by legal or other obstacles, to take the entire economic rent; that is to say, the whole of the produce except what is sufficient to keep the cultivator alive and at work. Now a "fair" rent may best be described as a rent sufficiently below the economic rent to leave an adequate incentive to the best efforts of the cultivator. When there is no such incentive, that is to say, where the landholder tries to secure the economic rent or something like it, the cultivators become disheartened–as may be seen on too many estates at the present day; they know that any increased produce obtained by their labour or skill will shortly be absorbed in the enhanced rent; and instead of striving to increase the divisible produce they devote their energies to a barren struggle with the landholder regarding the division of the produce that exists. Then arises what is known as an 'agrarian question:' the landholder is at logger-heads with his cultivators. Even if he succeeds in collecting more rent the increase is consumed in collecting-staff and in legal processes, and the one legitimate source of increased rent is cut off.

The alternative open to the landholder is to set to work to ensure and increase the produce of the land by providing the cultivators with all that is needed for efficiency, and gradually to take a fair share of the increased produce that results. The Indian cultivator does not expect to keep the whole of the increase, certainly not when his landholder has contributed to its production, but he does rightly claim a fair share as his own recompense; and when cultivators are getting richer the cnhancement of their rents so as to give the landholder his share of the increase can ordinarily be effected by harmonious arrangement.

Now everything that has been said regarding the landholders interests applies equally to the position of the state. The state and the landholder are jointly interested in getting as much rent as they can; and the first condition of lasting success in this respect is the provision of that incentive which is necessary to call forth the best efforts of the cultivators. From the economic point of view, the state, the landholder and the cultivator are members of a productive partnership, and it thus becomes the first interest of the state–the member of the firm that can look furthest ahead–to see that the other members give their best energies to the common object of the partnership. This principle will be found to provide the economic and financial justification for the various activities of the revenue administration and the allied departments of Government in India, and it furnishes the best touchstone by which suggested developments may be tried.

Now as regards the landholder's interest. It has been ascertained by experience that the present terms of settlement, securing to Government half the net assets calculated for terms of thirty years, leave the the landholder in ordinary cases sufficient incentive to administer his estate to the best advantage of the parties interested, in the economic circumstances which have prevailed during the period in which this experience has been gained. But there is no finality in decisions of this kind, and changes in the economic environment may at any time render it desirable for Government to re-consider the terms on which it permits landholders to engage for the revenue so far as can be seen, there is no present necessity for re-consideration, but when the time comes the question will have to be examined in the light of the fundamental principle that has just been stated.

The assurance of the cultivator's interest is a more complex problem, and the history of tenancy legislation in the provinces must be glanced at in order to show what has been attempted and what has been attained.

Broadly speaking, there was no possibility of tenancy problems becoming acute before the period of British rule. The conception of landholder and tenant was being gradually worked out by the people, and wherever a cultivator paid more than reached the treasury, there were at least the rudiments of a tenancy system since the excess payment was of the nature of rent. Disputes as to the amount of these payments doubtless occurred between the cultivators and the intermediaries; but the cultivators were then relatively in a strong position, because at that time land was competing for cultivators, and tenancy questions can become acute only when there is not enough suitable land to go round. But as internal order became established under British rule, the land filled up with that repidity which is characteristic of most reactions from periods of anarchy or disorganisation, and competition for land was not long in making its appearance, local at first and gradually spreading until it is now the normal condition in all parts of the province except the districts south of the Jumna and the unhealthy country lying along the foot of the Himalayas. Meanwhile the high revenue fixed in many of the earlier settlements, and the efforts of speculators to pay the revenue for which they had engaged, combined with the growing competing for land to bring tenancy questions for the first time into prominence. The landholders were naturally raising rents to the highest point, and were turning out those cultivators who refused to meet their demands. Now the recent economic conditions had given no scope for ejectments, and there seems to have been no customary law regarding them, so that they were resented by the people as a breach of their customary rights and were objected to by government, partly as providing recruits for the still common profession of gang-robbbery, and partly as imperilling the stability of agriculture. A long period of enquiry and controversy followed as to the actual rights of cultivators under precceding rules. Naturally there was no very clear evidence of rights established or respected by law, but it was fairly made out that, as a matter of fact, cultivators had enjoyed continuity of possession so long as they paid their dues and did not make themselves objectionable in other ways. There enquiries terminated in the passing of Act X of 1859 which for the first time gave legal recognition to the conception of *a right of occupancy* in the province of Agra. This Act did not extend to Oudh, which has a history of its own in these matters.

The Act provided that all cultivators who had held their present land for twelve years should be deemed to have *a right of occupancy,* and that cultivators admitted in future and allowed to hold for twelve years should acquire the same right on the conclusion of that period. The idea was thus to put all new cultivators on probation for twelve years, and during this period the landholder could eject them at pleasure; if he were satisfied with them then they acquired the right of occupancy. The right entitled them to remain in possession of the land so long as they paid the rent, and limitations were at the same time imposed on the power of the landholder to enhance their rent. We thus come to the two interdependent conceptions, continuity of tenure and external regulation of rent, which are the staple of all agrarian discussions, and it is well to get a clear idea of what they involve in Indian conditions.

Agriculture is by no means an easy business by which to make a living. Even when the standard practice of the locality has been mastered, it will be found that almost every field has peculiarities of its own, which can be studied only by experience, and which must be either taken advantage of or corrected if a farm is to yield a profit as a whole.

Again, the condition of a field can be injured easily and quickly, while its improvement is in many cases a tedious and difficult affair. A cultivator then requires the prospect of holding land for a reasonable term of years if it is to be worth his while to study its peculiarities and to improve its condition. He will naturally not take the trouble to do this if he is liable to be turned out at short notice, but will merely try year by year for the greatest immediate return that he can get, and thereby almost inevitably cause the land to deteriorate. When therefore there is in practice no security of tenure, the style of cultivation will be such as to diminish the poductivity of the soil–in other words, to threaten the stability of the income of the country: while given security of tenure and cultivators with the requisite standard of character, there is a reasonable hope that the soil will at least remain constant, or even slowly improve, in productive powers. These considerations are of general application, but the circumstances of the province give them particular weight. The whole character and tradtions of the ordinary cultivating classes lead them to treat their land as a source of income for the future as well as for the present, and therefore to work steadily for its gradual improvement; while, on the other hand, their intellectual limitations make the process a very slow one. A fair prospect of continuity of tenure is thus the first essential for the maintance of the productive power of the country.

It will be understood that the assurance of continuity for an indefinite period is not essential ; the land will be fairly treated under either an indefinite system, such as the right of occupancy, or under a leasehold system ensuring continuity for a fixed term of reasonable length. It is uncertainty from year to year that is the great evil from the cultivator's point of view, though under a leasehold system he will naturally be tempted to let the land run down in the last year or two of his term if he has no prospect of securing a renewal of his lease. As we shall see later on, the leasehold system was adopted for Outh, while the indefinite system is in force in Agra.

Continuity of tenure necessarily involves some external regulation of rents, for if the landholder can raise rents to any sum he thinks fit, he can, where competition is active, drive out any cultivator by fixing his rent impossibly high. The two conceptions are therefore, as has been said, interdependent, and any administration which undertakes to secure continuity of tenure in the face of competition for land finds itself compelled to assume the regulation of rents. In Agra this duty was assigned to the revenue officers, who are invested with the powers of a rent court to decide most matters in dispute between landholders and their cultivators. Enhancement of rent must be sued for on certain definite grounds unless the cultivator agrees to it, and when rent has been enhanced it cannot be altered again for a certain term of years.

The provisions of Act X of 1859 were re-enacted in 1873, and again in 1881 with amendments in detail intended mainly to check evasions of the law. For unfortunately the whole occupancy system proved to be unpopular with large numbers of landholders, who set themselves to evade its operation by a variety of ingenious devices. It would be most unfair to suggest that a considerable proportion of the landholders objected to a reasonable degree of independence assured to the occupancy-tenant: so long as he paid his rent he could almost do what he liked, and it requires only a slight acquaintance with the social conditions of country to realise what this independence meant to the landholder. The unpopularity of the system was manifested partly in taking any pretext to get rid of existing rights of occupancy, and partly in ensuring that no fresh rights should accrue. An occupancy tenant could be ejeted for failing to pay arrears of rent after they had been decreed by a rent court, and so it became an object with some landholders to involve their cultivators in litigation, to snatch decrees against them, and to manipulate the accounts of their payments-all of which processes were injurious both socially and economically. And to prevent the growth of fresh rights, a regular system of ejectments was organised on many estates, a formal or actual ejectment being made of every cultivator in the eleventh year of his tenure, so that a fresh period of probation began to run. In some cases, cultivators were actually compelled to leave their land and were provided with other land in exchange, but in the majority of cases the proceedings were purely formal. Ejectment notices were served and were not contested: the cultivator was formally dispossessed and promptly re-admitted (with sometimes a slight enhancement of rent, and usually a present to the landholder's agent); and in many cases there was practical continuity of holding because cultivators trusted their landholder. The evils of ejectment were not therefore in practice so great as the statistics of their operation suggested, but they still existed, and the growth of the system of nominal ejectments tended to bring the law into contempt.

The present Tenancy Act (Act II of 1901) was designed to remedy these evils. Its aim was three – fold – to remove objections raised by landholders in matters of detail, to put a stop to nominal ejectments and other evasions of the law, and finally to provide an alternative to the whole system of occupancy rights. The first object need not detain us. Landholders raised objections to point such as the freedom of sub-letting and their wishes were met so far as Government considered desirable. As to ejectments, apart from alterations of procedure, the main provisions were intended to secure that no process could interrupt the currency of the twelve years of probation unless the cultivator was actually deprived of possession for at least a year. The difficulty of making this provision effective may be judged from the complexity of the definitions of the terms "continuous holding" and "same land" contained in the Act. Then by changes in procedure ejectments during the term of probation were made more difficult and more expensive, while the trouble and money are thrown away unless the landholder is sufficiently in earnest in his desire to get rid of the cultivator to drive him out of the village by depriving him of all land for at least a year.

But the most interesting portion of the Act is that which provides for a leasehold system as an alternative to the right of occupancy. If a cultivator takes a lease for seven years or more, the time does not count as part of the probation, that is to say, it does not lead to occupancy rights, and thus landholders who object to the growth of these rights can avoid any risk by giving leases of sufficient length to secure the minimum of continuity essential to the cultivator.

Criticism of the provisions of this Act would be out of place, but readers may be reminded that practically no legislation affecting the land can be judged on the experience of a few years. The economic forces that have to be allowed for work slowly, while the adaptations in the social relations of different classes are effected more slowly still. Such general remarks as are called for in connection with the whole question may be postponed till we have sketched the history of the parallel development in the adjoining province of Oudh.

The history of tenancy in Oudh is, as we have said, entirely different from that of Agra. After the Mutiny and the period of somewhat acute controversy which followed, it was eventually decided to entrust the fortunes of the bulk of Oudh to the great landholders or talukdars, and all branches of the administration combined to emphasise the importance of their position in every possible way. Such special cultivating rights as could be found in existence were recognised and defined in the formation of the record of rights, but the area they affected was relatively small, and apart from them the soil and the cultivators were placed practically at the disposal of the landholders, subject only to the condition inserted in the grants which form their title-deeds, that "You will, so far as lies in your power, promote the agricultural prosperity of your estate, and that all holding under you shall be secured in the possession of all the subordinate rights they formerly enjoyed."

This condition was honourably observed by not a few landholders, but on the other hand it was ignored on some of the larger estates, while from the nature of the case it was ineffective on the smaller properties directly the progress of the country ensured effective competition for land. The rise in rents was consequently rapid, and ejectments were sufficiently numerous to destroy the feeling of security which, as we have seen, is essential to the success of the cultivator: on some estates indeed the treatment of the cultivators was such that Government considered seriously the question of cancelling the landholders' grants for breach of the condition which has just been quoted. It thus became apparent that tenancy legislation could not be any longer avoided, but there were particular difficulties in the way. It was necessary to safeguard carefully the position, and the susceptibilities, of the talukdars. and at the same time to recognise that in the existing social conditions it was nearly useless to give cultivators rights which the talukdars would not willingly concede, for the idea of an ordinary cultivator having the courage or the resources required to fight his talukdar in the courts was then–as indeed it still is–repugnant to the feelings and traditions of the province. On the other hand, allowance had to be made for the facts that though Oudh is a province of large landholders, a considerable part of the land is held by cultivating communities and small zamindars, while the practice–common in some parts–of managing estates pukhta, that is of leasing the rents ot thekadars, puts the cultivator in relations with men who cannot be counted on to be loyal to talukdari traditions, After protracted negotiations, the decision arrived at was embodied in Act XXII of 1886, which is still in force; and when the somewhat anomalous and illogical provisions of this Act provoke criticism, it is wise to remember that it is essentially the embodiment of a compromise between the talukadars on one side, and the Government representing the cultivators on the other; in fact the Act may be described without much exaggeration as a treaty or agreement, and its successful working is dependent to a great extent on the co-operation of the parties.

The main provisions of the Act affecting ordinary cultivators are as follows:

(1) A cultivator admitted to a holding becomes thereby a leaseholder for a period of seven years, during which the rent cannot be altered;

(2) after seven years his rent can be enhanced to the extent of one anna in the rupee, but not more, and any enhancement must be followed by at least seven years' rest;

(3) if the cultivator is ejected, the rent of the new cultivator is limited to precisely the same sum, while the landholder forfeits six months' rent to Government in the form of court fees. Each cultivator then is assured continuity for seven years, provided he pays his rent, and is free in theory from arbitrary enhancement of rent at the end of the term; the landholder has no advantage in ajecting a cultivator, as he cannot thereby enhance his rentroll, while he forfeits a substantial sum on each ejectment. It is thus the landholder's interest to retain a satisfactory cultivator, and he would only eject a man whose ejectment was worth paying for. So far then as the Act is adhered to, the cultivator has in practice an adequate degree of protection. Its weakness lies in the fact that if the landholder breaks the law nothing happens to him. In theory he can be sued for penalties for excessive enhancement, but no ordinary cultivator can sue his talukdar, and the kurmi or chamar holding land from a resident thakur zamindar or pukhtadar is perhaps in even worse case: he could not possibly stay in the village after taking his thakur into court. The success of the Act then, and with it the entire agricultural prosperity of Oudh, depends on its loyal acceptance by the bulk of the landholders, and on the gradual development of a public opinion sufficiently strong to coerce the dissentients. As we have said above, the lasting results of tenancy legislation take time for their manifestation, and it would even now be premature to pronounce the Act either a success or a failure; but its working requires the continued attention of all who are interested in Oudh, whether merely as students or as officials or landholders.

The classes of tenure in Agra differ in some respects from those of Oudh in accordance with the different tenancy laws in force, but the main heads of the khatauni are similar for both provinces. All the land of a mahal is grouped in Part I as (a) held for cultivation; (b) waste land capable of cultivation, and (as a rule) retained in the landholder's management; (c) barren land; while intermediate between (a) and (b) is the record of miscellaneous income of the mahal which is treated as rent. Under the first head come in succession landholders' cultivation, tenants' cultivation, and rent-free grants, these three heads comprising all the land that is held for cultivation. Part II shows the subordinate rights in land already included in Part I, mainly those of sub-tenants, that is, persons who have taken land from a tenant.

Landholders' cultivation in both provinces is of two classes-sir and khudkasht. If a landholder cultivates land of which he has proprietory possession it is khudkasht (or in Hindi nij-jot, both terms meaning personal cultivation); but certain khudkasht lands are classed as sir, and the landholder has special privileges regarding them. Sir is rather an intricate subject; the term is elaborately defined, in the Land Revenue Act, and it carries special privileges both under the assessment rules and under the tenancy law; like some other institutions we have mentioned it is gradually disappearing because land can cease to be sir, but no new land can become sir.

The origin of sir is two-fold. In a cultivating community it is the land which by the custom of the particular community is recognised as the special holding of one of the sharers; that is to say, in the internal arrangements of such a community it is usually the case that certain lands are recognised as the sir of cach sharer, for which he either does not account to the community, or if he does it is at a customary rate much below the current rental-value of the land. If the sharer cultivates land in addition to his sir, his position towards the rest of the community is that of a tenant, and he has to account for the rent at something like the letting-value; it is his khudkasht but not his sir. Thus sir cannot be distinguished by any objective considerations: it is what the community has in the past treated as sir, and nothing else, and Government's only concern has been to find out what the community treated as sir and to record it accordingly. The second kind of sir seems to have originated in the practice under which zamindars (that is intermediaries between the State and the cultivator) were allowed to cultivate certain land on specially favourable terms as part of their remuneration for acting as intermediaries. The right was recognised in the early settlements on the basis of possession for a term of years, and landholders were allowed to acquire it by continuous occupation of land (for twelve years in Agra, and for seven years in Oudh) until a comparatively recent period. Here again there is no clue to sir except a knowledge of what the State has treated as sir in the past.

The right of sir is very highly valued by the landholders: it has a sentimental value and also practical advantages. In assessment, its valuation is usually reduced by something like one-fifth or one-fourth before the revenue is fixed, thus maintaining the idea that sir is special remuneration to the landholder for his services; while if it is let to tenants occupancy rights cannot accrue in Agra nor do the terms of the statutory lease apply to it in Oudh. Thus a landholder is practically free to do what he likes with his sir land; he can cultivate it himself, or can let it to tenants for any term, and for any rent that they agree to pay.

Thus land standing in the name of the landholder as sir is a valuable asset; other land which he cultivates as khudkasht has fewer privileges; it is often treated leniently at settlement, but if it is let to tenants the ordinary tenancy law applies and the fact that it was once khudkasht is irrelevant. It must, however, be remembered that the patwari is not entitled to record land as sir: this can only be done at a revision of records, and where a revision has not recently been made, it is necessary to remember that land recorded as khudkasht may be sir if it was recorded as cultivated by the land-holder–in Oudh for seven years continuously before 1886, and in Agra for twelve years continuously before 1901.

In practical work it is convenient to know that sir is often, perhaps usually, the most productive land in the village as the early holders (of either kind) naturally chose the best land. Khudkasht, on the other hand, is often inferior: sometimes it consists of lands thrown up by tenants as unremunerative or of land which is–strictly speaking–on the margin of cultivation; it just pays the landholder to work it if he has time and stock to spare, but given no surplus which a tenant could pay as rent.

Holders of land in sub-settlement have sir in the same way as ordinary landholders, and in Oudh much of the underproprietary land has the same privileges as sir and goes by the same name; indeed in rural parts of Oudh the term sir is used to describe an under-proprietor's holding, so that it is necessary to be on one's guard against confusing the legal and the popular senses of the word.

With khudkasht it is usual to class land taken into his own cultivation by a lessee of rents (thekadar); a thekadar sometimes like to take up land to add to his profits and he sometimes cultivates holdings that have fallen vacant, but he does not thereby acquire the ordinary rights of a tenant.

We may now turn to the classes under which is grouped the land held by cultivators who are not landholders in the mahal. These classes are as follows:–

Agra.	**Oudh.**
Permanent-tenure holders	Occupancy tenants.
Fixed-rate tenants.	Ex-proprietary tenants.

Ex-proprietary tenants.	Other tenants.
Occupancy tenants.	
Tenants on seven-year leases	
Other tenants.	

The first two classes in Agra are found only in the permanently-settled tracts of the Benares division. It will be remembered that the early English administrators looked on the land revenue as a land tax of the kind with which they were familiar in English-that is, a tax fixed once for all. Accordingly, the revenue was permanently settled in Bengal and in the Benares division which came under British rule at an early period. The intention to settle the revenue of the rest of Agra in the same way was stated on several occasions, but action was postponed owing to the disorganisation of the country, which made it impossible to estimate a fair revenue; and by the time when adequate data had become available, truer ideas of the nature of the land revenue had found acceptance, and the idea of a permanent settlement passed out of practical politics. In Benares, however, it existed, and it was decided that the old tenants (those who had held continuously since settlement) should share in its benefits: they were therefore declared to be fixed-rate tenants; that is to say, the landholder cannot enhance their rents (except in very special cases), or eject them so long as they are not in arrears, while they can transfer their holdings at pleasure. The permanent-tenure holders are a very small class of persons who at settlement were recognised to have rights intermediate between the landholder and the tenant. They pay only a fixed sum to the landholder and receive the tenants' rent. Their position is therefore analogous to that of holders in sub-settlement, and possibly this would have been their position had the Benares settlements been made at a later period.

The ex-proprietary tenant is purely a creation of English law. Administrators have always felt compassion for the landholder who lost his land, either by being sold up for arrears of revenue or by getting into debt for other reasons; such men have no other source of livelihood, and in practice they usually developed into gang-robbers or dakaits. The law now is that a landholder who poses his proprietary rights becomes *ipso facto* a tenant of his sir, of any khudkasht which he has cultivated continuously for twelve years; his rights are those of an occupancy tenant in Agra, and in addition he pays a reduced rent. The arrangement is highly unpopular with the classes who purchase land, because a bankrupt landholder is usually a bad cultivator and almost invariably a bad rent payer;

it is also at variauce with the interest of Government in keeping the land at a maximum of productivity because it keeps highly productive land in the hands of inefficent producers, it is in part a concession to the unfortunate, and in part a measure of police.

The ex-proprietary tenant is found both in Agra and in Oudh. In Agra he was recognised formally by the seriés of tenancy acts, but the Oudh Rent Act took no notice of him until 1901, up to which period the rights rested on an incidental provision in another law (section 25 of the Oudh Laws Act of 1876). The Oudh occupancy tenant is also an ex-proprietor, but one of a limited class of persons; the creation of this class is due to historical causes and admission to it no longer possible.

The origin of the Agra occupancy tenant has been explained in section X; it is unfortunate that the expression occupancy tenant, which in Oudh means a particular class of ex-proprietors, in Agra indicates the mass of the established tenants; but the use of the term dates from the period when the two provinces were distinct, and it is too late now to alter. One point of importance connected with the Agra occupancy tenant is that the patwari is not perimitted to record the formal accrual of the right; this is done only at a revision of records, or under the order of a court in a particular case; in the meantime the patwari goes on recording the number of years during which the tenancy has continued, so that in cases where the records have not recently been revised entries may be found of non-occupancy tenants holding for thirty years or more. Of course the courts recognise in all such cases that occupancy rights have come into existence, and the record is sufficient for all practical purposes. The point is important as illustrating the principle on which the work of the patwari is determined–he has to record plain facts and not to think about their legal significance. The same principle is found in the prohibition of new entries of sir, the record of khudkasht continuing until the records are revised.

Thus in Agra the list of other tenants includes both the tenants who are still in the probationary period and those who have passed through it but have not yet been formally recorded as holders of occupancy rights. (The new class of leaseholders recognised by the Act of 1901 are, of course, grouped by themselves.) Similarly in Oudh the class of other tenants includes all those who have not ex-proprietary or occupancy rights. The great majority of these tenants have what are called statutory rights; that is to say, their rights and liabilities are those stated in the Oudh Rent Act as the ordinary conditions of a holding.

There are a few cases where these conditions do not apply, but the patwari is not required to concern himself with them: here, too, he has to record the bare facts only.

It must, however, be understood that in any place a tenant may be found who has (whether by his lease or by custom) special privileges in addition to those common to his class; for instance, an Agra occupancy tenant may have special privileges regarding the amount of his rent, or an Oudh tenant may not be liable to summary ejectment at the end of seven years. Such privileges are, of course recognised by the courts: the patwari is expected to note their existence in his khatauni, but the record cannot be regarded as complete in this respect, and a tenant who alleges such a privilege is entitled to a careful investigation since the allegation would not usually be made without some sort of justification.

Following the various classes of tenants, the khatauni shows the holders of land under rent-free grants. These are of two classes-free grants (muafi dádá zamindar) and service grants (muafi khidmati or chakurána). The free grants are usually of a religious or charitable nature, given to priests or mendicants, or for the support of places of worship, so much so that they are commonly spoken of a charitable grants (muafi khairati) : when given to a priest, however, they usually connote the idea of worship for the religious benefit of the grantor. Once given, such grants cannot be resumed at pleasure, but they can be resumed or assessed to rent, or converted into landholding rights in the circumstances laid down in Chapter X of the Agra Tenancy Act, the provisions of which Chapter have been incorporated in the Oudh Rent Act. As we have seen, these provisions of law are necessary to prevent any divorce between the land and the revenue due from it; but there is usually a distinct social stigma attaching to the resumption of such grants, and proceedings under these sections are rare. It is important to see that land is not recorded as grant unless it is the landholder's intention to grant it. It is very common is some parts of the country to find fields cultivated by men who do not know what rent they have to pay–sometimes they are trespassers and at other times they have been satisfied with leave to cultivate and have left the rent to be settled later. Such holdings are properly recorded under "other tenants," the land being shown as "unrented" (bila lagan) or "rent undertermined" (bila tasfiya lagan), until an arrangement is come to regarding the rent.

The second class–that is of service-grants–approximates more closely to tenants' holdings; the practice of giving them reaches far back into history, and it is the traditional method of remunerating (in part at least) certain artisans and servants who are required for the convenience of the village. Thus a potter may be established in a village by the grant of a few fields to cultivate, and he will then supply earthen vessels to the village at customary rates; or the village-messenger (gorait) is always available for odd jobs in return for the land he is allowed to cultivate. Such grants are valid only so long as the services are performed, and the holder can be ejected if he fails to render them.

The foregoing classes will be found to account for all the land of a village which is held for purposes of cultivation, whether by landholders, by tenants or by grantees. The next item in the records is the miscellaneous income of the mahal, known as sayer or siwai, and described more or less correctly in English as manorial dues. It is variable in amount and its sources are very miscellaneous, and for this reason it is an interesting subject to discuss with an old zamindar. The income may accrue from the products of uncultivated land- timber, firewood, berries, thatching-grass, grazing-dues, fisheries, kankar (lime), saltpetre, etc.; or from strangers (that is persons other than cultivators) using the conveniences of the village, *e.g.*, market dues, rent of houses or camping grounds, ferry-tolls and the like. The settlement rules indicate what classes of miscellaneous income are regarded as assessable to revenue, but the present tendency is to leave them to the landholders unless they are considerable in amount and regular in their nature, as, for instance, the yield of a substantial area of jungle kept for firewood.

The next main group of entries in the khatauni comprises the lands that are suitable (theoretically) for cultivation, but are not at the time let for that purpose; the classification is fallow, waste, and groves. Fallow (parti) is land which has been cultivated, but is now unoccupied: for three years it is classed as new fallow (parti jadid), and thereafter as old fallow (parti kadim). Some of the new fallow is usually of value, consisting of fertile land that has fallen vacant owing to accidental causes, but the old fallow is as a rule land that has failed to pay for cultivation. The waste (benjar) is the land that looks culturable, but that no one has yet tried to cultivate; it is very rare except in the thinly populated areas on the outskirts of the province. Such land is occasionally let for grazing and treated as a tenant's holding; more usually it is open free to the people of the village, but where the extent is sufficient outsiders also are allowed to put on cattle at a fixed fee which is treated as siwai.

Groves call for rather more detailed mention. The more enlightened governments of the past seem uniformly to have approved of the plantation of trees like the mango and the mahua, which yield fruit for a long period of years, and the predilections of the people are all in the same direction. Members of cultivating communities have in most cases maintained a considerable grove-area, individuals planting up portions of the waste with the consent of the other sharers. These landholder's groves do not introduce many complications in the administration, though the village customs affecting them, which are recorded in the wajib-ul-arz, are usually interesting and sometimes of practical importance. But difficult questions often arise regarding groves planted by tenants (bághátriaiya). Village-customs differ greatly regarding these, and the wajib-ul-arz must always be consulted. It is hard to generalise amid the divergency, but it is perhaps safe to say that in the greater part of the province a tenant who has obtained leave from the landholder to plant a plot as a grove is entitled to the produce of the trees so long as they stand, and to their timber when they fall, and also to occupy the soil on which they stand (cropping it or using it for grazing). Disputes are not uncommon as to what happens to a grove when a tenant is ejected from his cultivated land, and these have to be decided on the recorded custom of the village; but in some parts of Oudh, the holding of a grove gives a man a moral claim which it is unusual to disregard to hold enough land in the village for his support. Even where this is not the case, the sentimental value attached to groves is such that people will fight for them even more keenly then for their cultivated land.

In the khatauni the holder of the grove is named and the plots described. The rent is also shown in the exceptional cases where rent is charged. The rules do not require a record of the ownership of separate trees, because such a record would be very intricate and the patwari could not frame it without committing himself to some interpretation of legal relationships, and, as we have seen, one main principle of the record-system is to avoid making the patwari into a lawyer. The question often arises: What is a grove ? and it is not always easy to answer. The safest course is to ascertain the characters which in the locality are regarded as essential to the existence of a grove and then see how far the plantation in question conforms to this ideal. The commonest criteria are perhaps (1) that the land should be enclosed by a hedge or bank, (2) that the trees should have been planted with some degree of regularity, (3) that there should be some mature trees in existence. This last criterion sounds rather absurd, but a tenant holds to the idea of his grove even when all the trees have disappeared from the land; the right to replace dead tree's is common but not universal.

and the operation is one that is apt to be put off. Naturally the question whether a given plantation constitutes a grove is often one of degree; no one would call a single mahua tree a "grove," and no one would deny the term to a carefully fenced plot planted regularly with mature mangoes; but when a dispute exists the only workmanlike way of adjusting it is to go and look at the land in the presence of the villagers.

Groves have to be distinguished from orchards of smaller fruit-trees, such as guavas or oranges, which are cultivated mainly from commercial motives and are treated as cultivated land. Plantations of grafted mangoes, kept for profit, cannot logically be distinguished from guava-orchards, but from the revenue point of view the practice is to treat them as groves. The point is practically important because cultivated orchards are assessed to revenue, while groves are exempted. Until a few years ago, the principle of exemption of the groves was strictly enforced: reduction of revenue could be claimed as soon as a new grove was established, while the land was assessed as soon as a grove was cut down. The numerous petty proceedings for assessment and exemption were felt to be a nuisance to Government and to the people, and a few years ago they were abolished, and the matter left to be adjusted at the periodical revisions of settlement; but many authorities hold that the result of these changes has been to diminish the incentive to maintain groves, and a reversion to the former system is under consideration.

The existence of scattered trees not constituting a grove is noted in the khasra, but is not recorded in the khatauni, nor is any attempt made to record the ownership. Custom in regard to them differs, but as a rule trees on waste land, fieldboundaries and the like belong to the landholder, and the methods by which he exercises his rights in this respect have a considerable influence on his popularity. A good landholder does not insist on a full price for such timber: he usually gives enough to burn bricks for a tenant's well, or allows a babul to be cut when required for making agricultural implements; and the enforcement of strict rules in this matter is usually bad management because it may drive a whole village into opposition.

The third main group of entries in the khatauni refers to the unculturable land-barren land (usar), land covered with water (zeráb), and inhabited sites (abadi). As regards barren land it is well to bear in mind that the classification of waste as banjar or usar is a question of degree. There is no obvious distinction, and as neither class is assessed to revenue, Settlement Officers have not wasted much time on the matter. Questions regarding the distinction very seldom arise, but if they do, the records cannot be relied on to decide them. Land covered with water may be the bed of a stream or of a jhil or lake, and does not as such give rise to disputes, though difficulties may arise regarding the rights to fisheries (jalkar) or to take wate for irrigation; these are usually dealt with fully in the wajib-ul-arz. The inhabited site, too, has numerous customs. Perhaps the most ordinary rule is that a cultivator holds free of rent the land on which his house stands: he is entitled to occupy it while he cultivates in the village, but in the event of his leaving the village the house reverts to the landholder, and the tenant usually pays a fee on building or rebuilding. Tradesmen and artisans however commonly pay ground-rent (parjot) for the land on which they are allowed to build, and this is treated as siwai income.

Thus Part I of the khatauni contains an entry of every plot in the mahal under its proper head, and the areas in all the mahals should total un to the recorded area of the village, a check which the patwari: has to apply annually to ensure that the khatauni is complete. Part II is set aside to show rights existing in regard to plots which have already appeared in Part I : thus sir or an occupancy holding is in Part I, while the tenants to whom some of it has been sub-let are in Part II. As we have seen, it is desirable to show tenants of sir land as a class apart, because their rights are much less than those of a tenant of ordinary land; similarly sub-tenants have a minimum of rights and a maximum ofliabilities.

In conclusion, a few words may be said about sub-leases and transfers of tenant rights. Sub-letting is generally regarded as perfectly legitimate when the tenant who sub-lets is, for any reason, unable to cultivate the land. Thus the land may come by inheritance to a widow, a minor or a lunatic, and it is obviously the best arrangement to sub-let it. A similar case, that used to be very common in Oudh, is where the tenant is serving in the army, and sub-lets his land during his absence. More temporary emergencies are also recognised as valid grounds for sub-letting for a year or two, as for instance when a tenant's plough-cattle die and he is unable to replace them before the ploughing season. What landholders in Agra object strongly to is seeing an occupancy tenant sub-letting his land at rents which the courts would not enforce as against the tenant, and sitting down to live on his rents. The provisions of the Agra Tenancy Act regarding sub-leases are intended to meet these views: sub-leases are permitted only as temporary arrangements, except in the case of tenants who are unable to cultivate. Similarly, landholders object very strongly to seeing an occupancy holding pass under the control of a money-lender and the right is definitely made non-tranferable by law. But occupancy tenants continue to mortgage their rights, and capitalists continue to lend mòney on them, taking the risk that the landholder may enforce his legal remedy of annulling the right as against both parties. Whether it is on the whole desirable that tenants should be able to transfer such rights as they possess is a very large question, presenting many analogies to the question of transfer of landholders' rights, which has been debated for many years; it would be going too far to enter on it here, but we may just remark that it has to be studied from various sides–political, social and economical. India is a poor country, and it is for the benefit of the country, as well as for the Government, that her productive resources–and the land is by far the greatest of these–should be in the hands of those who are most competent to use them; but on the other hand, the social and political results of a system of easy teansfer may produce lasting as well as temporary difficulties, and all these factors must be taken into account by anyone who wishes to discuss the question.

The first step in the development of rental systems seems to have been the transition from actual division (batai) to estimation (kankut) of the amount of the crop. The change simplifies work as it takes less time to estimate than to measure the produce field by field; and the practice existed in the case of revenue during the Mohammedan period. In itself it is not favourable to the landholder as the estimators are apt to be influenced by conscious or unconscious bias in favour of the cultivator, but is has convenience in its favour. We have seen however that there was a strong tendency to collect the revenue in cash, a tendency that will arouse the sympathy of every collector, and the practice of estimating the yield seems to have brought with it the idea of cash payments, the share of produce due being valued in money and the value paid instead of delivering the produce. It seems probable that it was through this process that the idea of paying cash for the occuption of land first made itself familiar, but there can be no doubt that Akbar's revenue administration gave it a greatly increased vogue and that the conception was (so to speak) naturalised at the time when the English assumed the administration. The revenue had to be paid in cash, and it was natural for the landholders to take their rents in the same medium. Thus at the present day cash-rents are the rule and grain-rents the exception.

There are, however, traces in particular localities of other steps in the evolution. They are interesting historically, and it is essential that the rent courts should be on the look-out for their existence. In some places, for instance, while the rents of the staple crops continue to be paid in kind, cash-rates are charged for certain particular crops, notably sugarcane and fodder. In this case the change was no doubt convenient, as the delivery of such bulky or perishable produce would be a nuisance and the landholder would not always be in a position to make use of it when received; and the same system seems to have been extended to crops (notably potatoes) recently introduced into the locality. In this way arose the system of zabti-rents, which is common in parts of the Agra and Rohilkhand divisions. When land held on grain-rents is used for growing sugarcane, fodder, potatoes, and occassionally a few other crops, it pays for that season only a cash-rate at so much a bigah, determined by the custom of the locality; the next year the rent of it is paid as usual in grain. A Similar system is described in parts of the eastern districts by the word jinspher. In places again the rent of a field, payable in cash, varies from year to year according to the crop grown on it. A particular field may yield four rupees when under wheat but only two rupees when under barley. In a few places, too, the rent is determined in the same way by the crop of the previous season. In both these cases the mode of transition from grain-rents to cash is obvious.

Another type of system is that in which a cultivator pays a rate for each plough he works, without reference to the area he brings under cultivation, a system which must go back to the time when land was plentiful, and the means of cultivation the most important question. Again in parts of Bundelkhand the rent of a cultivator is regulated by the amount of irrigable land in his possession, and is not affected by the quantity of dry land he cultivates. In this case irrigation is the most important factor of production, and so groverns the rent.

Special customs, too, have to be watched for. In the alluvial lands of Ballia, for instance, there is a custom (which has been recognised by the Privy Council under the term balpanchit) that no rent is paid for land in a season when it is rendered unproductive by a deposit of sand or other action of the river. In parts of Muttra again, where the landholders and tenants are really members of the same community, there are no rents at all: the tenants pay only the amount assessed as revenue.

The foregoing instances are sufficient to indicate the anomalous rental systems which an official may come across. They are wonderfully persistent in the face of changing agrarian conditions, but they must be classed as survivals and doubtless in process of time cash payment will become almost the universal rule.

Cash-rents are not fixed everywhere by the same methods. They may be calculated by recognised rates on each unit of area, or each field may have its own recognised rent, or the rent may be fixed for the holding as a unit. The tendency seems to be for the last-mentioned system to gain ground, but the others are very common, and officers who have to administer the rent law or assess the revenue must be familiar with their working. In the first case, the land of a village is divided by tradition into areas (usually called *har*) according to variations in productive capacity, and for each area there is a recognised rate of so much per kachchha bigah. Where this system prevails, a cultivator, if asked the rent of his land, will say so many annas per bigah, and the village thinks of rent in these terms. A change in the rete per bigah in such cases is difficult for a landholder to carry out and it certainly shocks the feelings of his cultivators; hence as we have seen it may be thought more convenient to effect an enhancement of rent by reducing the size of the bigah, a more indeterminate unit than the rate stated in cash. In other places, the people know nothing about rent-rates, but recognise a definite sum of money as the rent due from each field: here a cultivator, when asked the rent of his holding, will reel off the rents of each field, leaving it for the listener to add up the total; or finally a cultivator may think, and speak, of the rent of his holding as a whole; he will know nothing of field-rents, or of rent-rates, but will state his rent at a lump sum of money.

One of the great difficulties in testing the accuracy of the rents recorded in the khatauni is to obtain from the cultivators a clear statement of the rents they pay, and it is often necessary to be very patient with men who have the essential facts in their heads but have difficulty in making them plain: a knowledge of the prevailing rental systems is a great help in this work, so that an officer can meet the cultivator half-way. Sometimes confusion arises because a cultivator has more holdings then one. He thinks then of the total rent he has to pay, and not of the items recorded separately for *(e.g.)* his occupancy and non-occupancy holdings. Things are worse when a village has recently been partitioned and a holding has been split among several mahals : it takes a long time for a cultivator to become familiar with the fraction of his rent due to each mahal, though he knows the total well enough. In all such cases patience and consideration for the cultivator will be found to secure the best results and save time in the long run.

It is necessary to remember that one of the results of our tenancy legislation has been to create a distinction between the rent legally due and the rent claimed in practice. Thus in Agra an occupancy tenant's rent can be enhanced legally only by a suit or an attested agreement, but a landholder, especially a small landholder exercising partiarchal authority in his village, does not as a matter of fact worry about such formalities but raises the rent of a tenant by varbal command, and the tenant may not be prepared to enter on a contest. The landholder could not of course recover the extra sum in court, but then he does not rely on the courts in such matters, and the higher rent is claimed and paid. In such cases it might be thought that a Government record should show only the legal rent, but it has to be remembered that for a just assessment of the revenue it is essential to know what the landholder as a matter of fact claims from his tenants, and not merely what the law will enable him to recover. In the Agra khatauni therefore the entry of rent is divided into two columns to show the legal rent and the excess demand; a cultivator's statement of his rent will ordinarily be the sum of these two colomns. It is of course desirable to educate the landholders into compliance with the law regarding enhancement, and something can be done by urging individuals to regularise their claims by getting an agreement to pay the enhanced rent attested by the supervisor-kanungo; but the process will be gradual. Illegal enhancements are perhaps as common in Oudh as in Agra, and theory would suggest that the record of them should be made on the same lines. In practice, however, consideration for the feelings of the Oudh landholders has prevented the introduction of any such record in that province ; there only the total amount claimed is shown in the records, without reference to the legality or illegality of the demand.

We have indicated in a former section that landholders fully appreciate the advantage of having their rent-rolls understated in the records. It must be said in justice to them that the great majority allow the patwari to record the rents which they in fact claim, and that in many cases where errors exist the error is the result of accident or negligence. In most districts, however, a minority of landholders persist in making the patwari under-state their rents, or in technical language "conceal their assets," and it is a practice which the revenue administration must fight by every means in its power, both because it undermines the records which are the foundation of the revenue assessments, and because it produces a feeling of dissatisfaction among landholders whose records are accurate when they see that such fraudulent practices result in an under-assessment of the revenue. It is not of course easy to detect the practice when carried out efficiently: the cultivators willl be taught to state glibly the amont of their rent as recorded in the papers, and at first sight it may be thought that there is nothing else to go on. But a conspiracy of this sort must be known to many people, in particular to the patwari and frequently to the supervisor-kanungo, and its disclosure is very largely a matter of the degree of discipline maintained among the staff. We have seen that the patwari tends to regard himself as the servant of the landholder, and it is obvious that the supervisor also will be tempted to stand in, unless he has just grounds for believing that honesty is in this matter the best policy. Probably the most effective method of ensuring correct records in the long run is the maintenance of discipline among the record-staff.

In conclusion, a few words may be said regarding the law of distraint for rent, one of the features of our tenancy legislation which at first excites most surprise. We have seen that the conception of rent as a share of the produce is dominant among the people, and it is a natural conclusion that the recipient of rent should have power to prevent any disposal of the produce which might defeat his claim. In Mohammedan times it seems to have been a recognised practice to post watchers (shahna) over the crops of probable defaulters, so that they could not be removed until satisfactory arrangements were made for the revenue, and the practice came into general favour among zamindars in times when they could not look for much assistance from an organised government. The present law is then a systematic statement of the ancient practice of the country and a limitation of its abuses. Under it a landholder can distrain on the produce by notice, the effect of which is to prevent the cultivator disposing of it until the rent is arranged for, and if no such arrangement is made, it can be sold by a public officer known as kurk-amin.

2

Ryotwari Land Tenure

(I)

One of the unfortunate things about the abolition of Zamindari is that whilst we are agreed on the necessity of the abolition we have no common policy as to what we should do on an All-India basis after the big estates are abolished. Some Provincial Governments have remained dangerously silent whilst other are still groping in the dark with the best intention to do something really good. On the whole, however, there is a definite tendency to accept Peasant Proprietorship as a solution and many of us have fallen into the trap of thinking that since Zamindari is bad Rayatwari is good. The Prakasam Committee in Madras, the Flound Commission in Bengal, Dr. Naidu's Report on Indebtedness (Madras) and many individual writers and legislators have all recommended Rayatwari tenure and peasant proprietorship as a solution. Acharya Kripalaniji had also raised his influential voice as President of the Congress (in 1947) in favour of peasant proprietorship.

The Universal Popularity of the Idea of Small Holdings.

The idea of small holdings has had a big hold on the minds of people throughout the world, its praises having been sung by both revolutionaries and conservatives. Ever since the French Revolution its praises have been sung by Jacobins and Jesuits, Nazis and Communists, radicals and reactionaries alike. The re-shaping of land on this basis after the first world war in Denmark (1919), Poland, Czechoslovakia, Rumania and Germany is well-known. At a later date the reactionary Nazis, and to-day the Communists in some contries, have upheld the idea.

Advantages Claimed in Europe for this System.

The popularity of a small holdings policy rests on certain advantages claimed for it, the following being the most important of all:

(1) It promises relief of unemployment.

(2) It increases productivity.

(3) It is conducive to socil stability.

(4) It gives us a powerful slogan, "Land for the Masses."

(5) It increses population.

One of the principal motives in the adoption of a small holdings policy has been that of creating employment and though this is of special importance in countries which are not industrially developed it has had great effect also in countries like Great Britain. Agriculture through small holdings is expected to create employment without the desadvantage of much competition, the small holding creating in itself both a home for the worker and a source by which he could feed himself and his family, thus relieving the State from the burden of having to import food.

The idea that peasant proprietorship leads to the highest productive developments in agriculture has been accepted by many. The example of Danish agriculture is sometimes cited to show this for whilst in 1861 about 88 per cent. of the cultivators were tenants by 1925 about 88 per cent. of the cultivators were occupancy owners. The fact that Denmark is the one country where the majority of land owners are opposed to private property in land is rarely if ever noticed. The advantages of greater productivity on small-sized farms, which are more manageable by a limited number of owners or cultivators as compared to relatively big farms which are not manageable with the same efficiency, are sometimes identified with the advantages of peasant proprietorship because small holdings and peasant proprietary holdings are erroneously supposed to be the same.

A large number of writers from Toynbee to Turnor have felt that as the increase in productivity raises the status of the worker, peasant holdings make for social stability and independence of mind. The Yeomen of England of old have been looked upon as the backbone of popular resistance to Stuart absolutism for they are regarded as having been fearless men who could look the whole world in the face with courage and with faith in God. Not all supporters of peasant proprietorship however, have connected social stability with independence of thought in this sense. It is also believed that the establishment of a peasant community creates social stability through the development of groups of people who are self-contained and who have a strong sense of property. Such people as these are supposed to be beyond the control of ordinary trade-unions and connot be brought together for mass action or for any communist or other revolt. This was the foundation of the German Nazi idea of peasant proprietorship working as an instrument of social stability.

In all periods of turmoil and reorganisation the slogan "Land for the Masses" has never failed to create great enthusiasm and the political utility of this is tremendous. The idea of abolishing big landlords has a lesser appeal for untrained human nature then the idea that land will be distributed among the masses. Whether we take France of 1789 or China of 1947 we find the same thing. Much ofthe enthusiasm of the revolting masses springs from the promise that after they are freed from their feudal burdens land will be given to them. Many communist programmes of Agrarian Law aim at making land "the individual property of each person" to whom it is redistributed. All communists in India likewise are by no means opposed to the redistribution of land on a similar basis

Arguments of the Indian Champions of Peasant Proprietorship.

The advocates of peasant proprietorship in India are even more emophatic about its utility than the European writers like Warriner, Karl Brandt, or Dr. Spiegel whom they quote. The following are some of the important arguments put forth in favour of the system in India

(1) It will give maximum employment to the labour available.

(2) It will bring about economic decentralisation and give an independent means of support to the majority of producers.

(3) It will preserve liberty and a democratic rural society and establish social stability and self-respect.

(4) It will give the greatest possible yield per acre, maintain maximum soil fertility, and also help to intensify livestock production.

(5) It offers no hindrance to technical progress whilst it suits our social structure and satisfies the Indian peasant's love of land.

Advantages of Peasant Proprietorship are not for all Countries and at all Times.

The advantages claimed for peasant proprietorship have been mentioned at some length, and could have been discussed at even greater length if space permitted, because only a thorough analysis of these advantages can enable us to see why the idea of small holdings is popular and also how far it is likely to be useful when applied to India. **Some people seem to imagine that we can expect to enjoy the theoreticaladvantagesofpeasantproprietorshipunderallcircumstances and at all times in all countries. This is the fatal blunder which we have to avoid in India.**

Peasant proprietorship is very attractive indeed but what determines its workability and makes it suitable for a country is the presence of certain conditions favourable to its growth. These conditions are not always present in every country nor in any one given country can they continue to remain the same at all times. These conditions are not present in India and as we proceed we shall see why to accept peasant proprietorship to-day is to hug illusions and ignore the stark realities of the economic situation.

There is not enough Land in India for the Success of Peasant Proprietorship.

Almost the first question the supporters of peasant proprietorship should ask and answer is whether the area of land available for cultivation is sufficient to provide economic peasant holdings for all the cultivators to-day, and also whether this area of land will continue to be sufficient for our increasing population in the next 50 years? There is no magic in the phrase "small holdings policy" and such a policy would be ridiculous in the face of a raising man - land ratio where all our energies have to be devoted not in encouraging but in fighting the evils of small-holdings.

In a country like ours where land is limited whilst population is not, where fertility is more the characteristic of the population than of the land, where holdings are too small to be profitable or to remain profitable in the future a system of peasant proprietorship based on decentralisation would be just as ineffective as the use of cottage made rifles for defence against enemy bombers. The abolition of Zamindari is the first barricade we have to storm in our advance towards prosperity but behind it and supporting it are other evils of which the most important are the growing pressure of population on the soil and the uneconomic cultivation of subdivided holdings. The abolition of Zamindari must not be followed by a substitute or a solution which does not take into account these fundamental evils for we can no longer afford to substitute Zamindar King Log by a Peasant Proprietary King Stork.

If we take the whole of India we find that we have some 1000 million acres of land of which the cultivated area is about 280 million acres. This gives us an average holding of between 4 to 5 acres only for each cultivator in addition to one acre kept as current fallow. On a 'per capita' basis the area under cultivation including fallow, would be no more than 0.85 of an acre which compares very unfavourably with the minimum of 1 acre to 2½ acres regarded by different authorities as absolutely indispensable for the nourishment of man. Despite all our separations and divisions, and all our Provincial differences, our main task everywhere is to provide a programme of reconstruction for millions of men all over the country. If we take the old British India alone we have some 500,000 villages with a population of more than 300 millions scattered all over in the 243 districts of the old 11 Provinces, an average district having about 200 villages, each village having about 500 souls. It would be an under estimate rather an over-estimate to say that the number of cultivated holdings comes ot over 60,000,000.

The Increase in Total Population.

We must consider the paucity of land in relation to the frighful rapiditywithwhichourteemingmillionshavemultipliedandarecontinuing to multiply. From 100 millions at the time of Akbar's death (1605) to 150 millions only by 1850, then a sudden increase to 208 millions by 1872, about 303 millions by 1911, and 389 millions by 1941. Between 1800 and 1900 our population increased by about 150 millions in spite of 30 famines which killed off 32.4 millions. The rate of increase has varied ofcourse from 0.9 per cent. (1911-1921) to 15.1 per cent. (1931-1941). It is hardly any consolation to us to be told that our rate of increase between 1870 and 1930 (31 per cent.) was much less than the increase in the same period in England and Wales (77 per cent.) or Russia (115 per cent). U.S.A. (125 per cent.), and Japan (113 per cent.). Those who take this lightly should consider the facts a little more seriously.

In ten years we added to our population more human beings

than the total population of Canada, Australia, New Zealand and the Union of South Africa put together, though we have got here only 22 per cent. of the total area of these countries. In this one country of ours we have more population than that of about 30 countries of Europe put together. It has taken some thousands of years for the populations of Britain and Wales, France, Greece, Belgium, Denmark and Finland to increase to their present level but in India more human beings than this total population of all these countries put together were born within 40 years. In fact during the decade 1931-1941 more than the total population of Canada and New Zealand put together were born every year in India.

The possibilities of increase in our population in the immediate future must not be overlooked. The National Planning Committee thinks that we shall be about 450 million by 1951 and that today (1947) we are more than 420 millions. Professor Fisher has anticipated that we shall be 500 million in 20 years and Professor A.V. Hill thinks that we will be over 650 millions by 1970. Some scientists like Dr. H.L. Richardson are of the opinion that we should consider the present rate of increase to be 6 millions a year and even if we take no more than the present rate of increase the population of India would be doubled in sixty years. What shall we say of other estimates which, though more moderate than that of Professor Hill, tell us that we will be 600 millions by the end of this century, about 1300 millions in 2100 A.D., about 3000 millions in 2200 A.D. and after three centuries we will be nine times as many as to-day? It is of course not necessary to accept all these figures but we cannot escape from the logic of the position as it is today.

Provincial Figures of Man-Land Ratio.

Provincial figures of cultivable area and population pressure are not more encouraging. If we take Bengal in about 1940, we find that for a cultivated area of 30 millions acres there was an agricultural population of 34 millions. The 1931 Census showed that 6 million families (each of 5.2 persons) possessed only 28.9 millions acres of cultivated land, formerly each family having had a bare 4.8 acres. The average cultivated area per family as calculated by the Floud Commisson came to less than this. This can be compared with the size of economic holdings which was not supposed to be less than 5 acres in eastern and northern Bengal and not less than 8 to 10 acres in the rest of the Province.

Enquiries made by the Director of Land Records and Surveys showed that 41.9 per cent. of the agricultural families in Bengal had holdings of 2 acres or less. The figures given by the Flound Commission showed that more than 70 per cent. of the cultivators were in a desperate condition. According to Khan Bahadur S.M. Hosain, a member of the Commission, the average income of this large majority of cultivators could not be more than Rs. 10 to Rs.14 per head per annum (pre-war price level). The Commission's conclusion was that "already the area of land available for cultivation is insufficient to provide economic holding for all........ and the situation will become steadily worse if the population continues to increase at the present rate." The Census of 1941 has shown that the rate of increase has been more than this- about 20.3 per cent., which is greater even than the All-India figure. Within 50 years (1891 to 1941) the population has increased from 390 lakhs to 603 lakhs. The pressure of this population on agriculature can be seen from the fact that the percentage of population dependent on agriculture has increased continuously from 53.83 per cent. in 1881, to 63.19 per cent. in 1891, 71.5 per cent. in 1901, 75.4 per cent. in 1911 and 77.3 per cent. in 1921.

The situation in other Provinces is not of course much better. The average size of a holding in the United Provinces was estimated to be about 6 acres in 1931 but the average condition of the agricultural classes there is even worse than in Bengal–a fact admitted by the Floud Commission. The United Provinces Banking Inquiry Committee itself reported that a large proportion of the holdings were only 2½ acres or less when the minimum economic holding could not be less than 4 to 5 crores. In several acreas in the East and the North the holdings are small beyond imagination. In certain parts of Gorakhpur the average holding at the time of the last Settlement was only 1.3 acres, in parganas like Hata the average was only 0.9 of an acre and in Salimpur 0.6 of an acre. A village survey of district Hadoi showed that one-third of the cultivators had holdings of only 3 bighas whereas in a village in district Gorakhpur the average holding was only 0.29 of an acre the average cultivated area per individual being only 0.27 of an acre. In Bihar and Orissa taken together (excluding the old Chota Nagpur) the average holding is even less than in U.P. and in fact the pressure of population in relation to land was felt even as early as 1901.

There is very little difference between Zamindari and Rayatwari areas so far as this paucity of land is concerned. In Madras, 74 per cent. of the Ryotwari holdings have an average size of not more than 2.4 acres, whilst if we put 94 per cent. of the ryotwari holders together their average mean holding is no more than 3 acres in size. If we include all the estates of all the ryotwari owners, big as well as the small, we find from the Settlement Reports that the average size of land (per patta) has been reduced from 6.85 acres in 1900 to 4.13 acres in 1940–41. The net cultivated area per head of the population was only 0.76 of an acre in 1943–44. The Madras Government has admitted that "a substantial number of holdings in the Province are uneconomic and their produce is not enough to maintain the ryots'family and the minimum livestock required for cultivation purposes." The total population has increased during the last 50 years from 337 lakhs to 493 lakhs (46 per cent.). To-day while the population is increasing by one million every year the number of holdings is increasing by about one lakh every year.

The Province of Bombay is supposed to have holdings of a bigger size than most other Provinces, but on the other hand the yield per acre of net area sown is the lowest in India -about 0.19 of a ton per acre. Besides this though the average ryotwari holding is about 11 acres, nearly 50 per cent, of the holdings are below 5 acres in size, while as many as 78.5 per cent. of the holdings are below 15 acres. The number of holdings increased from about 12 lakhs and 72 thousand in 1904-05 to over 23 lakhs in 1942-43.

The situation revealed by village surveys in far from satisfactory. Non-official investigations have shown that there are villages in the Bombay Deccan where there has been no increase in the area cultivated during the last 100 years and yet the agricultural produce of the village has to support 700 or more inhabitants compared to about 250 people in 1832. Official investigations made more thoroughly have shown a more gloomy picture than this. Dr. Mann's conclusions are known to everybody. If he found more than 30 years ago that 81 per cent. of the holdings were uneconomic (Village: Pimpla Soudagar) the proportion of such holdings to-day can be imagined.

The results of an investigation made by the Professor of Agricultural Economics, College of Agriculture, Poona, in one of the most prosperous of the agricultural regions of India – Charotar, in Kaira District, Bombay- -showed that the size of the net cultivated holding for the tract was only 6 acres and 36 gunthas. Charotar is known for its intensive farming and Mollison regarded it as one of the most fertile of all agricultural areas in the whole of India, yet the holdings of the farmers whose conditions were examined were so small that they could provide employment only for 57.9 per cent. of, the available time of the male workers and 32.4 per cent. of the available time of bullock labour.

World's Highest Rural Density Records.

A study of population density shows the seriousness of the problem equally well. It is true that density may have very little meaning when we consider industrial countries. Where there are great facilities in transporting food a density figure loses much of its significance, as in the case of London City or England as a whole a few years ago. But in India density is an important consideration. If we ignore a couple of very extreme cases like that of the Nile Valley with a density of over 11,000 persons to every square mile, it can be said that we have in India a rural density which is unknown in most other parts of the world. In some parts of this country we have reached the world's higest conceivable density records of this type.

For several decades on end we have had in the rural regions of Bengal, Bihar, etc., a density of 1,300 persons per square mile which even more than 20 years ago was regarded as four times the rural density that could be supported in Western Europe. It is held that agriculture in Europe cannot support more that 250 persons per square mile. In several parts of Bengal itself, such as the south-western part of Dacca, the adjoining strip of Mymensingh, central portion of Faridpore and Bankurgunj, etc. we have had a population density renging from 1,000 to 3,275 per square mile which is practically the world's highest record. In parts of Bihar (like Saran sub-division) a density varying from 985 to 1077 per square mile was reached more than 56 years ago.

We have here areas of great fertility like the Indo-Gangetic plain. The necessities of life of our people are also much less than in Europe. Both these factors make it possible to support more than 250 people per square mile. But there is a limit to this and the present density leaves no doubt as to the fact that we are living on a more unbalanced diet than any other European people. A density like ours can only be attained at the sacrifice of proteins for carbohydrates and a more or less complete absence of fruits or milk. This is the inevitable result of a dietary forced on the people by paucity of land.

The land situation in relation to the density in the Ganges Valley--covering large portions of the United Provinces, Bihar and Bengal is serious indeed. In some areas there has been serious soil erosion, agricultural decadence, and denudation of forests. We have extensive double-cropping in some of these regions but those who have studied this closely look upon it as a sign of improvident husbandry and subsistence farming. The encroachment on land necessary for fodder crops and pasture and the denudation of forests are tragic facts. Expert opinion tells us that the area under forest should be 20 per cent. of the total area of a Province but except in C.P. and Berar the area is much below this. In the United Provinces the forest area is only 5 per cent. of the total. In Sind, N.W.F. Province and the Punjab it is even below 4 per cent. For India as a whole we require on this basis about 102 million acres of forest but actually we have only 68.1 million acres. We thus require millions of acres of land for **re-afforestation** alone.

The land per capita of population, as compared to other coutries, reveals the paucity of land here. We have less than one acre per capita as compared to 6 1/3 acres in Argentina, 4 2/3 acres in Canada and 31/3 acres in the United States of America. There are countries like Germany which have the same area per capita as we have and there are also countries like Japan where the area per capita is supposed to be even less than ours, but these countries are highly industrialised and also have much more intensive and scientific farming than we have. In many parts of our overpopulated country the land per capita is only half or less than populated country the land per capita is only half or less than half an acre. In Dacca for example we have only 14.4 lakh acres of cultivated land for a population of over 42 lakhs which means that the area available per head is only 0.34 acres. In Faridpore district there isnot even a single acre of forest or cultivable waste left to-day and the acreage per head is reported to be only half an acre. The same story is repeated in several parts of other Provinces.

A comparison of our density with that of the most over populated region of Europe is equally significant. Density figures of Europe's 42 most overpopulated and poor rural regions given by the League of Nations show that only in one case (Ardino-Stara Zagora) was the density as high as 483 per square kilometer (or about 1236 per square mile) whilst in the majority of cases (22 districts out of 42) the density was less than 100 per square kilometer (very roughly about 256 per square mile). It is true that cultural and natural conditions differ from country to country and international comparisons are not likely to be very useful but we do not want here any great precision and the wide differences between the density here and in overpopulated Europe ought to be significant.

Are Zamindari Estates Large Enough for Proper Re-distribution of

Land?

The above study of our man-land ratio and our fast increasing population and high density ought to show that it is fallacious to presume that there is enough land for the success of peasant proprietorship. This fallacious presumption however has received support largely on the understanding that the present Zamindari and other big estates are large enough to permit a proper re-distribution of land after we abolish all the big estates. Besides this there is also a general belief that we can increase the area of cultivable land as well as the productivity per acre on the basis of a system of peasant proprietorship.

It would have been a good thing of couse if the amount of land in the possession of the big landowners had been so extensive as to permit us to increase the average size of a peasant farm upto the level of a reasonably sized economic holding based on a proper conception of the standardof living of our masses in the future. But the actual facts do not warrant such a presumption. We cannot deny that the present distrubution of land in Zamindari areas is very bad. But though land is very badly distributed and in certain areas a very large percentage of the total land is in the form of big estates–as can be seen from the size of individual jagirs and Zamindaris referred to in a previous chapter--the total land available is much less than necessary for a proper redistribution in the form of prosperous individualistic peasant farms.

It is true the apart from the big Zamindari estates, land has been very badly distributed also in the raiyatwari areas. The bad distribution of land in ryotwari areas leads us however to the same conclusion as in Zamindari areas–that bad distribution cannot and does not in itself mean that there is enough land to distribute among all. After all the limit is set by the total amount of cultivated and cultivable land available. The idea that we can increase the area of cultivable land by bringing into cultivation all our waste lands on a peasant proprietary basis is even more fallacious than the idea of re-distribution our present-day big estates. We shall discuss this more fully later when we shall see how impossible it is to bring more waste culturable land under cultivation under the present system. We may however note here that even in exceptional cases such as in those of the two districts of Malabar and South Kanara in Madras, where extensive new areas were brought under cultivation under the present system the heavy pressure of population could not be relieved by the extension of cultivation and there has been no improvement of any kind whatsoever.

The advantages of Small Holdings have no Meaning for us in India.

The supporters of peasant proprietorship in India waxeloquent about the theoretical advantages of family farming or small holding. In actual fact the question of the paucity of land in relation to our population makes this talk of the advantages of family farming quite meaningless. Phrases like "small holdings", "peasant ownership", etc. are very misleading when applied to India without a due consideration of the paucity of land. We forget that the small holdings of India are not and cannot be the same as the small-holdings referred to by European writers when they speak of their advantages.

The word "peasant" itself is not a very exact term and a peasant farm in Europe does not mean a very small farm. No doubt a "peasant farm" or a "family farm" may very in size, depending on climatic and economic factors, but this does not mean that it can be of any size howsoever small . Our supporters of peasant proprietorship make the same mistake as has been made by some continental agronomists regarding the minimum size of small farms. Our writers do not hesitate to quote authorities like Warriner in support of small holdings but they do not seem, to have read Warriner and other carefully. Warriner and P.Lamartine Yates have made it clear that the continental idea that a peasant farm can be good under all conditions, whatever its size, is "an ingrained illusion." We seem to love such illusions.

It seems a "peasant family farm" can be of any size upto 300-400 acres, though the most successful of such farms are not always as big as this. The most successful of peasant farms doing dairy business are much smaller than this but not smaller than 50 acres. They are supposed to vary from 50 to 150 acres in Holland and Denmark. Likewise it is necessary for us to know when a small farm necessarily ceases to be really. P.L. Yates and Warriner feet that no family farm should be below 10 years, though even 10 acres, according to these writers are not enough to keep the family fully occupied.

The average size of a normal peasant farm even in Eastern Europe is not below 12 acres and it seems any size smaller than this would be regarded as absolutely undesirable even in this poor and overpopulated portion of Europe. If we take the "small holdings" of U.S.A. or England the size of course is considerably bigger and these small farms would be the equivalent of very big or large farms here. In only those farms sizes in general writers like Warriner describe only those farms as "large farms" which are over 50 hectares or 120 acres in size.

Dwarf Holdings must not be Mistaken for Small Farms.

Those who speak of the advantages of peasnt farming generally refer to farms well over 12 acres in size, in fact to farms which are by no means "small farms" in our traditional Indian sense. When we compare the size of these prosperous European farms with the size of average peasant farms here we find that our "small holdings" are really no better than the "dwarf farms" of Europe (under 2 hectares or 5 acres). The advantages of small farms are not the same as the advantages of "dwarf farms" for the latter have no advantages. All great writers have been quite emphatic in asserting that dwarf farms are the weak point in a peasant economy, unless ofcourse they are in the possession of industrial or other workers who cultivate them as a subsidiary occupation.

The Small and Dwarf Farms of Europe.

There are ofcourse a large number of "dwarf farms" in Europe but everywhere their existence is looked upon as a tragedy. Holdings under one hectare are not even included in national statistics in some of the countries and it is difficult to find the number of holdings from 2½ acres to 12 acres in any classified form. However we have consolidated figures showing the percentage of holdings in the group 1-5 hectares. It seems that Greece, Spain, Roumania, and Yugoslavia have the largest number of holdings below 12 acres. But holdings upto 12 acres can be far better than anything we know of here in India.

Southern Poland (formerly Galicia), Yugoslavia, and Bulgaria are probably the poorest among the rural overpopulated regions of Europe but no one sings the unrealistic song of the advantages of small farming there. Yields per acre have been decreasing in Galicia and huge areas have been denuded of the very soil in Yugoslavia where children suffer from rickets and "almost every family has its cripple," Bulgaria is more dependent on agriculture than any other European country and reminds us of India for its implements are primitive, capital is scarce and there is little manuring of land due to burning of dung as fuel.

Dwarf Farms can be Harbingers of Communism.

Western Europe is ofcourse happier than Eastern Europe and the praise of small family farming is supposed to emanate from there more than from overpopulated Eastern Europe. And yet there are parts of Western Europe also where small farming would have been a definite cause of ruin and poverty but for the saving factors of high intensive farming and industrialisation. Switzerland, Germany, Belgium, France, the Netherlands, etc. may be happier than Poland or Bulgaria but this is by no means due to small farming by itself.

In Switzerland holdings are very small, as small as in South-East Poland but here and also in Germany and in Czechoslovakia the peasants are side by side employed in industrial work. Swiss cottage industry is well-known of course. The existence of dwarf farms thus dose not mean poverty and starvation in countries like these because these farms are in possession of industrial or other workers. In Germany about 27.4 per cent of the farms are only about 5 acres each, as in India,but most of them are located in highly industrialised parts of the country and the farmers work in the factories also. These farms of 5 acres each are not supposed to be self-sustaining and are only a means of improving the diet of industrial and other wage-earners.

In some countries such as Norway the small size of holdings is compensated by the rights of pasturage or timber which help considerably. In most other cases in the past there has also been a partial escape through emigration. Where there are no compensating factors of these types or where these factors are inadequate there is unrelieved poverty and one can perceive a definite drift towards communism as in Poland or Bulgaria or Yugoslavia to-day.

A study of the European countries having dwarf farms has convinced advocates of small farming like Karl Brandt himself that if our ideal is to get the best return from land the size of the holdings must be capable of utilising to the full the available man power. If we ignore this we will only be planning the pauperization of our masses which will soon develop into political chaos and end in communism. The view of men, who are normally opposed to any kind of joint cultivation, that peasant proprietorship will help us to utilise our man-power more fully than other alternatives is tragically fallacious as we shall see as we proceed further.

The Causes of the Success and Failure of Peasant Farming Abroad.

Any impartial study of peasant farming abroad ought to open our eyes to the realities facing us before it is too late. If peasant farming has succeeded in certain countries it has also failed in many others. The success of peasant farming in certain parts of the world has been due to a combination of economic, technical and marketing conditions which cannot exist here under peasant proprietorship. The extensive use of mixed farming, the presence of conditions which could encourage both milk and meat production, the possibilities of animal husbandry and of investment of extra crop production in extra livestock, and above all, factors like sufficient land and rainfall and absence of a high agricultural density seem to have been the principle factors responsible for the success of this system.

It will be noticed that peasant farming has failed to succeed in most conuntries like Rumania, Yugoslavia etc., where the holdings have proved to be too small due to high agricultural density in particular. The creation of small peasant units in grain-growing areas in some of these countries was a definite mistake and some authorities on peasant proprietorship have admitted that large-scale methods would have proved of greater benefit than the land reform which created such peasant farms in these countries.

When we talk of small farming we must not ignore the importance of animal husbandry which is its very foundation. But not all countries have the requisite conditions suitable for livestock farming. As in the case of cereal production so in the case of animal farming we must have enough land, apart from other things like adequate capital, proper irrigation etc.

Can we in our complacency forget that animal husbandry is as essential to our small farming as elsewhere but to make it successful our small cultivators must be rich enough and lucky enough to have plenty of capital, irrigation facilities, and a reasonably heavy effective demande for livestock products including milk, meat, etc.? Unless cattle can be used for more milk as well as meat production there is a tendency towards the development of an excessive number of working animals on the small peasant farm. This system of farming also requires in all areas adequate rainfall considered in relation to animal husbandry and mixed farming.

Warriner tells us that is was the inadequacy of rainfall that made peasant farming in Russia less successful than in Germany. The inadequacy of rain-fall in many parts of Bombay, N.W.F.P., Sind, Rajputana, Western India States etc. cannot be lightly brushed aside by saying that where rainfall is inadequate we can have artificial irrigation. The latter would be like the advice to eat cakes given to people who have not even bread to eat.

Peasant farming cannot succeed anywhere where there is not enough land to distribute but this is most obviously true in predominantly cereal farming areas where reinfall is inadequate. In such areas it would be almost suicidal to ignore the importance of large-scale production on the basis of co-operative and even collective farming. It is important to note that some such solution as the use of machinery and large-scale production is regarded by more than one writer on peasant farming as the only practical solution in such areas. Because of this we find that the idea of collective cultivation has received good support in the Balkans. This is very understandable.

The Tendency to Ignore the Question of Uneconomic Holdings.

It is time for us to understand that it is impossible, even for the short period of the next 50 years, to establish any system of peasant proprietorship on the basis of proper economic holdings. We can, if we want, make the same mistake as the made by the land reformers in countries like Rumania and Yugoslavia but a starving peasantry based on a small-scale peasant system will give us neither political stability nor econmic prosperity.

Most of those who prefer the status quo that is, do not like the idea of changing the present system or at least do not wish to go beyond the ryotwari tenure in general, have tended in the past to ignore the question of uneconomic holdings. There have been of course important references to the evil of subdivision of land in Reports and letters written in the last century by officials such as Sir Charles Elliott and Sir Edward Buck, Mr. J.G. Lumsden, Rao Bahadur G.V. Joshi and others and in recent times the Agricultural Commission as well as several experts like Mr. Keatinge and Dr. Mann have also drawn our attention to this evil, but on the whole there has been a strong tendency to ignore the evil as if it was not vitally important. The Provincial Governments before August 1947 did not care to collect statistics regarding the different sizes of holdings cultivated and not many noticed this or even protested about it. As late as in 1944 the Government of India issued its Second Report on Reconstruction Planning and though this was a critical period in the history of our food production there was no reference to uneconomic holdings.

The Supporters of Ryotwari Tenure and Peasant Proprietorship have no Final Solution for Uneconomic Holdings.

The silence about uneconomic holdings is now of course a thing of the past but still we find that there is (a) a very inadequate appreciation of the need for scientific agriculture and of the capital investment required to make agriculture profitable and (b) the absence of a clear-cut solution for the evil of uneconomic holdings, the seciousness of which has not been fully grasped.

If any proof were needed of the inadequate appreciation of the capital investment required for our agricultural development it is furnished by the Tata Plan itself. If made a provision of only Rs. 250 crores for the working capital which it thought was necessary for introducing improved methods of farming all over India. As this sum was to be spread over 15 years it meant an annual provision of less than two and a half rupees per cultivated holding or about half a rupee per head per year of the village population.

The inability of the supporters of ryotwari to give a proper solution for uneconomic holdings is a very serious matter. The Bengal Land Revenue Commission looked upon the pressure of poputation as the ultimate cause of Bengal's economic troubles but it had nothing to suggest as solution for it. It avoided facing the logic of the situation by saying "it is the most difficult problem which we have to face but it is virtually impossible under present conditions to suggest any remedy for it."

It is interesting to see that the Government of India, before the recent transfer of power, had also shirked the issue. In one of its war publications entitled *400 Millions to be Fed,* it was mentioned that our population had increased greatly but when the discussion came to the question of the stabilising of an adequate ratio of the cultivated area by the total population, the only conclusion given was "That is a problem that has to be solved". As we shall see below, many people to-day want the control of sub-division of land by legal methods but even these men have to add in conclusion an honest note of pessimism and they can by no means be regarded as sure of their remedy.

Peasant Proprietorship Encourages Sub-Division of Land.

The honest supporters of peasant farming who admit that it is difficult to find a final remedy for the uneconomic size of farm business should go a step further if they want to know where the difficulty lies. We have still to learn the truth that if subdivision of land is an evil the ryotwari tenureof land is also an evil for this land tenure actually encourages the processes of sub-division. It was the bread-up of our village communities and the making of individual ryots responsible for the payment of their quota of land revenue which considerably encouraged the sub-division of land. Like wise the settlement of individual cultivators on the same basis as this on small plots of land, whether as a method of helping demobilised soldiers or otherwise, has not helped to check the evil.

How can anybody escape the fact that the trouble about the subdivision of land seems to be even more rampant in ryotwari tracts than in the non-ryotwari areas? Legislative action to stop this evil was found to be first necessary in the ryotwari areas. The history of small peasant farming in Europe also shows that the subdivision of land among the children in each generation is the principal evil of this system and the principle obstacle to progress. With it of course there is also the other evil of fragmentation, a curse which is no less serious in Europe than in India. The evil of fragmentation has been described as "the biggest curse afficting European farming to-day."

Why Consolidation of Holdings is no Real Solution.

Many people are under the impression that we can have peasant proprietorship and avoid the evil of sub-division and fragmentation by adopting the remedy of Consolidation of holdings for fragmentation and the principle of Primogeniture for subdivision of land. Some people seem to have taken to the idea of Consolidationof holdings with almost blind faith and are not even aware of the fact that subdivision of land and fragmentation of land are two different evils requiring two different remedies.

We have been trying to bring about cosolidation of holdings for the last many years. There is no reason why we should not realise that not only have the attempts at consolidation been a failure but there is very little possibility of consolidation being an effective solution for uneconomic holdings. We can consolidate, even under the most favourable circumstances, only our present fragmented holdings but if these holdings are too small they will continue to remain uneconomic even when they are consolidated. Where existing holdings are very small they can be unprofitable or uneconomic even if we have no evil of fragmentation at all.

The second main shortcoming of consolidation is that it is a solution at the best only for the problem of fragmentation but not for the more serious evil of sub-division of land. For this reason it had not succeeded much even in Europe under more favourable circumstances than our own. For example, after the last war the French Government succeeded in consolidating all the strips of fragmented farms in North-East France, but within 20 years all this work was undone by the evil of inheritance subdivision of land. The results of consolidation in other countries under other conditions such as in Switzerland or Germany, or the Netherlands, have not been more encouraging either.

The creation of "pocket handkerchief strips of land" is a tragedy and a curse everywhere but the evil of sub-division of land is even more serious than fragmentations. Even if we cannot think of anything better than the present system, which is by the way a completely untenable view, we have at least to create economic holdings out of the small holdings of to-day and also to preserve those holdings which are large enough to be called economic and prevent them from being sub-divided. It is easier however to prevent further subdivision than to create new economic holdings.

The adoption of the principle of Primogeniture and measure usually connected with this reform can help us only to prevent further sub-division. Even this simple and onesided reform however has not been readily accepted and will be difficult to put into practice under the conditions created by our present system. Normally, it is presumed that if land is inherited only by the eldest child the other children should be paid some compensation by the inheritor. The problem of finding this money is regarded as insurmountable by some. Others, in sheer desperation, have proposed that there should be no compensation except the obligation on the part of the inheritor to maintaion the excluded minor heirs, if any, till they attain majority. There are other more serious difficulties to be faced besides that of compensation such as the question of the employment of the dispossessed heirs and that of a possible fall in land prices.

Those who have faith in peasant proprietorship and expect reforms like consolidation of holdings to brings about a prosperous agriculture in this country are doomed to disappointment. We cannot stop the uneconomic cultivation of our small farms and we cannot create new economic holdings so long as we do not decide to introduce far reaching changes in our land tenure system and in our farm organisation itself. Joint cultivation of our small farms on a far-reaching co-operative and collective basis is our only solution.

Those who do not want to give up their illusion about individualistic peasant farming may do well to notice that those who believe in consolidation and similar remedies are not sure of the results. Land revenue experts like Mr. Fawcus, late Commissioner of Dacca Division, and Mr. F.W. R. Robertson, who was also a Commissioner (and later became Chairman of the Federal Public Services Commission), have openly stated in their evidence before the Floud Commission that they cannot regard consolidation of holdings as a practical method for checking subdivision and fragmentation. The stoutest supporters of peasant proprietorship who have accepted consolidation of holdings as necessary have added at the end of all their lengthy support of these remedies that "before leaving the subject we must admit that a final or perfect remedy for the too small or uneconomic size of a farm business is difficult to find."

The Supporters of Peasant Proprietorship are not very logical.

One would expect that those supporters of the peasant system who are honest enough to say that they have not enough confidence in the possibilities of finding a final remedy for the uneconomic size of farm business would gladly support joint cultivation of holdings on a co-operative or collective basis. But surprisingly enough some of these honest men are the most opposed to any such joint farming operations. They are, we are told, moved by the ideological consideration of liberty, democracy, etc., but this attitude is not very logical.

The principle reason put forth by several supporters of peasant farming and ryotwari tenure for their opposition to any kind of joint farming or anything resembling the Russian system of collectivised agriculture is their abhorrence of force or compulsion. But not all of these opponents of force are quite logical. A very prominent young leader recently denounced in an Economic Conference, the Russian system on the ground that the use of force was bad. But when it was pointed out to him that voluntary consolidation will not succeed he agreed that force may have to be used even under peasant proprietorship. His attitude did not show that he felf (a) that if the use of forcewas bad for purposes of collectivisation it must also be bad for purposes of consolidation of holdings, or (b) that on the other hand, if force was inevitable it was definitely mischievous to start terrifying people from now by drawing horrible pictures of the use of force in other countries.

It is true that several eminent writers are still in favour of voluntary consolidation and even as late as to-day have expressed a desire to win over the countryside by "persuasive demonstration of practical advantages." Compulsory consolidation is looked down upon by these men since" acts of ejectment and forcible expropriation" involve, in their opinion, a violation of "the very fundamental aspects of the institution of private property." This is certainly more logical than believing that if force is bad for collectivisation it is not bad for consolidation but when we examine the view of these peace-makers on earth we find that they too in their own way seem to believe in force after all. They begin by suggesting voluntary co-operation and end by suggesting a combination of compulsory and co-operative consolidation. Their logic teaches them that if " a section of cultivators agree to consolidation, compulsion may be used against the rest".

It is also worth noticing that one or two writer who hate compulsory consolidation on the ground that it involves ejectment and forcible expropriation which violate private property do not hesitate to recommend compulsory exclusion, without any compensation, of all except one heir to the succession of land. This latter suggestion is justified on the ground that individual interest must yield before national interest and that such deprivation involves no question of justice or injustice. These writers do not see that if national interest requires the exclusion of all individuals from private possession of land such a thing should also be welcomed rather than opposed on the ground of sanctity of private property. To place private property interests above the national interest and then talk of national interest being above private individuals in comparatively insignificant matters is unreasonable.

Equally illogical is the attitude of those who suggest ryotwari and peasant proprietorship as a good substitute for Zamindari and admit at the same time that the economic evils of ryotwari tenure are even worse than the economic results of Zamindari. This is more or less the attitude of the Floud Commission itself. While it recommended Ryotwari as a solution it also admitted that in predominantly ryotwari areas the economic situation was actually worse than in Bengal. Referring to ryotwari Madras, for example, the Floud Commission showed that in every way conditions were much worse there than in Zamindari Bengal-the number of labourers was more, the poverty ofthe sub-tenants was greater, rents were higher, the amount of debt per head of the population was more, the average area per farming family in relation to the yield of crops was less. Even for the Punjab it admitted that the peasant proprietors there were exploiting the tenants and the condition of the tenants there was worse than that of Bargadars in Bengal.

Peasant Proprietorship is no Solution for Fighting the Evils of

Landlordism.

Just as the peasant system in itself cannot solve the problem of uneconomic hodings due to the pressure of our teeming millions on the soil it cannot also solve the problem of the other principal evils associated with landlordism such as sub-letting, rack-renting, parastism and bad distribution of land. If we start with things as they are to-day we notice that since landlordism is found everywhere in India, the parasitic rent-receiver and the exploited tenant cultivator are also found everywhere-like pain in a diseased body. In all ryotwari areas the exploitation of the real cultivator is a normal feature of our agricultural life and this exploitation is not less serious than the evils in Zamindari areas just because the landlord goes by the glorified name of a peasant proprietor.

One has only to look at the extensive process of subletting of land, the increase in the number of rent-receivers, and the large areas of land which have lapsed into the hands of money-lenders in all ryotwari tracts to realise that these evils cannot be stopped by the adoption of "peasant proprietorship" as a solution. In India as a whole 70 per cent. of the total area is cultivated by non-owners whereas in Bombay Province as a whole 60% of the area is under non-cultivating owners. According to Pearson at least half the land in Western India is now leased by landlords who do nothing for the tenants. It is also to be noted that at least one-third of the holdings in the ryotwari areas are sub-let to-day.

In the Punjab the landlord goes under the glorified name of a peasant proprietor but the number of persons living on rent increased from 626,000 in 1911 to 1,008,000 in 1921. This evil has not been checked to-day nor can we expect such a miracle. To-day in the Punjab as a whole about 52% of the soil is cultivated by crop-sharing tenants-at-will. It is reported that there are districts where the percentage of the total area cultivated by such tenants-at-will is unbelievably high. In Multan it comes to 74.1% and in Montgomery about 62.9%. The tenants-at-will have not even the ordinary legal protection given to other tenants in Zamindari tracts like Bengal.

Law Cannot Prevent the Evils of Rural Landlordism if it Continues to Protect Private Property in Land.

The supporters of peasant proprietorship presume that they can prevent by law most of the evils of landlordism mentioned above. This presumption ignores the fundamental fact that if these evils are the natural results of monopoly of land where the demand for land is considerably more than its supply, to protect that monopoly by law and prohibit its misuse is not possible. The misuse of economic power by a small group of privileged people cannot be prevented. We might as well give rifles to a small group of men tempted to be irresponsible and then prohibit them from using them.

It is easy to conceive of legal remedies such as primogeniture, compulsory cultivation of land by its owners, etc. but the fact is that whilst such legal prohibitions will have to be supplimented by a whole host of other legal bans and will ultimately have to be as revolutionary as the abolition of private ownership of agricultural land itself, they will fail in their purpose so long as the source of the evil continues to be protected by law. If we permit the private ownership of land to continue it will be totally impossible to prevent subletting of land for example. To ignore this is to ignore reality. After a certain limit is reached it is more profitable to sublet the land and rack-rent the tenant than to cultivate land as its owner. At this stage no law can prevent the real evil. Legal evasions of any law against any kind of tenancy and sub-letting or against the taking of rent in any form whatsoever are easy and manifold.

Hidden Forms of Tenancy.

Hidden forms of tenancy can easily be visualised. The tenant may appear as a nominal partner of some kind. If all kinds of partnerships and ordinary tenancy are prohibited the tenant may appear as a mortgagee and the owner may enjoy very high rents first in the form of high land values and then in the form of interest obtained through a bank deposit or other investments. If there is a legal ban on this too and on any kind of transfer of land the tenant may appear in the form of an employee (permanent or temporary) on the farm. If even the employment of hired labour on a farm is then declared illegal, the tenant may appear as a member of the family–he may be a relative of some kind who can be regarded as member of the family though in economic relationship he is a tenant. It is well high impossible to put a stop to this unless of course we produce a Dictator who has the temerity to ban the joint-family as an institution.

It is not necessary to visualise such developments however since the banning of the use of any kind of extra or hired labour itself will lead to a breakdown in agricultural productivity. Outside help of some kind is indispensable for operations like harvesting, weeding, transplanting, etc. and a legal ban or hired labour may make even the cultivation of proper economic holdings an impossibility. There is also the othe fact that a large number of our landowners, whether they be the Jotedar in Bengal or the Brahmin in Madras or even the Lingayat in Bombay, have given up the plough. The Brahmins as a class, the large number of middleclass people who own land in Bengal etc., do not cultivate land without hired labour. Besides there are the widows, minors, invalids, charitable and religious institutions, who own land but cannot cultivate it themselves.

Attitude of Willing to Wound But Afraid to Kill the Evil of Non-Cultivatingowners.

Apart from the important fact that the legal prohibitions referred to above will fail in their purpose we have the other significant fact that the legal bans contemplated are not acceptable to all champions of peasant proprietorship. We have permitted the growth of such a large class of non-cultivating owners that many supporters of ryotwari now even shrink from the logic of the necessity of fighting the evil of non-cultivating landlordism. Writers like Dr. Narayanswamy Naidu have been frank enough to admit that their support of ryotwari does not imply any immediate abolition of even absentee landlordism. It is admitted of course that the non-cultivating landholders form a high percentageoftheagriculturistsand,itisalsoadmittedthatonlya"socialistic state"can make possible the complete abolition of the present evils, but instead of fighting the evil these writers come to the conclusion that to-day we can do nothing better than just try to wean these landowners from their uneconomic ways of cultivation and make absenteeism as unattractive as possible.

The Support of Peasant Farming is More Sentimental Than Scientific.

Any impartial study of the reasons given in favour of establishing a system of peasant proprietorship will show that the supporters of the system are more sentimental than scientific on this question. We may analyse some of the so-called scientific reasons usually put forth in support of this system to see why they become just ordinary sentimental half-truths.

Peasant Proprietorship as the Salvation of Rural Labour.

We are told that "a system of peasant ownership can serve to keep on the soil a comparatively larger number of people in conditions which render them reasonably happy and to make the soil yield greater output." It is also added that, "small holdings limit the use of machines and lead to intensive agriculture which finds employment for manual labour in far greater numbers than does extensive agriculture or large farms worked by machines."

Statements like the above are quite scientific and unexceptionable when considered in the abstract as general principles. But when they are put forth as principles applicable to India at all times and under all conditions of the type prevalent to-day they cease to be scientific and become mere sentimental hald-truths. A great deal of truth is usually mixed up with a great many dengerous generalisations in statements like these.

The author of the above quotations is convinced that "production diminishes in the proportion in which the size of the agricultural undertaking increases." To say this, and also to express the ieda that we can give maximum employment by not using machines and not having large farms, may appear to be quite scientific but these are general principles which ignore completely several fundamental truths regarding productivity, employment, and size of farms. It is certainly true that production does not go on increasing in proportion as the size of the farm increases. But where we have dwarf farms as in India production will certainly increase in proportion as the size of the farm increases. Similarly maximum employment is not always secured by means which restrict output per acre or by perpetuation of small farms.

It is true that peasants like to stick to old methods of production rather than use machinery because of their fear of unemployment. But we have to balance the fear of unemployment with the necessities of more production. The questions of mechanisation in relation to productivity and the low productivity of our peasant farms will be taken up in the next chapter. It is necessary to realise here that where there is an ample labour supply and very small holdings we have a considerable amount of hidden unemployment and we cannot complacently talk about giving maximum employment to all under system of peasant proprietorship. Such a dream as this of giving maximum employment to all in our small peasant economy will end in nothing except low production and stark poverty for all.

It is utterly fallacious to support peasant proprietorship because of the fear of overpopulation and unemploment. Peasant proprietorship is supposed to increase population rather than decrease it; and as to agricultural unemployment we are already so overpopopulated that even without the use of machinery or large-scale farming we have almost double the population required for the cultivation of our fields by the traditional methods of our peasant proprietors. Our salvation lies in more production through technical progress. To have small farms and to limit the use of machinery with the false idea of giving full employment is to prevent all technical progress. To limit output by not using machines is also to limit support to more workers. To increase output per acre by modern methods is thus a far better remedy for the evil of overpopulation than that of stopping the use of machinery and large farms. Where output per acre increases the land can and will support more workers than is possible now.

It is quite possible and proper to agree that family farming is better of course than capitalist farming so far as employment of labour and maintenance of soil fertility are concerned. But it is difficult to believe that our dwarf farms can be better than joint farming for full employment or for maintaining fertility or for other like purposes. On the peasant farms of the size that will be forced on us by the paucity of land it will be impossible for labout to get decent wages or even for the State to fix minimum wages. This aspect of the problem has been almost completely ignored by the lovers of peasant proprietorship.

Since small holdings cannot solve the problem of poverty they cannot also solve the problem of labour employment, housing, or wage agreements. The system of cultivation of small holdings being uneconomical our present-day peasant proprietors are openly talking of resisting any attempt on the part of the State to fix a minimum wage. The desire of Government to do justice ot the labourers and prevent them from becoming communistic-minded is thus likely to be thwarted by the inability of the samll farmer to pay a decent fixed minimum wage. It is not possible to help rural labour and at the same time continue the present system of land ownership under which the employers of labour are themselves poor. European experience shows us that when the supply of labour exceeds the demands of small holders of land no minimum wage contracts can be enforced even if the State were to fix such minimum wages. If there is no redical change in our conceptions about ryotwari and small holdings no great reform in the direction of fixation of hours of work, or unemployment insurance or fixation of wages can be expected.

One of the so-called great justifications of the adoption of a small holdings policy is that it is supposed to enable rural workers to rise to the independent position of farmers and the proportion of labourers who rise to such positions is believed to be higher in agriculture than in any other industry. This was actua''y the case in England not many years ago. Unfortunately an examination of conditions in our ryotwari tracts will show that far from many labourers rising to the position of farmers a very large number of our farmers have been reduced to the level of labourers and this process has been continuous. Ownership of land carries with it great power over the person of the landless worker. Though theoretically it may be true that where we have small properties and a large number of landowners rural labourers have good chances of buying land, in India this does not happen for our landowners are too poor to give wages high enough to enable labourers ot save any money to buy land of any reasonable size.

Peasant Proprietorship and Decentralisation.

An exceedingly strong argument in favour of peasant proprietorship is that it will help us to establish decentralisation in production, an ideal put before us by Mahatma Gandhi. One can well appreciate a man like Gandhiji advocating decentralisation as a part of his programme of 1921 which should be accepted as a logical whole. In this programme the use of non-violence of defensive purposes was the very foundation. Unfortunately many of those who advocate decentralisation are by no means logical. They reject non-violence, expect the country to be organised for armed defence with the best mechanised equipment and talk of central planning in several directions including food production. The fact is that there is some scope for decentralisation but not for decentralisation which must necessitate peasant properitorship.

Gandhiji's greatness consists in his life and work considered as a logical whole, but those who want peasant proprietorship for the sake of decentralisation are unable to show how we can talk of things which are contradictory to one another. Most people agree that we need planning of our economic life, that we require a new agricultural policy based on crop planning and scientific rotation to ensure economic use of land and animal power, that intensive cultivation on scientific lines is necessary, and yet when it comes to actual production they desire complete decentralisation. It is not realised that all our present talk of democracy and decentralisation cannot and will not help us to fight the anarchy of our present agricultural system and that a predatory individualist agriculture and proper planning cannot go together. Planning necessitates strong centralisation and social control whilst its effectiveness depends not on a multiplication of independent units of production but on as small a number as possible of large units of a workable size.

One of our principal tasks in the future economic reorganisation is to increase productivity of labour by supplying labour the material basis of large scale industry-fuel, iron, chemicals, engineering, etc., and by instilling in labour a new sense of discipline and new incentive for work. If we abolish Zamindari in the interests of more production we have also to abolish the other causes of low production such as bad work, indiscipline etc. The Indian worker is supposed to be a bad worker compared with workers of more advanced countries. This was so also in Russia and just as it had to be remedied there we have also to set this defect right here. For the purposes, of supplying the material basis of more wealth through methods of modern technology as well as of instilling a sense of discipline and incentive for hard work, we shall require proper centralisation rather than decentralisation,

Peasant Proprietorship and Democratic Liberty.

Another argument about peasant proprietorship is that it will safeguard and preserve liberty. This land tenure system is supposed to be the only one which will give independent means of support to a maximum number of small cultivators. The arguments used in favour of this view by some writers on land tenures in India somehow savour of a theoretical study of the typical American attitude. They overlook several important aspects of the question whilst studying Economics in American Universities. In America, "Independent proprietors of the soil", were deemed desirable as early as in 1787 and important Americans ever since have accepted the view that ordinary farm tenancy is unfavourable to freedom, destroys love of country and weakens the spirit of independence. In contrast to this the free holder is regarded as "the natural supporter of a free government."

The American view was the result of conditions prevalent there. Where there is enough land the adequate rainfall one can well speak of the essential goodness of private property in land but this cannot and should not be regarded as a great political truth in itself. Where land has been limited in relation to population, ownership of land has not been looked upon with the same social esteem as in America. In many European countries, for example, farm tenancy rather than ownership has been looked upon as necessary for agricultural progress. Tenancy rather than peasant proprietorship has been used as a means of land settlement in Estonia, Holland, England and Italy, as pointed out by experts like Henry W. Spiegel. Prof. Spiegel tells us that there are no farm economists in Europe to-day who would generally and unconditionally condemn farm tenancy. In fact European economists like F. List have regarded the argument that every cultivator must also be owner of land as very absurd. The English economist Pigou has even tried to vindicate farm tenancy by pure economic reasoning.

Since the amount of land here is limited, it is ridiculous not to see that we cannot have both independent means of support as well as such support for maximum number of men. We have to choose between the end and the means. if our end is material prosperity our means cannot be peasant proprietorship or the theoretical talk of liberty which is a poor country is nothing more than the liberty to die of starvation. There are countries where the end has been sacrificed for the means. This is what the great economist Marshal is actually believed to have thought about France and the French peasantry in that country of peasant proprietors. But France has at least the advantage of a population which is not increasing as our own and which in fact is showing trends which are the exact opposite of our population behaviour here.

The argument that peasant proprietorship is essential for liberty is not so sound as it appears. In England the Liberals rejected it long ago when they took up the policy of establishing a State tenantry. On the other hand peasant proprietorship was accepted by the relatively more reactionary conservatives who wanted it to rainforce the voting strength of property. Those who support private ownership of land are by no means always those who want independence of mind and spirit in the people. The basis of true freedom is not ownership of land and if the Yeomen of England are regarded as an example of independent men we may with equal truth show that the Nazi support of peasant proprietorship was not means to encourage real independence of mind but its exacy opposite.

The supporters of peasant proprietorehip believe that this system will be good for social stability Unbelievably exaggerated panegyrics of the system have been sung and it has been held that the system will secure peace on the land, abolish litigation altogether and create an almost classless society. Our experience does not justify these hopes of a system with the peasant, "standing in rags still, yet standing upon his feet..... with his head erect which will bow to none." Where the stomach is empty the head cannot be erect. It is security which gives confidence and acts as the basis of prosperity and activity, and security is what the cultivator lacks to-day and will always lack if we confuse the right to own land with the security of a planned organisation. The right to own land no larger than a family graveyard will be the graveyard of all the high hopes about our peasant proprietors being either contented or independent minded.

Peasant Proprietorship as Means to Self-Sufficiency.

A large number of people imagine that peasant proprietorship will help us to establish a self-sufficing an self-contained society. Several of these men also imagine that all talk of raising the standard of living of the masses is bad, if not a fad of the supporters of mechanised farming. This attitude ignores several fundamental truths both about self-sufficiency as well as about the low standard of living.

Peasant-proprietorship can really have no charms in a society where the standard of living of the cultivators is very low. Low standards of life are often associated with low output per acre even under climatic conditions which are favourable to increased output. It is often said that peasant farming furnishes a great incentive to produce more but in reality the growth of population and continuous decrease in the size of holdings makes this incentive meaningless. It is not possible to sustain any incentive to increased agricultural efficiency unless we can raise the standard of living of the masses. The truth about the impossibility of expecting a permanent increase in food production without a permanent increase in the standard of living has been noticed by English experts but, strangely enough, it has been ignored by us.

We want our cultivators to produce more food but the farmer will not farm better till he is sure of the need of producing more and the inducement to better farming requires fundamental changes in our conceptions about life. Underconsumption is regarded as the effect of under-production but it is equally a cause of low production. Large masses of people lack ambition to rise in life, are ignorant, have faulty methods of farming and are isolated from each other and from the world. The ideal of subsistence farming and self-sufficiency is fatal to the development of any backward people and we cannot perpetuate it in the name of peasant proprietorship, liberty, democracy, etc.

It has been found from the experience of backward subsistence farming in Africa, for example, that even a simple change like sale for cash can induce cultivators to go in for improved methods of production. Even simple improvements in the structure and equipment of the home have proved to be a powerful inducement to better farming since improved methods of production are essential to "support" the more expensive homestead. We may not be as backward as is implied in African farming but the basic principles of progress remain the same none-the-less. To bring in improved methods of production, to use modern knowledge in the service of the masses, to overcome the dependence of the vast masses upon their own petty environment, to increase trade and communications, to break the barriers that separate one group of men from another–is a national and international duty.

A certain amount of self-sufficiency may be desirable but to refuse to use modern scientific knowledge, and to go within our own shells in the name of self-sufficiency, will not only drag down the large portion of the population, of the world which is in India to unnecessary exclusiveness and poverty but it will also have a disastrous effect on the world as a whole. We must strive our best to promote an active exchange of ideas and commodities among the different parts of India as a whole and also between India and her neighbouring countries. It is the exchange of ideas which quicken the mind and break down traditional modes of life and production. International inquiries have shown that unnecessary and excessive protection given to peasant farming and to obsolete methods of farming have prevented all real progress and have served to retain an unnecessarily low standard of living for the rural masses.

We shall see in the next part why we cannot expect any substantial increase in this country's productivity and prosperity on the basis of peasant proprietorship and why the hopes about any such increase in productivity are doomed to fail if we stick to our traditonal but out of date ideas as a solution.

(II)

The supporters of peasant proprietorship belive that the present scarcity of land in relation to the population can be ignored because of the possibilities of developments in two important directions-increase in the area of cultivable land and increase in productivity per acre of the lands under cultivation to-day. Some even add to this the optimistic hope that our birth-rate will also decline due of factors like education of women, late marriages, etc.

Prospects of a Check to Population Growth.

The hope that there will be a fall in our birth-rate even when we continue the system of small farming seems to be very unrealistic. We can of course have changes like education of women, late marriges, improvement in public health measures, etc. but these changes are likely to decrease our death-rate rather than the birth-rate. We know that at present factors like the reduction in infantile and maternal mortality have been increasing rather than decreasing population. As the Census of 1941 points out "even if the infant mortality rate continues to be 160 per mile for the next two decades substantial additions of 6.5 and 11.1 millions are likely to result by 1951 and 1961." Similarly if maternal mortality is reduced from 20 per 1,000 to 10 per 1,000 live births the saving in female life would be over 6 milions in one decade. The ultimate increase in the population would be much more as most of these women would marry and beget children.

We cannot also be too sure that a factor like late marriages of girls will necessarily lead to a decrease in population growth. In fact it is more probable that if our girls do not marry early at about 13 or 14 years their health will improve and this will be favourable to fecundity. As Kuczynski tells us, an improvement in living conditions can expand the child-bearing period and intensify the childbearing capacity. Similarly if we expect improvements in nutrition we cannot expect any decrease in the capacity to bear children, for our famine experience has shown to us that this capacity is kept in check to-day by dietary deficiencies such as of Vitamin E for example.

It would be most improper to expect an automatic fall in the birth-rate in predominantly agricultural country like our own specially if we reject the possibility of necessity of developing an urban industrial environment. It is very risky to ignore the truth that small farmers are inclined to have more children than other, Warriner has tried to argue that it is the families or farm employees rather than farm owners which show the highest reproduction rates. Apart from the fact that this conclusion has been successfully challenged we cannot look upon the question of farm employees and their families as something distinct from that of farm owners.

It may be of some interest to note here some of the findings of the pre-war German Census Bureau as given by Dr. Spiegel . It was found that in Germany fram laboures in general have a few more childern that fram oweners. But, in all occupations, married couples who own land have more children than those without land. Among farm owners, the size of the farm has a definite effect upon the number of children, the number increasing with the size in size groups under five hectares (12 acres). Owners of farms of 5 to 50 hectares have most children whilst the number of children decreases with farms of a size beyond 50 hectares. In the light of facts like the above it is dangerous to ignore the trends of our population growth and keep on believing that peasant proprietorship will solve the problem of population pressure and unemployment. It we want to solve the problem of unemployment we can hardly accept as a solution a remedy which is supposed to increase population not decrease it.

Prospects of Cultivation of More Land.

One of the commonest of fallacies in India is the belief that even if the amount of land at present is not enough to give us substantially large-sized peasant farms we can increase the area under cultivation by developing all the cultivable waste lands of to-day. More irrigation and better manuring of our waste lands are regarded as quite adequate for bringing these lands under the plaugh.

It is of course true that a very large part of our agricultural area lies uncultivated every year both as current fallows as well as culturable waste. Taking both these together we have about 150 million acres on the old British India alone or more if we take the whole of India. If most of this area can be cultivated we can increase the total area under cultivation by more than 50 per cent. The National Planning Committee holds that if we bring under the plough all the culturable waste, including fallows, our total cultivated area in British India alone can be increased by more than 60 per cent. It is wrong however to take it implicitly that the mere existence of all these areas implies that we can bring them immediately under the plough. We have to face the fact that very little of all this extensive area has actually been brought under the plough during the last 30 or more years in spite of the tremendous pressure of population on the land. The percentage of net cropped area to the total area, of old British India, has decreased rather, than increased between 1908-10 to 1937-39 and the maximum point of extensive cultivation was attained in India more than 40 years ago.

We have it on very good authority that most of our so-called cultivable wast land is really uncultivable under present conditions. We cannot make these lands productive and profitable without deep ploughing, adequate irrigation, and extensive use of power-driven machinery for pulverising the soil. The wooden-plough and even the ordinary ironplough of our cultivators would be of no use at all over millions of acres of such lands. Our small holders have neither the resources nor the knowledge and incentive required to cultivate such lands.

The question of capital resources required is vitally important. Where much capital has been and could be invested our cultivable wastes have become really profitable and productive. The late Sir Ganga Ram of the Punjab is reported to have made even his desert land productive through capital expenditure. There have been cultivators even in the Deccan who have made such waste lands cultivable by the use of power-driven machinery that could conquer and pulverise even the hard stones on the land. Such investment of capital is however completely beyond the means of the millions of the owners of to-day.

It is rather unreasonable to expect the small owners of land to bring more wast-land under cultivation when we actully find that these small owners are unable to cultivate properly even the land which is already under the plough. Millions of acres of cultivated land have been left completely neglected .There are very larg stretches of land which are so neglected that they yield to-day only about 1/10th of what they can be made to yield. All such lands as these could produce much more than they do if we had even simple land improvements like proper drainage or irrigation but such improvements also are entirely beyond the means and the initiative of the peasant proprietor.

The under-cultivation, neglect, and misuse of land under private ownership is of course no new thing. It is a very common phenomenon even in advanced countries like U.S.A. and England. It is said that in U.S.A. less than 50 years ago more than 50 per cent. of the land was not properly cleared or reclaimed or irrigated, wherease in England even to-day, and perhaps more to-day than 50 years ago, the neglect of land has almost become a national scandal.

We admit that the proper use and improvement of land is of public interest but we allow individual owners to regard land as private property with the result that such owners prevent others from using and improving what thay do not use or imporve themselves. In most countries valuable land remains unused just because speculators and other individual owners want to sell such land for building and other purposes when prices rise. We find such plots of land in the very heart of prosperous rural areas in India. As Henry George pointed out long ago. "If the best use of land be the test, then private property in land is condemned, as it is condemned by every other consideration."

Prospects of Increase in Productivity Per Acre.

The hope that we will be able to increase productivity per acre under a system of peasant proprietorship is another illusion which is as groundless as the hope about a stabilisation of population without any industrialization or increase in our standard of living. Our average yield of some of the principal crops like rice is the lowest in the world or very near that. It is also true that our low productivity is not entirely due to pressure of population or the size of our average holdings for in population and size of holdings we resemble China and Japan and yet the yield of some crops in Japan is three times and in China twice as much as our own. It would be wrong however to presume that because of this we can expect a great increase in productivity without any change in the present technique of production and in the present system of private ownership of agricultural land.

Some people imagine that if it was possible to increse food production in other countries like Britain by 70 per cent. or even more, we can also increase our production without any change either in technique or in the ownership of land. The improvements normally suggested are the use of better seed, better and more adequate manures, more irrigation, and control of crop pests and diseases. It is expected that whilst better seeds, manure and crops protection will increase the yield of some of our principal crops by about 30 per cent., more irrigation will increase the yield further to about the same extent-which means that all these put together will increase the yield by at least 60 per cent., if not more, over the present level. This expectation is even supposed to be below the real possibilities.

The optimism about the technological possibilities of more production is justified normally by a reference to an excellent Report issued on the subject by Dr. Burns who was Agricultural Commissioner with the Government of India. This optimism however is not justified at all and becomes meaningless when all the views of Dr. Burns are put together and his conclusions are analysed very carefully.

Dr. Burns's Report on Technological Possibilities in India is in reality a study of the failure of agriculture in India during the last three decades to develop on the basis of individual initiative and freedom. The Report reveals the tragedy of a country where there were no restrictions on individualistic predatory agriculture and no real policy to shape the course of production. It shows a continually declining yield per acre of the principal crops like rice and wheat. During two decades (1921-1942) the cultvated area under major food grains declined by over 2 million acres and the production of major food grains by as much as 8.6 million tons.

Dr. Burns' Report must be read with greater care than what is devoted to it by certain technical experts who believe that economists are a nuisance and what is required is just nothing more than better seeds, better manures and a few other technical advances of this type. No doubt Dr. Burns refers tothe need for utilising the services of Zamindars and Talukdars for land improvement but if he can be blamed for not being a little more of an ecomomist himself he at least felt the need for compulsion and controlled collective action much more clearly than many other. In his words "most of the anti-waste measures can only be carried out by collective action......Even in activities where individual effort would seem to be most rewarded.....there are great advantages in collective action .... We must mot be afraid of invoking a certain degree of compulsion." He clearly pointed out that modern technological methods required for more agricultural productivity "the increase in the size of productive units." It was not his fault if he felt that it was we who were not prepared to accept the full implication of this.

Dr. Burns emphasised the great need for mechanisation also. If on the contrary we stick to our fad about peasant proprietorship we must admit that in a system of small holdings and subsistence farming mechanisation can have no real place. It is not for nothing that Dr. Burns has quoted approvingly the appreciative remarks of such an impartial British authority as Sir Daniel Hall regarding Soviet Russia and her new system of agriculture.

Apart from the implications of Dr. Burns' Report one must not ignore the simple reasons why too much of confidence in the ordinary use of things like better seeds, manures, etc, will result in great disappointment. A large number people have great faith in the possibility of using better seeds in the immediate present. It is felt that this should be the easiest possible thing to do. But even this socalled simple reform is not so simple as it appears. With the exception of wheat, the main food crops are grown for the most part even to-day with non-improved seed. The introduction of improved varieties require higher fertility of the soil and if we do nothing to improve fertility of the soil the use of such improved varieties may result in a lower yield than before. This is what several experiments have shown. It is necessary to note before it is too late that things like use of better manure, irrigation, or improved plants through selection and cross-breeding are not possible without a considerable change in the present technique of cultivation.

The question of more production cannot be divorced from that of cost and the question of cost in turn cannot be divorced from that of the general organisation that we want to set up. More production involves extensive State help and State control which cannot be objected to on grounds of democracy or liberty. According to the Food Plan for India about 4½ maunds of paddy per acre is the average increase in yield which we may expect from an improvement like the use of fertilisers. The use of improved seeds is expected to increase yield of paddy further by about 3 maunds per acre. The Food Plan tells us that if we take the minimum total increase in yield to be only 3 maunds of paddy per acre, then the calculations of cost of the normal cultivator to-day show that it would be necessary to subsidise production and distribution of fertilisers unless the price of paddy is not allowed to fall below a certain level (Rs. 2 per maund).

Problems of increase in productivity are much more complex than we imagine. We cannot consider simple things like better seed, irrigation, manures, etc. in isolation from each other. When we consider the inter-relation between all these and then consider the question of cost we realise the enormity of the problem. If we take the cost of irrigation to begin with here, how can we ignore the fact that we have very high irrigation costs and very low percentage return to Government in certain parts of the country, such as Bombay Province. C.P. and Berar, Hyderabad, the Central India States, etc.? It has been estimated that the annual capital cost per acre irrigated in Bombay Province to-day comes to Rs. 501 and Bombay must spend about Rs. 160 crores if we want irrigation facilities all over the Province. If we take India as a whole we will have to invest about Rs. 1,300 crores for bringing about 125 million acres under irrigation. Even if we ignore the question of this cost, more irrigation means less fertility for the soil unless we have enough soil to keep fallow or enough manure to restore this fertility.

Just as we do not have enough soil to keep fallow we do not also have enough manures to keep the soil highly productive. The most improtant manure is farmyard manure but its supply is limited. It is extremely difficult to-day to increase farmyard manure without increasing the number of farm animals on land. To-day we need land for growing as much food for human beings as possible rather than for growing fodder. The methods of use and collection of farmyard manure are defactive and these defects cannot be easily rectified. We cannot stop the present use of farmyard manure as fuel unless we have enough wood to use as fuel which is another impossibility as it requires the existence of at least 60 acres under fuel trees in each village or about 42 million acres all over India. One of the main types of manure we can use in provinces like Bombay is ground-nut cake; but developmetns in ground-nut cultivation itself require irrigation apart from the fact that such development may lead to the use of ground-nut cake more as food than as manure to produce more food. Regarding other manures we do not have even 25 per cent. of the oil-cake we require whilst the chances of an extensive use of composts and chemical manures are equally limited.

Proper irrigation and introduction of improved strains in crops like sugarcane and cotton are not so advantageous as we suppose when the size of holdings is small and the chance to use manure is still smaller. So bad has been the effect of these on the fertility of the soil in the case of the small holdings in the United Provinces for example, that in many areas during the last few years the percentage of double-cropped to cultivated area has actually decreased. Larger holdings could at least be given some rest but the growing of sugarcane and cotton on the small holdings has robbed the soil of its fertility and decreased the total returns. The peasant has no other choice there except to decrease his double-cropped area "although this means a still lower standard of farming and living."

There is a tendency to ignore the fact that when we plan for more productivity per acre what we want is a change in quality as well as quantity. It is comparatively easy to produce more of the inferior varieties of food than we do but what we really require is not exactly this. A reasonably careful calculation made shows us that if we take the food shortage of Bombay Province to-day be about 800,000 tons of food grain and pulses, it is possible to produce through the two methods of counter-bunding and better seeds alon this much extra quantity of Jowar and Bajree. But this can hardly be set of against the real needs of a shortage of 440,000 tons of rise and 240,000 tons of wheat. An extra increase of these inferior cereals is meaningless if we accept the contention that even to-day about 400,000 tons of Bombay's cereals are so inferior that they are not fit to be included even in the present dietary of the people.

It is clear that if by more productivity per acre we mean better food production to satisfy the standards prescribed for minimum healthy nutrition, we will require extensive State irrigation, improvements in plant breeding, and a host of other changes which are impossible without improvements like better methods of cultivation, intensified manuring and farming, crop-planning based on scientific rotation and the like.

Low Productivity and Capitalization of Small Farms.

Those who expect that productivity per acre will increase under peasant proprietorship and small holdings should remember that small farms and increasing productivity do not go together. Careful studies of the productivity of small farms made by individual writers like Sir A.D. Hall and by other experts on behalf of the League of Nations like Mr. Wilbert E. Moore have shown that there are many disadvantages of small farming. The fact that the small owner of land is not able to provide sufficient capital and attention to land so as to increase production is now recognised as a universal evil.

There are people in India who still believe in and quote Arthur Young's dictum that the magic of property turns sand into gold. They do not know that this dictum has been proved to be false even in England itself. Though Sir A.D. Hall is inclined to believe that the small holders of land in some cases have shown greater progress than the big owners he tells us equally clearly that there is no more deceptive half-truth which has ever found acceptance than the above dictum of Sir Arthur Young. Inquiries made during 1914-1918 in England have proved that many of the worst cases of neglected farms were found to be in owner occupation.

The main factor which has made private ownership of land in England almost a national scandal in of course the inability of the landowners to spare much capital for land improvements. The landlords of England, both small and big, have lost their old love of the land as agricultural enterprise has become a liability for them. There has been a tendency to sell away lands to their tenants but the tenants have not been so willing to acquire ownership as is imagined. Ownership is sometimes acquired to prevent the sale of the holdings to new landlords but the shrewd English tenants know that they have no financial means to undertake improvements and increased productivity. If even big and rich landlords as in England have not been able to provide capital for land improvement what hopes can we have of our poverty stricken owners of dwarf farms to increase productivity through more capital investment ?

Evidence collected by the League of Nations shows that all over Eastern and Southern Europe where small farms have been encouraged low productivity of agriculture is one of the most serious of all results. This is due to many factors of which the most important is relatively low capitalization. The small farmer there, as in India, has not much liquid capital while the need for such capital is very great. The prevalence of high indebtedness relative to assets and income are sure signs of a very slow and very low self-capitalization in agriculture. In India far from accumulating capital our farmers have lived largely on their borrowings and repidly depleting resources. European experience shows us that when due to capital depletion we have soil exhaustion, poor equipment, and increasing indebtedness, "the process may be a spiral escaped only by capital originating outside of agricultural organisation."

Low capitalization can also be in the form of low fixed capital. In small holdings things like buildings, farm animals, ploughs, etc. are much below the quantity and quality required and so is also the expenditure on irrigation, drainage and other means for improving the soil. Where holdings are very small we may also have on the other hand overcapitalization in relation to the small area of the holding. The farmer may have a pair of bullocks and a plough which he may not be able to use fully. We find from research done by the Agricultural Economic section of the Agricultural Department, Bombay, that even in prosperous tracts like "Charotar" (Kaira District, Bombay) the farmer is not able to use fully even one bullock and plough and that the bullock remains unemployed for 60 per cent. of its employable time. It is easy to see that when fixed costs are heavy in relation to the area cultivated they decrease profits and thus affect the accumulation of liquid capital. This is proved also from European experience which has taught us that on the whole the large farm is better than the very small one for the simple reason that on the former the cultivator can derive a higher unit yield from his livestock and equipment costs. On the whole, therefore, liquid capital accumulates more on the large than on the small agricultural holding.

High Capitalization and Accumulation of Farm Capital on Small Farms depends on Animal Husbandry and Abundance of Land.

One of the principal methods for rapid accumulation of farm capital on small holdings is the development of mixed farming with a definite emphasis on live-stock products rather than the cultivation of inferior cereals and pulses as is the case to-day. Where livestock farming is introduced the small farmer tends to put his savings into more livestock which is a real productive asset. On the other hand when we have only grain farming, the peasant has either no savings at all or he invests his savings, if and when he has them, in more land which does not increase his productive assets but merely raises land prices.

It is generally presumed that peasant farming is more successful in Western Europe than in Eastern Europe. According to experts like Yates and Warriner what justifies this peasant farming there, is the much greater amount of capital per head in the form of more land and livestock than in Eastern Europe. This may even make peasant farming more justifiable than large-scale mechanised farming. But this is not possible everywhere for the chances of having animal husbandry depend on the amount of land available, apart from other facts. Where therefore conditions favourable to capital accumulation are not ther one can hardly go on dreaming of great prosperity under peasant farming.

Absurdity of the Belief that Small Farming in India is Good for Intensive Production and Soil Fertility.

Those who advocate peasant proprietorship often do so on vague feelings that peasant farming is good because it carries "more cattle to the acre than the large farm, that is to say, more capital," that "it promotes intensive production through investing in farm livestock," that "only the family farm can be relied upon to maintain soil fertility" and so on. There is also a definite tendency to accept blindly the viewpoint of writers like Warriner that the total volume of savings in a peasant economy is greater than in a system of large estates. How fallacious most of these beliefs are will be easily realised from what we have noted above. The viewpoint that the peasant can accumulate more capital than is possible in a system of large operating units has been challenged effectively by writers like Wilbert Moore and Carl Brinkmann.

The fallacy in the belief that family farms are a good means for maintaining soil fertility, will be noticed at once by any one who realizes that the small farmer of dwarf holdings is forced throughout the world to deplete his capital which not only prevents him from adding farmyard manures and other fertilizers to the soil but forces him to get the highest yield at the lowest cost irrespective of the harm done to the soil. Small farming both in Eastern Europe and in India involves shallow ploughing by primitive equipment, complete neglect of soil erosion, and the use of manure as fuel. Even where manure is not used as fuel its quantity is limited as usual due to the difficulty in developing livestock farming as we have seen.

We may note a few other disadvantages of small farms which have been pointed out by authoritative writers already mentioned before. Peasants on small farms are unable to weather short-term crisis. Similarly the position of the landless farm worker "is most acute not in those countries where the large estates occupy a large proportion of the agricultural land but in those countries where the family farm is the usual agricultural undertaking." Due to low productivity and absence of diversification small farming has led to a low level of living and great poverty, diets are poor and lack protective foods and housing facilities are also very poor.

The Need for Understanding the Implications of the Opinion of Mr. B. Seebohm Rowntree and Professor Marshal.

Those who are too optimistic about improving the lot of the peasant proprietor may do well to note the judgment of no less a person than Mr. B. Seebohm Rowntree, a world famous expert on Belgian agriculture. "Belgian experience has shown that it would be quite possible to have a country consisting almost entirely of peasant proprietors, obliged to work very unreasonably hard to maintain a comparatively low standard of comfort. We cannot then hope to materially improve the lot of the small agriculturist by the mere creation of a class of peasant proprietors."

We are too often prone to associate prosperity with peasant proprietorship and we think that because this system satisfies the peasant's love for possessing land it must also make him happy. The reality may be that where we have both prosperity and peasant proprietorship the former may be largely the result of reasons other than ownership of land itself. Writers like Turnor have admitted that the causes of prosperity are many and it cannot be implied that ownership itself is the only cause of such prosperity. Similarly, if peasants are proud of their possession of land, as in France, this does not necessarily mean any real prosperity. It was reported some years ago that the French peasants subsisted on the worst possible diet and lived in their kitchen for economy. Many travellers in France, and other authorities have been of the view that the paid farm labourers of England earned bettter incomes and led happier lives than the proprietary peasants of France. The great economist Marshall himself believed that the French peasant proprietors were even poorer than the English tenant farmers.

Small Farming is the Enemy of our National Goal of More Production.

Our national goal in the immediate present according to the chosen leaders of the people like Pandit Jawaharlal Nehru and Sardar Vallabhbhai Patel is more production in every field of our economic life. If this is our goal we cannot afford to neglect the tragic lessons of the failure of peasant proprietorship in Eastern and Southern Europe. Practically throughout these regions, which resemble us in poverty and relative overpopulation, the solution of peasant proprietorship has ignored the improtance of an overall increase in agricultural production. In fact an increase in oproduction was not a primany goal of the institutional changes in agriculture introduced there. The purpose of the land reform in most of these countries was to distribute wealth rather than to produce it. Those who doubt this may refer to important publications of the League of Nations, Geneva. This purpose of the land reform was probably a great mistake but whatever we may say about the wisdom or unwisdom of what has been done in Europe, we cannot afford to make similar mistakes here. If our ideal is more production how can we accept a solution which has failed to increase production ? It is gratifying to see that many, if not all, of those who are really serious about increased production in India, admit that a system of small holdings will not be capable of producing the food which the country requires. Among these men we have many high officials of the Government of India.

It is unfortunate but true that non-official opinion in India has not proved to be very realistic on this question of land tenure. Though this many be an exception to the general rule the official experts seem to show a greater sense of reality at least on this question. One may expect in a democracy men who are more rich than learned to beat the big drum of their own publicity but this becomes dangerous when the public are not fully conversant with the intricacies of a technical subject like this. There has been too much of a tendency among a few non-officals to rush in where even the real experts on world agriculture would fear to tread.

We have to note that even where there are more favourable circumstances than our own the great authorities on family farming are by no means unanimous or over-confident about its utility. It is true that some authorities, like Karl Brandt, are not enthusiastic about large-scale farming. Professor Brandt tells us : "We warn most solemnly against toying with the idea of destroying the existing rural structure of family farms." There are others however who have warned us equally seriously about toying with the idea of family farming. Sir A.D. Hall tells us. "Men toy with the idea of a rural community that will be approximately self-contained, one that farms to feed the family rather than to earn money." Besides not even men like Karl Brandt have been able to ignore the importance of economic progress which is the only realistic approach to the solution of the population problem in countries like ours. The book by Warriner and Karl Brandt are the bible of the blind supporter of the Indian peasant proprietary system. But these two writers are by no means so over-enthusiastic as some of our Indian writers. It is certainly a mistake to think that Warriner regards peasant farming as the only solution to the farm problem even of Europe with a population problem less acute than of ours. She is inclined in fact to accept a redistribution of the farm population to regions outside Europe as the only solution if economic progress and political stability are to be attained.

Where Population Cannot be Reduced Production Must be Increased.

The question before us is very clear. Do we expect to have only a self-contained rural community of poverty stricken peasants or do we also want to take advantage of science and of all other organisational large-scale imporvements based on both mechanisation and industrialisation ? Situated as we are we find in all countries there are really speaking only two real solutions. We have either to reduce population or increase production. We may of course have both these but where population cannot be reduced or stabilised production must be increased with all possible speed with the help of all that science can give us.

We have seen in the early part of this chapter that we cannot hope to see any substantial decrease in our birth-rate if we adhere to the plan of small - farming and all its implications in the orthodox sense of the term. It is true that Emigration is another powerful weapon for fighting the evil of relative or absolute overpopulation. It has been used extensively in Europe in several countries. It provided an effective escape in the past for rural populations of some of the overpopulated European regions. Previous to the first World War there was a transoceanic emigration from Poland to the United States, Canada and Argentina. There was emigration also from countries like Scotland, Ireland, Spain, Yugoslavia, etc. The question of emigration has however become very complicated during the last few years and to-day it is fit only for academic discussion. After the first Great War overseas emigration fell off and restrictions were imposed everywhere in the countries which used to receive outsiders. Problems of assimilation of alien elements and cultures are great obstacles even for the European countries.

If the only other solution is more prodution our main task to-day is to increase the size of our cultivating units and to make labour more productive in relation to the land that is cultivated. If we want to increase production we cannot resist the use of scientific agriculture and industrialisation considered in relation to the cultivation of all our waste lands, the use of intensive and mixed farming and large-scale investment of capital in land improvements of all kinds. We must set aside all the academic talk of peasant proprietorship as a bulwark of liberty and democracy. We require constructive positive planning by the State with the power to set aside ruthlessly all who come in the way of national prosperity by the meaningless talk of freedom and private initiative. We have had too much of freedom and initiative for the food hoarder, black marketeer and landlords who have used them freely to destroy all real freedom.

The Real Solution of Our Problem.

In the succeeding chapter we shall see how co-operative and collective cultivation will help us to solve the problem of our small uneconomic holdings. Before we go to that we may note here the absolute necessity of three things–positive constructive planning by the State, the introduction of scientific agriculture based on as much use of machinery as possible and, thirdly, the introduction of large-scale industrialisation. If the lessons of the world are to be of any use to us we should remember the warning given by the European Conference on Rural Life, 1939, regarding the problem of overpopulated rural regions. So far the methods of relief applied have been imperfect and the results of partial legislative reform have been inadequate. Nothing has so far been done to rescue the population from extreme poverty and chronic deterioration. The problem of rural reconstruction of over-populated regions is very complicated and no piecemeal treatment will succeed.

Both the abolition of Zamindari as well as the reconstruction of land tenure require the setting up of a strong executive authority with centralised powers of co-ordination and compulsion. The warning expressed before must be repeated. Our legislatures must not learn merely to talk before our executives learn to act. A strong executive ant the setting up of Planning Boards, regional if necessary, is our first great need. The question of mechanisation is closely connected with strong State control and nationalisation and deserves a chapter by itself. We also require heavy investment of capital per acre and large-scale industrialisation.

The neglect of the need for more investment of capital per acre and of the question of industrialisation has been a very serious cause of our inability to do anything really substantial. Since the amount of land in India is limited we must make up for this by considerable increase in the investment of capital per acre specially when we know how the low productivity of our agriculture is one of the direct results of the very low capitalisation under peasant farming.

The Question of Industrialisation.

From the pure economic point of viwe it is impossible to conceive of any great developmet in our agriculture without a general economic and industrial development. Industrialisation is practically the first and the most important necessity in all overpopulated countries and is regarded as such all over Europe wherever conditions are similar to our own. It will be noticed that even in the so-called "non industrial" countries of Eastern and Southern Europe we have got a fair degree of industrialisation. We have been told that some of these countries were expanding their industrial production between 1919-1939 more rapidly than the older industrial countries of Western Europe. This applies also to the most backward of countries like Yugoslavia, Bulgaria and Poland. Copper and bauxite mines have been developed in Yugoslavia, and Poland has witnessed much development in her coal-mining and textile industries.

Industrialisation is not only necessary for armed defence but even more necessary for farming itself and for improving our agricultural technique and efficiency. Industrialisation will help to absorb out unemployed surplus farm labour whilst mixed farming and cultivation of protective foods and other like developments in farming require wide markets with high purchasing power which urbanisation will create.

Those who underestimate the importance of industrialisation in India forget that from the point of view of production, labour is more effective in industries as compared to agriculture. About 67.2 per cent. of our total working population is engaged in Agriculture but produces only a little more than half of the national dividend (53 per cent.) whereas 10.2 of the working population engaged in Industry and Mining produces 17 per cent. of the national wealth. It is also believed that there is a wide selection of industries in which our comparative disadvantage in production is less than in agriculture. An Indian cotton mill, or an iron factory, equipped with modern machinery and working under other advantages such as the procurement of raw materials at home, etc. is likely to suffer less by comparison with corresponding mills or factories in Europe than our badly equipped average small cereal producing farm does by contrast with the farms of the New World or even of Western Europe.

One of the most important of the economic effects of industrialisation is on the pressure of population of the soil. It reduces this pressure and helps to maintain a more balanced occupational distribution of population. We have before us the example of Japan with conditions similar to our own. The proportion of agricultural workers to the total there in 1872 was as high as 84.8 per cent. which through industrialisation was reduced to 71.8 per cent. in 1887, 61.5 per cent. in 1912, 53.5 per cent. in 1920 and 50.3 per cent. in 1930. Industrialisation may not help us to reduce our population pressure to these limits or even to the extent we desire. There are economists who feel that mechanisation and industrialisation will have to absorb 30 millon workers in 10 years time and they think this absorption is not possible. We have the example of Soviet Russia where in spite of her gigantic 5-Year Plans for industrialisation 66 per cent of her population is still rural. However, it is very important to note that in spite of her rural character the growth of the population on the land has been arrested in Soviet Russia and the country has now reached a point at which the number of people engaged in agriculture is beginning to fall. So far as India is concerned much depends upon the amount of industrialistion that we have but even it industrialisation is not very rapid and it does not work wonders all at once it will at least make us less rural than we are.

Besides the economic advantages, industrialisation will have great and beneficial effects in our reproductive behaviour, a fact which should induce us to accept it even if it had no other result of any kind. We have already seen before something of the relationship between fertility rate and urbanisation. Whilst the great authorities on depopulation like Rivers, Raymond Pearl, Buxton, Roberts, Baker, etc. differ somewhat among themselves there is a general agreement on the point that environmental factors (like standard of living and education) are more important than genetic factors. The higher the degree of urbanisation and industrialisation that we have the lower will be the fertility and growth rate of our population. This is a world truth and India is but a part of this world.

Another most valuable effect of industrialisation in India will be that it will teach us to establish a more secular life than we have. Through a decided secularisation of our social structure it will divert our attention away from narrow communalistic and religious conflicts which are used to-day to hide the real evils of the land problem and the urgency of their abolition. In conclusion we can say that if in a country like ours, reduction of population or increased production are the only two possible solutions of overpopulation the development of industrialisation should be doubly welcomed because it helps to bring about both these desired objectives.

3

The Meston Settlement

It is not quite correct to give it that name, but it may, since it has become current, be used to describe the present allocation of fiscal resources between the Central and Provincial Governments. The introduction of this settlement was a new departure in the development of Provincial finance, and was necessitated by a redical change in the conception of the place of the Provinces in the Indian political system. It was an integral part of the process 'of devolution, of drawing lines of demarcation, of cutting long-standing ties', which was the foundation on which the structure of the Reforms was erected; and it was pivoted on the abolition of the 'divided' heads. The fact that the financial settlements were based on Provincial needs was taken as the cause of the Central control of Provincial expenditure, and as the Government of India took a share of the proceeds of certain taxes, they were considered to have a direct motive for interfering in the details of administration. In view of these considerations, it was taken for granted that the Provinces could not become self-governing unless they adjusted their expenditure according to their income, and there was a definite and complete separation of resources. The new settlement was, therefore, to be based on revenues and not on needs, and made completely free from the 'taint of the divided heads'. There was to be not only separation but also what the Americans call segregation of resources, and expenditure on Provincial subjects from Central revenues was to be completely banned. There was to be no overlapping between the domains of Central and Provincial taxation, and each authority was to have not only independent sources of revenue, but also an exclusive right to use them for its own purposes, and the other authority was not even to enjoy concurrent powers with regard to them. This was the new doctrine of the financial 'clean cut' which determined and circumscribed the allocation of resources in the new settlement.

The new scheme was, therefore, a corollary of the new system of government which the authors of the Reforms sought to establish in India. It was sketched by them in paragraphs 201-210 of their *Report,* and its fundamental principles were later on accepted as sound by the Government of India, the Functions Committee, the Joint Select Committee of Parliament, and the Financial Relations Committee. These principles, as stated above, started from a new standpoint. The Provinces were to be given the largest measure of independence of the Government of India, and could attain the higher political status which they were to be given only when they had their own financial resources and final powers over their budgets. The Central Govenment was to have resources for the upkeep and development of services of all-India importance, and all other resources were to be handed over to the Provinces. This did not mean that on the financial side the Provinces were to be granted all residuary powers, for in paragraph 210 of the *Report,* in view of the ultimate responsibility of the Government of India for the security of the country as a whole, the authors of the *Report* definitely provided against proposals which might trench on their field of taxation or in any way impair their supreme authority. But the Provinces were to have large and buoyant sources of revenue for the development of the functions appertaining to their spheres, the vital importance of which for the well-being of the nation had of course to be taken as an admitted fact. The introduction of wide measures of legislative and administrative devolution rendered it necessary that the Provinces should be given distinct and growing sources of revenue.

This decision regarding the disposal of the divided heads gave rise to the difficult problem of their allocation. It was solved mainly by the consideration of administrative convenience or what Seligman would call efficiency. Each Government was to be given the sources of revenue which properly beloged to it, i.e. those which could be conveniently and efficiently administered by it, Customs, salt and opium were already Central heads, and it was taken for granted that they should be allocated to the Central Government. Land revenue and income-tax, however, were divided heads, and it was necessary to assign them either to the Central Government or to the Provincial Governments. It was proposed to make land revenue a Provincial head on account of its intimate connexion with administration in rural areas. This consideration was held conclusive, and the soundness of the proposal was taken as self-evident. As regards income-tax two reasons were urged in favour of making it a Central head. The first was the necessity for maintaining a uniforms rate throughout the country on account of the inconvenience of having different rates in different Provinces. The other was the necessity of avoiding multiple taxation in the case of ramifying enterprises. The complications arising from the difficulty of reconciling the conflicting claims of domicile and status were anticipated by centralizing this important source of revenue. Excise was made Provincial on grounds which cannot be considered adequate in themselves, but were accepted as sufficient by the authors of the scheme. It was stated that excise was to be made a Provincial receipt as it was already Provincial in Bombay, Bengal and Assam, and there was no valid reason why it should not be not made Provincial throughout India. The fact that it has been assigned to the central government in all federal countries should in itself have suggested a doubt regarding the soundness of making it a Provincial head in India, but this consideration was not taken into account owing to the horizon being limited by Indian conditions. Stamps were to be Central on account of the advisability of avoiding discrepancies of rates, while court-fees were to be assigned to the Provinces and court-fees were to be assigned to the Provinces and regarded by them as a means of augmenting their resources. Irrigation was also handed over to the Provinces on account of its close connexion with land revenue. Forests and registration were already Provincial; and, as in other cases, it was assumed that it was not necessary to disturb the existing arrangements.

This scheme was based on two other assumptions, which were not explicitly stated, but were taken as essentially valid for the division of resources. One was that the interest of equity required that all the Provinces should be given the same sources of revenue; or, in other words, uniformity was considered necessary for equality of treatment. Till 1920, as already stated, there was no uniformity as regards the percentage of each divided head of revenue allotted to the Provinces in spite of the fact that the Government of India had laid down the principle of uniformity in 1904, and it was endorsed by the Decentralization Commission in 1909. Now, however, the soundness of the principle was accepted as obvious, and it was not felt even necessary to formulate it. In the second place, it was assumed that the resources assignd to the Provinces gave them revenues which were theirs by right, and also that they should adjust their expenditure to them; and it, of course, followed that the receipts from the Central heads were the property of the Government of India and could be used only for all-India purposes. It was held that the scheme gave to the Provinces what was of the Provinces, and gave to the Government of India what was of the country as a whole. By a coincidence, the strangeness of which did not even strike the authors of the scheme, a settlement dictated primarily by the considerations of administrative convenience also answered the needs of equity, and each Government got what was really its own. It was admitted that the scheme under which income-tax was a Central and land revenue a Provincial head would be somewhat unfair to the Provinces which had large industrial and commercial interests, for income-tax was recognized as only the industrial and professional complement of land revenue. But this consideration was not allowed to have any weight in the allotment of revenues, as it was thought that it was impossible 'to extend the principles of equality to individual heads of revenue'. It was claimed by the authors of the scheme that it secured equality of treatment between on Province and another, and otherwise provided a suitable basis for the new financial settlement.

To this comforting conclusion there was, however, one very important exception. According to this distribution of resources, the income of the Government of India fell short of the expenditure on services for which they were made responsible, and it was necessary to meet the resultant deficit. The authors of the Reforms were hard put to it to suggest methods by which this end could be achieved. They discussed three or four alternative methods, but rejected them all as they did not fit in with the existing facts; and they then proposed to make up the deficit by levying fixed contributions on the Provinces to be assessed as a percentage of the difference between the gross Provincial revenues and the gross Provincial expenditure, both to be calculated on the basis of the proposed scheme for the division of resources and functions. Taking the figures of 1917–18 as the basis of their calculations, they concluded that, if each Province contributed 87 per cent of its gross surplus, the Central budget would be balanced. This proposal laid bare the difficulty which was inherent in the whole scheme, but was not otherwise clearly perceived. The fact that some of the Provinces, under the plan, were to be called upon to bear a much heavier proportion of the Central deficit than others at once challenged attention, and had to be explained. The difficulty was got over by admitting that it was there already, and that there was no way of avoiding it. 'The plan,' it was stated, 'continues the disparity which is at present masked by the system of divided heads.' The worst that could be said against it was that it made the inequalities which were latent in the old settlement patent to the eye, but it was easier to put up with them in as much as the contributions were to be a transitional feature of an other wise even and well-balanced scheme of allocation of resources. This disparity among the Provinces, it was assumed, arose on account of the inequality of their contributions; and, with their cessation, they would all be put on the same footing and get the resources to which they were entitled by the dispensations of Providence.

The Provinces, which were prejudicially affected by the plan, thought more of the immediate burdens than of the distant gains and lodged vehement protests against it. A scheme by which Madras had to pay five times as much as Bombay, the United Provinces also about five times as much as Bengal, and the Punjab and Burma much more than other and richer Provinces obviously made very invidious distinctions, and could not be tolerated as a necessary evil even for the time being. The Government of India saw the point of these protests, and contended on behalf of the Provinces that an arrangement which undoubtedly disclosed their true position in the past did not justify the continuance of these inequalities in the future. They suggested that the initial scale of contributions should be treated as provisional, and steps be taken to fix a standard scale to be determinded on some equitable basis. As the whole question, according to them, needed skilled investigation, they urged that a committee of experts be appointed to enquire into the matter, and recommend the initial and standard scale of contributions, This view was endorsed by the Joint Committee of Parliament, and accordingly a committee consisting of Lord Meston, Mr. Charles Roberts and Sir E. Hilton Young was appointed to report on the question of contributions.

This committee, which we may henceforth call by its popular name-The Meston Committee-submitted its report with great expedition. The only question which was referred to the committee in the first instance was the question of contributions, and later they were asked to advise whether Bombay should be allowed to retain any share of the revenue derived from income-tax. The Committee found it difficult to treat this issue as applicable to one Province only, and upheld the objections of the authors of the Joint Report against the provincialization of income-tax. Their main task, however, was to suggest the initial and standard scale of contributions. It is necessary to bear this in mind, as generally it is assumed, that the whole financial settlement was brought under review and reported upon by them. They, as a matter of fact, stated definitely that since the scheme of re-distribution of resources proposed in the Joint Report had already been approved by the Joint Select Committee they considered it outside their duty to advise any alteration in it unless they found the strongest reason for a change. The only change, which they recommended, was that general stamps should be made a Provincial head throughout India, instead of a Central head, as proposed in the Joint Report. They gave two reasons in support of their proposal. The first was that it was necessary to make this change 'to secure a genuine and complete separation of resources', as otherwise stamps would continue to be divided head of revenue. The other reason given by them was that, without this change, some of the poorer Provinces would start with little or no surplus, and the initial distribution of the Central deficit would be difficult. They based their calculations on the revised estimates of revenue and expenditure of 1991-20, and fixed the deficit of the Government of India at Rs. 9.83 crores. This amount had to be distributed among the Provinces. They did not approve of the proposal to levy the contributions as an all-round ratio of the normal surplus of the Provinces. This, according to them, was not desirable as there was a difference of opinion regarding the normal standard of expenditure, and a uniform ratio would leave out of account the special needs of particular Provinces. They made allowance for very great disparity in the financial strength of the Provinces, and gave exceptional treatment to Burma, the Central Provinces, Bihar and Orissa, and Assam, and proposed to assess the initial contributions on the increased spending power of the Province, i.e. the additional income which a Province would acquire on the introduction of the new scheme of the scparation of resources. They also suggested a standard scale of contributions, which was to be worked up to in seven years, based on the taxable capacity of the Provinces. It is not necessary to say anything about the ideal scale of contributions as it was not incorporatd in the settlement approved by Parliament; but the fixed ratios suggested by them as representing an equitable basis of the relative contributions of the Provinces were based on considerations of a very nebulous character; and the committee, in assessing the relative taxable capacity of the Provinces in the short time which they had at their disposal, betrayed an utter lack of appreciation of the complexity of the task which they had undertaken. This fact, however, need not be stressed any further, as it has no bearing on the present financial position. It is of greater importance to point out the significance of the fact that the Meston Committee modified the original proposals of the Joint Report by attaching some weight at least to the general financial position of each Province, and the more imminent claims upon its resources; in other words they were, to a certain extent, influenced by the consideration of the needs of the Provinces in fixing the initial contributions, and accorded, as stated above, preferential treatment to four Provinces. They did not go far enough in making the adjustment of resources to needs to affect or alter the essential character of the settlement, but they had a dimunderstanding of the difficulties which the latter sought to evade in vain.

The change was, however, of a very inconsequential character, and the burden of Central expenditure was unevenly distributed in spite of a change in the basis of assessment of contributions. Madras, the United Provinces and the Punjab had to bear 35½, 24½ and 18 per cent respectively of the total initial contribution, making 78 per cent of the whole; while Bengal and Bombay contributed only 6½ and 5½ per cent of the levy respectively. The Meston Committee also followed the line of argument, which had been urged in the Joint Report, in meeting the objection that the scheme imposed disproportionately heavy burdens on some provinces. The contributions were not new or additional burdens. They were only a temporary expedient; and their weight was the best index of the amount of the gains of the Provinces, both immediate as well as eventual, under the new financial scheme. The Provinces which had to pay more were merely asked to forgo for a period the full enjoyment of their ulitimate advantages; and all, it was stated, would be well when the Government of India remitted the contributions, the reduction and the eventual cessation of which was to be the first charge on the improvement of their revenues. The problem of inequalities was considered only as a part of the problem of assessment of contributions, but the fact that inequalities of revenue and expenditure would continue even after the extinction of the contributions was not held to be of any consequence or importance either by the authors of the Reforms or by the Meston Committee.

The Joint Select Committee of Parliament considerd the Meston Committee's Report, approved of the fundamental features of the proposals, and were definitely opposed to the provincialization of income-tax. They rejected the scheme of stadard contributions, but recommended that the Provinces which had to pay heavy contributions in the beginning should be the first to be benefited by their remission, and laid down a formula according ot which the reduction was to be effected, On grounds of policy they gave the Provinces a small share in the growth of revenues from taxation of income so far as the growth was due to increase in the amount of the income assessed. The scheme, as modified by the Joint Select Committee, was embodied ih the rules made under the Government of India Act, and is now in operation.

The Provinces were also given powers to impose additional taxes for provincial purposes, and the taxes which could be imposed by they without obtaining the previous sanction of the Government of India were specified in Schedule 1 of the Scheduled Taxes Rules. They included taxes on amusements and betting, succession duties, a tax on non-agricultural land and taxes on advertisements, etc. The Government of India were given residuary powers in taxation as in all other matters.

After the introduction of the Reforms, the Government of India and the Governments of all the Provinces passed through a period of financial stress. The Government of India attributed their misfortunes to war, frontier expeditions, exchange and trade depression. The Provincial Governments were unable to find any natural calamities, except the failure of the monsoon, to account for their troubles, and fulminated against the Meston Settlement in their inability to balance their budgets. The Meston Committee held out the prospect of 'abundant general resources' and considered it an unthinkable sequel to the Reforms that the Provinces should embark on new taxation at the outset of the new era. They also saw no justification for the Government of India imposing fresh taxation for carrying on the administration of Central subjects. For the first three years of the Reforms all the Governments in India had to face enormous financial difficulties, and the efforts to overcome them involved a very great strain on their resources and good temper.

The Meston Settlement became a by-word for financial iniquity and injustice, and the frequency with which it was condemned both by officials and non-officials convinced the general public that the case against it admitted of no difference of opinion. The Government of India, pressed on all sides for assistance, found it impossible to afford any relief, on account of their own financial difficulties. They, however, made an exception in the case of Bengal, and in 1921, on the recommendation of the Finance Member, the Legislative Assembly agreed to the remission of the Bengal contribution for a period of three years. This concession gave the much-needed relief to Bengal, but did not improve the general atmosphere. The protests of the other

Provinces became more vehement than ever, and the tension of feeling over the question was increased on account of the prevailing political distrust and suspicion. A conference of Finance Members at Simla was called in April 1922. Various proposals for easing the situation were discussed and the whole position reviewed at some length, but no change was made in the financial settlement. The Government of India decided to uphold it, and once more repeated their promise to treat the abolition of the Provincial contributions as the first charge on the betterment of their revenues. Since the remission of the Provincial contributions, Madras, the United Provinces and the Punjab have adopted a more quiescent attitude. They consider their abolition merely an act of tardy justice, and feel that the financial outlook, so far as they are concerned, is quite hopeful. Their revenues can never be in excess of their needs; but they are sure to expand, and provide them with funds for the development of their vital services. But other Provinces still hold that, without the revision of the whole settlement, their future is far from reassuring, and expect that the next step in constitutional advance will not only give them wider power, but also larger resources to enable them to use those powers to the advantage of their people. There are not many who understand the Meston Settlement, its genesis and subsequent developments. But there is a general feeling that it is to go, and make room for a more generous and equitable financial arrangement. The psychological atmosphere is full of hopes of change for the better, and it is necessary to take this general expectation into account in making the financial re-adjustments. The prejudice against the Meston Settlement is very strong; and though, like all prejudices, it has very little rational basis, it cannot be summarily dismissed on that account.

It is necessary to examine the position a little more in detail to understand its full significance. This cannot be done without acquiring a closer acquaintance with the financial history of the Reforms poriod; but before dealing with this it is desirable to give an account of some of the concrete proposals which have been made during the period in order to get an idea of the general trend of subsequent discussions. The Reforms Enquiry Committee of 1924 considered the problem of finance, and expressed the opinion that the difficulties arising therefrom formed one of the main obstacles to the success of the Reforms. They urged the need of reducing the Provincial contributions; but as that in itself could not meet the needs of certain of the Provinces, they considered that a revision of the whole settlement was inevitable, and should be undertaken as soon as a favourable opportunity occurred. They themselves, however, did not make any recommendations owing to the absence of definite information which could be made the basis of a revision.

The question was again examined at some length by the Taxation Enquiry Committee. The Committee was not required to consider the equity of the Meston Award, but only to indicate the theoretically correct principles of distribution of taxes between Imperial, Provincial and Local. Sir Basil Blackett, in his speech in the Legislative Assembly on 18 September 1924, stated that the taxation enquiry was an essential preliminary to framing a more satisfactory settlement. The Committee was not expected to enquire into the expenditure side of the question. Their function was to suggest what may be considered as a scheme for the ideal division of resources. Being debarred from dealing with the practical issues, their treatment of the problem was lacking in precision, and conveyed an impression of their inability to come to close grips with its realities. They pointed out certain general tendencies relating to the division of taxes in other federal countries, but stated that there was no ideal system for the division of sources of revenue, and the allotment of taxes, owing to historical and other factors, had everywhere to be supplemented by further adjustments. They based their proposals on the assumption that all Provinces would be treated alike. Their object was to devise a satisfactory method by which the redistribution of resources could be brought about without disturbing the existing equilibrium. They did not recommend any change in the present allocation of land revenue, irrigation, fees including judicial stamps, import duties and revenue excises. They were in favour of general stamps, execise on country-made 'foreign' liquors and the whole of the revenue from opium being transferred to the Central Government ; and they also suggested the use of export duties, a 'basic' rate of restrictive excises and the probate duty as balancing factors, which presumably meant that export duties might be provincialized, and the probate duty and a basic rate on restrictive excises centralized, if it was necessary to introduce these changes in the interest of an equilibrium of revenues. But they wanted these balancing factors to be used only in case of real necessity.

As they advocated the transfer to the Central Government of general stamps, excise on country-made foreign liquors and oplum revenue on administrative grounds, they mainly relied upon the division of the proceeds of the income-tax for restoring the equilibrium. They also discussed the alternative methods by which the receipts of the income-tax could be divided, and recommended that the Provinces should be given the proceeds of a basic rate on personal incomes, graduated proportionately to the general rate, to which would be added a small fraction of the receipts from the corporation-tax, in order to give 'a partial recognition to the principle of origin' in assessing taxable capacity. The basic rates for the income-tax and the corporation-tax were to be determined, with a view to give the Provinces a share of the proceeds of these taxes equal to the revenues which the Provinces derived from the sources, which, under their plan, were to be centralized. They did not realize that the same basic rates would not do as compensating factors in the case of all the Provinces on account of the variations in the yield of these taxes in the different Provinces. But the Committee was not concerned with the effects of their recommendations on Central or Provincial finances. Their duty was to recommend an allocation of resources which gave to the Central and Provincial Government sources of revenue which appertained to their respective spheres, and could therefore be efficiently administered by them. The inequalities were to be adjusted by the use of balancing factors; and they took it for granted that the present distribution of the total revenues of India between the Central Government, on the one hand, and the Provincial Governments, on the other, was not to be disturbed, The scheme was of some theoretical value in the sense that it sought to carry further the principle of administrative efficiency in the allocation of the sources of revenue; but, as a practical solution of the problem of federal finance in India, its value was strictly limited.

The recommendations of the Taxation Enquiry Committee were carefully considered by the Government of India. They rejected the proposals to centralize the excise duty on country-made foreign liquor and the excise on opium owing to administrative and other difficulties. They were willing to centralize general stamps; but, on account of the opposition of the Provinces in which it had been an elastic source of revenue, it was ultimately suggested that only duties on documents which were of a commercial and quasi-commercial character should be transferred to the Central Government. The proposal of the Taxation Enquiry Committee to compensate the Provinces for the loss of revenue from general stamps by giving them the proceeds of the basic rate on personal incomes, graduated proportionately to the general rate, was not accepted by the Government of India. They considered that the adoption of a graduated rate would be in convenient both from the point of view of the Central Government and of the Provincial

Governments, since it would create complications in the event of a decision to alter the rates or to adopt a new system of graduation. They, therefore, suggested an alternative method for the division of income-tax, by giving the Provinces a share of income-tax, calculated at the rate of three pies in the rupee on personal incomes from all sources of assessees resident within each Province. This proposal was made on the assumption that domicile was a satisfactory criterion of liability to taxation so far as the Provinces were concerned, and a flat rate assessed on personal incomes would, therefore, be a suitable device for giving the latter a share in the proceeds of income-tax. There is nothing to be said against this as a make shift arrangement; but as the object of the proposal is not to disturb the equilibrium of revenues under the Meston Settlement, its intrinsic importance as a means of permanent re-adjustment is limited on that account. The Government of India also rejected the Taxation Enquiry Committee's proposal to give the Provinces a small share of the receipts of the corporation-tax, as the distribution of the tax on companies, according to them, could not be made without making assumptions of an extremely hypothetical character. These proposals were discussed in the Conferences of the Financial Representatives of the Provinces held in 1926 and 1927 ; but, as each Province wanted to get as much and give as little as possible, it was decided to put off the whole question and let its settlement await the deliberations of the Statutory Commission. The Meston Settlement, along with the constitution of which it is an integral part, is now in the melting pot; and there is, as stated above, a general expectation that it will be replaced by an arrangement which will provide ampler scope for the free play of the dynamic forces of national life. However that may be, it is clear that the theoretical scheme for the distribution of resources, suggested by the Taxation Enquiry Committee, has never received official countenance, and need not be further considered.

We now can undertake a review of the financial events of the Reforms period. The position of the Government of India may first be considered. The year 1921-22 opened in very unpropitious circumstances. It was the intention of the authors of the Joint Report and that of the Meston Committee that the Central Government should be given adequate revenues to meet the expenditure of the functions assigned to them; but the actual developments belied this expectation, and the equilibrium between revenue and expenditure, for the attainment of which they had incurred so much odium, could not be realized.

The budget, which the Finance Member presented in 1921, showed that the anticipated surplus of 10½ crores of 1920-21 had been converted into in an actual deficit of 11¾ crores by the Afghan War, the frontier operations, the trade depression and the vagaries of exchange and, what was worse, the estimates for 1921-22 revealed a deficit of 18¾ crores. The Finance Member held that the deficit was not solely die to temporary and transient causes, and that it was necessary to impose additional taxation if India was not to slip down 'the hell of financial demoralization' which had led so many countries to national bankruptcy. He proposed additional taxation, which was calculated to yield Rs. 19.17 crores and leave a surplus of 84 lacs after meeting the deficit of 18 crores. Next year, however, the revised estimates of 1921-22 showed that expenditure was in excess of revenue by 34 crores on account of the increase of charges and the falling-off of receipts, and the actual deficit for 1920-21 was 26 crores instead of 18 crores. The outlook for 1922-23 was not more cheering, and a deficit of 31¾ crores was anticipated. The Finance Member once again pointed out that their financial difficulties were not due to temporary causes. 'The problem before us,' he said, 'is one that cannot be shelved or left to look after itself.' The only way out of the difficulty was to levy additional taxation, proposals for which were put forward by the Finance Member and were expected to bring extra revenue of about 29 crores. Some of these proposals were very unpopular and were rejected by the Legislative Assembly, and the uncovered deficit was increased from 2¾ crores to 9 crores. In response to the insistent demand for economy in Central expenditure, a committee, commonly known as the Inchcape Committee, was appointed in the latter part of 1922 to recommend measures for effecting reductions in the expenditure of the Central Government. The Committee, after a careful scrutiny of the expenditure of every department, recommended reductions amounting in all to Rs. 19¼ crores.

The budget for 1923-24 again showed that the financial position and outlook were anything but reassuring. Sir Basil Blackett, who assumed the charge of Indian finances a few weeks before the introduction of the Budget for 1923-24, dwelt at some length on the unsound financial position of the country and pointed out how India had come perilously near the limit of safety on account of the deficits of five years in succession. The deficit for 1923-23, according to the revised estimates, was 17½ crores instead of 9 crores; and in spite of the fact that the Government of India proposed to effect economies to the amount of about 12 crores, as recommended by the Inchcape Committee, the anticipated deficit for 1923-24 amounted to 5.85 crores. The Finance Member proposed to cover this deficit partly by crediting to revenue the interest from the investments in the Paper Currency and Gold Standard Reserves, and partlyby doubling the salt-tax. The latter proposal evoked a storm of opposition, and was rejected by the Legislative Assembly. The Government of India being convinced of the imperative necessity of balancing the budget, the Viceroy certified the Finance Bill, including the enhanced salt duty. The reactions of this step on the political situation were distinctly disturbing; but what Sir Basil Blackett called 'the rake's progress' in Indian finances was thereby arrested, and budget equilibrium established.

The position continued to improve from 1923-24 onwards, and the Government of India have since then been enjoying a period of financial prosperity. The revised estimate of 1923-24 showed a slight deficit of Rs. 38 lacs; but the actuals of the year produced a surplus of Rs. 2.39 crores, exclusive of a windfall of Rs, 4.73 crores representing profits accruing to India from the sale of enemy ships. According to the forecast for 1924-25, a surplus of Rs, 3.36 crores was estimated. As this was regarded as a real surplus, the Government of India proposed to utilize a sum of Rs. 1.82 crores in reducing the salt-tax from Rs. 2-8-0 per maund to Rs. 2 per maund, and a sum of Rs. 1.5 crores in reducing the Provincial contributions. The Finance Member did not make any secret of the fact that he himself was in favour of applying the whole of the surplus to the reduction of the Provincial contributions, keeping the salt-tax at the higher level to which it had been raised in the previous year; but as he knew that this course would not commend itself to the Legislative Assembly, he proposed this compromise as a measure which would satisfy public opinion, or what he regarded as popular prejudice, and also make a beginning 'in dealing with this running sore of Provincial contributions'. The Legislative Assembly did not agree even to this compromise, reduced the salt-tax to Rs. 1-4-0 per maund, and pronounced (in the words of Sir Basil Blackett) 'a message of despair to all those who were looking forward to expenditure for the amelioration of the conditions of life and for improved educational and sanitary expenditure throughout India.'

Since 1924-25 there have been recurring surpluses. The next year brought a surplus of just under four crores instead of the modest balance of 18 lacs allowed for in the original budget; and the budget estimates for 1925-26 disclosed a surplus of Rs. 3.25 crores. The

Government of India decided to apply Rs. 2.5 crores for the reduction of Provincial contributions, and to keep 75 lacs as a margin against possible misadventures. The reduction of Provincial contributions was granted in accordance with the order of priority laid down in the Devolution Rules. In 1926-27 the surplus of the Government of India was Rs. 3.05 crores. They devoted Rs. 1.25 crores to the further reduction of Provincial contributions; and Rs. 1.75 crores were disposed of by the abolition of the cotton excise duty, which had already been suspended in December 1925. In 1927-28 the Provincial contributions were practically abolished. Though the remission of Rs. 2.58 crores was definitely declared temporary, it was known that, unless events took a very unfavourable turn, the contributions would not be revived. Sir Basil Blackett spoke of this achievement with very great satisfaction, and referred to the advantages which would accrue to the Provinces in having additional resources at their disposal. 'Ever since the Reforms have been inaugurated,' he said, ' the Provincial contributions have been a millstone round the neck both of the Central Government and of the Provincial Governments, poisoning their mutual relations and hampering their every action. Their quality more than their amount had strained the resources of the giver and the patience of the recipient. They have brought curses and not blessings, both to him who has given and go him who has taken. The year 1927-28 sets India free from their incubus'.

In 1928-29 the Government of India again anticipated a surplus of Rs. 2.63 crores, which enabled them to bring about a complete and final abolition of the Provincial contributions. Just now the margin between Central revenue and expenditure is not wide; but it may be assumed that it will continue to increase if the teadencies, which have been at work in recent years, are allowed to produce their full effect. Sir Basil Blackett expressed the view that, with the extinction of the contributions, it would be possible for the Central Government to satisfy the claims of the tax-payers. The Government of India have already reduced Central taxation by the abolition of the cotton excise duty, the reduction of the salt tax and several other minor changes. There are, however, other claims on the Central revenues which till now have been ignored. But the fact that the Central Government have climbed the steep hill of financial recovery is a great advantage in itself; and though it has, to adapt the words used by Sir Basil Blackett in his budget speech of 1925, brought us within a distant view of still higher peaks, it is possible to take an optimistic view of the future.

Improvement in the finances of the Central Government is not to be measured merely by the extinction of the Provincial contributions or the restoration of budget equilibrium, great as these achievements are in themselves. The Government of India have since 1924 secured several other important gains. The unproductive debt of India has, during this period, been reduced from Rs. 250 crores in 1924 to Rs. 178 crores in 1928. By the introduction of the Debt Redemption Scheme, definite provision has been made for the progressive reduction of public debt; and, though there is a difference of opinion regarding the advisability of adopting this ambitious policy, the introduction of the scheme must be counted as a major achievement of this period. The separation of railway finance from general finance and the institution of the depreciation and reserve funds have, besides emancipating the railways from the control of the Finance Department, been a source of strength to the latter, and made it possible for it to finance its ways and means programmes with greater ease. The balances have also been drawn upon to a considerable extent for capital expenditure; and the Government of India have, on several occasions, been able to find money for outlay chargeable to loan funds without fresh borrowing in India or in England. The credit of India has, as a result of these measures been raised; and the situation is otherwise well in hand. The victory of the Government of India over adverse circumstances in a great asset; and, now that we are straining our eyes to the vision of the future, we can do so with an assurance that reconstruction can proceed on sound foundations.

The only head of revenue, the yield of which has increased considerably during the period, is customs. This increase is due to the enhancement of the general tariff rate and the imposition of 'protective' duties, the receipts from the latter being about Rs. 1½ crores. The revision of the tariff schedule with a view to framing what may be called a scientific tariff, has been, as is well known, long overdue; but if the policy of maintaining taxation at the present level is to be adhered to and the duties as whole kept as high as they are now, the yield from customs can be expected to grow steadily. There is a great deal to be said against customs on account of their undersirable reaction on economic life in general, and their incidence on the poorer classes; but in view of the necessity of providing funds for development it will be short-sighted to reduce these duties in order to afford relief to the tax-payers. The other two important sources of revenue are the income-tax and the salt-tax. Income-tax has not shown much capacity for expansion on account of the trade depression, but now that the tax has been modernized and the administrative machinery brought to a higher level of efficiency, it should contribute to the expansion of the Central revenues. The salt-tax yields about Rs. 7 crores and is still an important source of revenue for the Central Government. If the present rate is maintained, its revenue will increase, though not very repidly. The contribution of railways to the Central revenues is likely to increase; but whether it can be depended upon to give greater elasticity to Central revenues will be determined by donsiderations of policy regarding which something will be said in Chapter VII. The net receipts from opium amount to about Rs. 2.5 crores, but it will disappear as a source of Central revenue in a few years on account of the stoppage of the opium export to foreign countries.

The only important function for which the Central Government is responsible is defence, and the expenditure on defence during this period has been reduced from Rs. 69 crores to Rs. 55 crores. The Inchcape Committee suggested a standard figure of Rs. 50 crores. It should not be impossible to reduce the military expenditure to that figure; and if the Government of India is responsive to public opinion, it should even be possible to attain the standard of 43 crores adopted by the Meston Committee as a basis of their calculations. The expenditure on civil administration has been slowly rising; but as prices are falling and increments to salaries have already been granted, it may be expected that this item of expenditure will not throw an additional burden on Central revenues unless the Government of India assumes new functions. The conclusion is, of course, obvious that the growth in the revenues and decrease in the expenditure of the Central Government will be an important factor in the financial re-adjustments of the future. The only consideration that can be urged against it is that the Central Government has to be prepared for war, and ought to have a sufficient margin for emergencies. With the general tariff rate at 15 per cent and the present rates of income-tax, which are by no means low, the margin for emergencies is very narrow; and the argument that, if the rates of these taxes are not appreciably reduced, there will be very little reserve for emergencies like war, is valid as far as it goes. But it cannot be pressed very far. The Government of India should, if they follow the policy demanded by enlightened public opinion in India, keep out of wars, the financial burden of which can be properly thrown on the Indian exchequer; but even if this consideration is not given the weight that it deserves, it will be wrong to shape the taxation policy of India to provide her with fiscal reserves for these emergencies. War has become such a big enterprise that no country can expect to meet its cost by taxation. It is necessary to have recourse to borrowing on a large scale for the purpose; and to delay the development of the country, by reducing taxation with a view to hold in reserve the potential taxable capacity of the people, is as useless as it is short-sighted. It is worth while to take a little risk in order to accelerate the rate of national progress so that the people may be able to rise to a higher level of achievement, and at the same time be better fitted to bear the fiscal burdens of war. A high level of taxation is, from this point of view, itself an insurance against wars and other contingencies.

Bengal, of course, comes first, and the peculiarities of its financial position lends to its study a special interest. Under the Meston award, the normal revenue of Bengal was fixed at Rs. 8.57 crores; and the conference of Provincial representatives, held in September 1919, fixed its normal expenditure at Rs. 7.91 crores. The Government of India, however, later on admitted the inadequacy of this scale and fixed it at Rs. 9 crores. The actual expenditure of Bengal in 1921-22 was Rs. 10.48 crores, and its revenue Rs. 8.32 crores. There was, in other words, a deficit of Rs. 2.16 Crores. Since then Bengal, but for a small deficit of Rs. 21 lacs in 1926-27, has been able to balance its budgets; and, according to the revised estimates for 1928-29, Bengal will have a revenue of Rs. 12.17, crores. an expenditure of Rs. 11.83 crores, and a closing balance of Rs. 2.53 crores. This seems to show that Bengal is doing fairly well; and its financial position, in spite of a very large deficit in 1921-22, has not been unsatisfactory during this period. This result has, however, been achieved by exercising rigid economy and imposing additional taxation. During the first two years of the Reforms, Bengal under took retrenchment to the extent of Rs. 89 lacs and Rs. 49 lacs respectively, and levied additional taxation which was expected to yield Rs. 104 lacs. The figures of expenditure show that the Bengal expenditure on education, sanitation and other beneficent departments has not expanded to any considerable extent. The increase of expenditure on education from 1921-22 to 1927-28 was 22 lacs, on medical services about Rs. 18 lacs, and on other departments Rs. 5 lacs. There was an increase of Rs. 13 lacs in expenditure on general administration, but on police and law and justice expenditure was practically stationary. Bengal has, since 1922-23, received a concession in the form of the suspension of its contribution to Central revenues; but the Government of Bengal has, ever since the introduction of the Reforms, maintained that the injustice done to Bengal under the Meston Settlement has nothing to do with the question of contributions, and that the extinction of the latter does not in any way weaken their case for a thorough overhauling of the whole settlement. They have never lost an opportunity of pressing their point of view on the attention of the general public and the Government of India, and have urged persistently that the financial settlement was wrong *ab inilio* and treated Bengal most unfairly.

The difficulties of Bengal are due to the inelasticity of its resources. The principal heads of revenue in this Province yield receipts which are quite inadequate for its needs and are not capable of expansion. Land-revenue is, it need not be said, an inexpansive source on account of the existence of the Permanent Settlement, and so long as the latter is treated as sacrosanct, it is not possible to impart elasticity to the revenues of Bengal. The increase under excise and stamps during the period is 47 and 73 lacs, respectively. In 1921-22 there was a sudden decline in excise revenue on account of an extensive propaganda against the use of excisable articles, and the revenue in 1922-23 exceeded that of the previous year by about 19 lacs; the net increase therefore, in excise receipts may be taken at about 28 lacs. The increase in stamps revenue is due to the revision of fees, judicial and non-judicial, and it is not possible to raise them much higher to augment the Provincial revenues. There has also been an increase of receipts under forests and registration. But these are minor sources of revenue, and cannot be used to develop the resources of this Province. Bengal has levied what are known as the scheduled taxes, and increased its revenues by Rs. 20 lacs, but it is very unlikely that there will be any substantial growth in the receipts from these taxes unless a succession duty, which is also a scheduled tax, is levied and fully developed. The Meston Committee referred to the inelastic revenue and low scale of expenditure of Bengal in their report; but, in view of 'its size, intrinsic wealth and general economic possibilities', they did not consider it right to differentiate in its favour in the assessment of the Provincial contributions. Its size, wealth and possibilities, whatever they were, are still there; but it is extremely doubtful whether they will help the Province to find a margin for development. Bengal has, since the inauguration of the scheme of decentralization, received much less than its due; and though it has partly itself to thank for its inadequate revenues, it has certain claims on the Government of India, which the latter will have to take into account in any equitable scheme of re-allocation of resources.

United Provinces

The Meston Committee estimated the normal revenue of the

Province at Rs. 12.32 crores, its normal expenditure at Rs. 10.75, including the Rs. 2.40 crores of the contribution to the Government of India, and its additional spending power at Rs. 1.57 crores. The actual revenue for 1921-22 was Rs. 10.02 crores, and the expenditure Rs. 11.49 crores; and there was a deficit of Rs. 1.47 crores. This year was followed by four years of deficits in succession, and the total deficit up to 1925--26 amounted to over Rs. 3 crores. This was, to a certain extent, due to falling-off of receipts; but the principal cause of tne financial difficulties of the Province was increase in expenditure, which in the first two years of the Reforms amounted to Rs. 2.84 crores. The revision of pay of services and establishment alone cost Rs. 1.52 crores, and there was an increase on all other heads of expenditure. The successive deficits were met from the Provincial balances and the funds obtained from a loan raised in the open market. The United Provinces Government put an unwarranted construction on the word 'productive' expenditure, used the loan funds for charges which should have been met out of revenue, and violated the letter as well as the spirit of the rules under which the Provincial Governments are allowed to raise their own loans. The Accountant-General pointed out this irregularity in his Appropriation Report, and the Government of India, had to warn the United Provinces Government that no loan would be sanctioned, whether raised in the open market or obtained through the Provincial Loans Fund, if its proceeds were applied in practice for meeting the revenue deficit. The era of deficits came to an end in 1926-27, and for the last two years this Province has been able to balance its budgets and make provision for considerable surpluses. This has been rendered possible by the remission of its contribution of Rs. 2.40 crores by the Government of India. The estimated revenue and expenditure for 1928-29 were Rs. 12.47 crores and Rs. 11.95 crores, respectively; and since the latter amount does not include the contribution, it means that expenditure in 1928-29 was estimated to exceed the actual expenditure of 1921-22 by Rs. 2.86 crores. The prospect for the United Provinces is now quite satisfactory, and its financial position fairly good. But its scale of expenditure is, as it has always been, low; and it has even now to make up what the Meston Committee called considerable arrears of administrative progress.

There has not been much additional taxation in the Province during this period, though court fees and water rates have been raises. The receipts under stamps, and irrigation in 1927-28 show considerable increase, as compared with 1921-22; but excise, which has, in almost all Provinces, yielded growing revenue, has not in any way contributed to the increase of the revenues of the United Provinces, and its total yield in 1927-28 was less than that of 1921-22 by about Rs. 10 lacs. The incidence of the excise duties in the United Provinces in 1926--27 was the lowest among the major Provinces, and it may be possible to increase the revenue from this source by revising the rates. This Province should to a certain extent be able to enlarge its spending power by developing its fiscal resources.

Madras

Madras, like the other Provinces, had to face great financial difficulties in the first two or three years of the Reforms; but its financial situation is now, to use the language of the money market, distinctly easy. The Meston Committee anticipated that it would have additional spending power of Rs. 2.58 crores, after paying the contribution of Rs. 3.48 crores to the Government of India. In 1921-22 it had a deficit of Rs. 99 lacs; and in spite of additional taxation of Rs. 77.5 lacs and considerable reduction of expenditure, there was an anticipated deficit next year of Rs. 42 lacs. During these years its protests against the contribution were vehement, and Madras was often spoken of as the 'milchcow' of India. In 1923-24, however, the position considerably improved; and since then Madras has been, in spite of the provision for fresh expenditure under various heads, realizing large surpluses; and its balances, which had been reduced to Rs. 17 lacs in 1924-25, have again risen to Rs. 4.85 crores in 1929-30. During this period large sums have been spent on the repayment of loans and on capital expenditure out of revenue. The estimated revenue of 1928-29 was Rs.16.97 crores and the expenditure Rs. 16.95 crores. The expenditure on education has increased by Rs. 72 lacs from 1921-22 to 1927-28, on medical services by Rs. 12 lacs, and on general administration by Rs.93 lacs. The improvement in the financial position of Madras is due to the remission of its contribution to the Central Government and an increase in the yield of taxes. The Meston Committee expected that Madras would, under their plan, receive 'a windfall so vast as would not be profitably employed for several years'. As a matter of fact, however, Madras could not, as stated above, even balance its budgets in 1921-22, but it is now the lucky recipient of a 'windfall' the spending of which will require a great deal of careful thinking. 'There has been,' as was admitted by the Finance Member in his Budget speech of 1929, 'a scramble for funds among the departments; every time that there was a remission in the contribution, money was allotted to them, with the result that, not having any far-seeing objective or well-planned programme, they spent away as best as they could. 'The Finance Member also spoke of' the immensity of the needs which have still to be met.' The unsatisfied needs of Madras, as of the country as a whole, are immense, and any amount of money can be usefully spent on progressive schemes; but the scale of expenditure in Madras cannot be described as unduly low, and it will be idle to deny that Madras now finds itself in possession of funds, the largeness of which is embarrassing for the time being, though they can certainly be used to very great advantage when well-considered and well-matured schemes are taken in hand.

There has also been a great expansion of revenue in Madras. It has increased from Rs. 11.75 crores in 1921–22 to Rs. 16.97 crores in 1928–29. Land revenue receipts increased from Rs. 6.07 crores in 1921–22 to Rs. 7.55 crores in 1927–28, stamps revenue from Rs. 1.09 crores to Rs. 2.45 crores, and excise receipts have also shown an upward tendency in the last two years. The financial position of Madras, both in respect of revenue and expenditure, compares well with that of the other Provinces, and the incidence of its burden in the early years of the Reforms is also the measure of its gains at the close of this period.

Bihar and Orissa

In contrast to the United Provinces and Madras, Bihar and Orissa is very unfortunate; and its position is now, as it has been since 1912--13, a complete anomaly in the scheme of financial decentralization. Judged by the figures of surpluses and deficits, this Province has not done badly as compared with the other Provinces, for, till 1925–26, it achieved what was not possible for most of the other Provinces, i.e. equilibrium between revenue and expenditure. For the last three or four years it has not been able to avoid revenue deficits; but these amounts are not large, and Bihar and Orissa has, on the whole, been able to make both ends meet. But to say this is to say very little, and that little has no significance so far as the real financial position of the Province is concerned. Among the nine major Provinces, Bihar and Orissa stands fourth in point of area and population, but both in respect of revenue and expenditure per thousand of population it stands lowest. It occupied that position in 1912–13, in 1920–21, in 1921–22 and 1928–29, and there is no prospect of its being able to make up the lee-way with the present distribution of resources. The origin of this disparity has already been explained, and it is impossible to view its future without dismay unless this Province is placed in a position to increase its fiscal resources. During the Reforms there has been some increase of expenditure. The total expenditure has increased from Rs. 4.58 crores in 1921–22 to Rs. 5.88 crores in 1928–29; the expenditure on education has risen from Rs. 55 lacs in 1921–22 to Rs. 86 lacs in 1927–28, on medical services from Rs. 21 lacs to Rs. 46 lacs and on other beneficent departments from Rs. 12 lacs to 24 lacs. There has also been a slight increase of expenditure on general administration, police and law and justice. This again appears at first sight quite satisfactory. This expenditure on education is up by about 60 per cent., and on public health and other beneficent activities by more than by 100 per cent. This compares well with Bombay, where the expenditure on education has risen only by 17 per cent, and on other heads not even in that proportion. In one way such a comparison is very misleading, but it has been made to show that progress in the industrial Provinces has not been as rapid as in the agricultural Provinces. In spite of the remarkable progress in Bihar and Orissa, the industrial Province of Bombay spends about four times as much per head on education, about three times on public health and more than twice as much on other beneficent activities. It is not necessary to make any comments. The facts speak for themselves. The inadequacy of public expenditure in Bihar and Orissa is obvious, and it is unthinkable that this Province should be doomed to stangnation while the other Provinces and the country as a whole are going ahead; but that is the only way in which its future can be envisaged if there is no substantial improvement in its present financial position.

This gloomy outlook is, of course, due to the inelasticity of the resources of this Province. Its total revenue has increased from Rs. 4.43 crores in 1921–22 to Rs. 5.74 crores in 1928–29. This increase is mainly due to the growth of revenue from stamps and excise. Revenue from stamps has increased from Rs. 58 lacs in 1921–22 to Rs. 1.05 crores in 1927–28, and excise revenue from Rs. 1.23 crores to 1.90 crores. There has also been an increase of revenue under the other heads, but that is not considerable. Revenue from stamps and excise cannot be expected to go up much higher. Excise revenue has, after reaching the highest point in 1927–28, been stationary for the last two years with a slight downward tendency. Stamps revenue also seems to have attained a position of stable equilibrium, and is not growing. The Permanent Settlement makes it impossible to obtain an expanding revenue from the taxation of land, and other sources of revenue do not possess any capacity for growth. The Province as is well known, is the richest Province in the country in respect of mineral resources; but the public right over them has already been alienated by the declaration of Lord Cranbrook, the then Secretary of State for India, in 1880, that, even if the legal right to minerals in permanently settled estates could be established, it would not be desirable to enforce it. The Province has, by this ill-advised decision, been reduced to a position of utter helplessness, and a right which could have been used to increase its fiscal resources has thereby been given away on account of an undue regard for vested interests. The postion, to repeat once more, is almost desperate. The Finance Member of Bihar and Orissa in his last Budget speech spoke of 'the bleak poverty' of the Province, and the imperative necessity of securing 'better terms and much better terms' under the new financial settlement. That Bihar and Orissa has not been fairly treated in the past cannot admit of any doubt; and that it is, on that account, entitled to special consideration, must also receive general assent if we take a really national view of the question. But it can vindicate its right to get'much better terms' only by its willingness to cultivate the qualities of self-help and self-reliance to a much larger extent. This is, however, a line of argument which will have to be developed at some length in a later chapter. It is not necessary to anticipate it here. This brief review of the financial position of Bihar and Orissa during this period shows that, in spite of the balanced budgets and the growth of revenue and expenditure under some principal heads, the Province is still in an undeveloped conditon, and special efforts will have to be made to accelerate the pace of its progress in all spheres of administration.

Punjab

The Province, which comes next in size of population, is the Punjab. Under the Meston Settlement, it has enjoyed a period of financial prosperity; and its revenues have, as anticipated by the Meston Committee, moved upwards with marked ease. Its revenue and expenditure have risen from Rs. 7.1 crores and Rs. 8.81 crores, respectively, in 1921–22 to Rs. 12.73 crores and Rs. 12.77 crores in 1928–29. It passed through a period of revenue deficits in the first two years after the introduction of the Reforms; but since 1923-24 the upward tendency of its revenues has asserted itself, and its revenue surpluses from 1923–24 to 1925–26 amounted to over Rs. 4.5 crores. There has been an increase in its expenditure on all heads except police, on which there has been a slight decrease. The increase on general administration from 1921–22 to 1927–28 amounts to Rs.13.32 lacs, on law and justice to Rs.11.83 lacs, on education to Rs.66.97 lacs, on medical services to Rs.25.65 lacs, and on other beneficent departments to Rs.25.41 lacs. This pace has been kept up since then; and from the details given by the Finance Member of the Province in his Budget speech of 1929, it appears that the allotment on education has increased since 1926–27 by 21 per cent, on medical services by 33 per cent, on public health by 19 per cent, on agriculture by 34 per cent, and on industries by more than 50 per cent. This is a remarkable expansion of expenditure, and has been accompanied by an all-round progress of the Province. It has also been in a polition to provide large funds for capital expenditure out of its revenue. In 1927–28 and 1928–29 the capital expenditure, financed from revenue, amounted to about Rs. 2.60 crores. It has also made a beginning in building up a Revenue Reserve Fund, and large sums have been credited to it to provide a stand-by for the lean years. Its relative position in the scale of expenditure has been considerably improved during this period, and it compares favourably with all the Provinces except Bombay and Burma. The Punjab cannot possibly have any grievence against the present financial settlement in view of this general improvement in its position.

There has been an increase of receipts from all the main sources of revenue. Land revenue, including the receipts from irrigation credited to this head, has risen from Rs. 3.79 crores in 1921–22 to Rs. 4.9 crores in 1927–28, and irrigation receipts proper from Rs. 1.74 crores to Rs. 2.57 crores during the same period. That means that land revenue and irrigation, taken together, account for an increase of over Rs. 2 crores. Revenue from stamps has risen from Rs. 81 lacs to Rs. 1.14 crores, and has thereby contributed Rs. 33 lacs to the growth of the Provincial revenue. In 1927–28 there was a temporary set-back in he receipts from excise, but there was steady increase in the excise revenue from 1921–22 to 1926–27, and the receipts rose from Rs. 1.08 crores to Rs. 1.24 crores. The Province has also been realizing very large amounts by the sale of land, and the total amount credited to this head till 1926-27 amounted to Rs. 5.49 crores. The remission of the Provincial contribution has, of course, increased its resources, and placed at its disposal an additional soending power of Rs. 1.75 crores. In irrigation this Province has a very valuable asset, which has great fiscal possibilities. Water-rates do not, according to the Irrigation officers of this Province, truly represent the obligation which should be imposed on the classes benefited by the provision of irrigation facilities made at the expense of the general tax-payer, and ought to be considerably raised. The tendency now at work is the other way; and already this Province has sacrificed an annual revenue of Rs. 25 lacs on account of the lowering, as a result of the pressure of the rural parties in the Provincial Legislature, of the occupiers' rates in 1925–26. But if the standard of civic ethics can be raised to a higher level, this Province can very well expect to expand its revenue still further by the revision of its water-rates; and with the completion of the Sutlej Valley project and the hydro-electric scheme, its non-tax revenue should, in due course, provide still larger funds for the development of the Province. The fiscal future of this Province is, therefore, very reassuring in every respect, and now that it is in a position to choose beween the development of services and the remission of taxation it can, by making the right choice, consolidate the position that it has won for itself, and become one of the most progressive Provinces of India.

Bombay

The equity of the Meston Settlement was questioned by Bombay before its introduction. Bombay had, like other Provinces, a heavy revenue deficit in the first year of the Reforms; and then, after having balanced budgets for three years and realizing a total surplus of Rs.1.20 crores, it has, since 1925–26, been having recurring deficits, and the future outlook is distinctly depressing. This unhappy result, is, in no small measure, due to the misadventures of this Province in its handling of what is known as the Bombay Development Scheme, which has proved to be an exceedingly bad business investment and has thrown an annual interest charge of Rs. 66.11 lacs on the Provincial revenues; nad a sum of Rs. 95.16 lacs had to be provided every year since 1921–22 for the sinking fund of the loan. The loss, which the Province has had to suffer, has nothing to do with the financial settlement, though it has hit it hard, and cannot be taken into account in evaluating the actual results of the Meston Award. There has been practically no increase of expenditure on any service except education, the expenditure on which shows an increase of about Rs.23 lacs. The apparent increase of the expenditure on general administration is mainly due to the re-classification of expenditure and not to its growth. There is an actual decrease of expenditure on police, law and justice and even medical services and public health. In spite of this arrested progress of expenditure, Bombay still retains its position of eminence as spending Province, and its scale of expenditure in 1927–28 is, as it has been since 1876–77, far above the Indian average. On education its expenditure per 1,000 of population is more than double that of every other Province except Burma and the Punjab; on medical services and public health, its expenditure is higher than that of all other Provinces except Burma; and on the other beneficent departments, the only Province which can claim priority over it is the Punjab. Its expenditure on police, law and justice and general administration, in spite of the retrenchment of the Reforms period, is far in excess of that of the other Provinces, the only exception being Burma, whose expenditure on police and law and justice is higher than that on Bombay. It is neither practicable nor desirable to ask Bombay to reduce its expenditure for the benefit of the other Provinces. It cannot even be expected to stand still till the other Provinces come up to its level. But the fact that it is in advance of the other Provinces is an important consideration in itself; and their needs must naturally have precedence over its needs when there is a question of providing for Provincial development at the expense of the Central revenues. Bombay has, in the new financial settlement, to be placed in possession of funds to meet its growing expenditure. That, however, cannot be done by an arrangement which involves a sacrifice of the income of the Central Government, when the less fortunate Provinces like Bihar and Orissa and Bengal, are in such financial straits. In 1919 the Meston Committee expressed an opinion that Bombay could without inconvenience forgo the greater part of its balances. Its balances have been reduced to a very low figure, having fallen from Rs. 306 lacs in the beginning of 1921–22 to Rs. 7 lacs at the end of 1928–29, and its new resources have not been sufficient even to meet its own expenditure. Now Bombay has to find new resources for itself; and its high scale of expenditure carries with it an obligation to rely to a greater extent than other Provinces upon its own efforts for enlarging its resources.

The revenues of Bombay, in the opinion of the Meston Committee, had a pace of expansion distinctly higher than in any other Province. They based their view on the fact that from 1912–13 to 1919–20 the revenue from excise had grown in Bombay by 102.57 per cent., from stamps by 119.13 per cent. from land revenue and other sources by 32 per cent, and from all Provincial heads taken together by 52 per cent. This pace of expansion has, however, not been maintained during this period. It would appear that from 1921–22 to 1927–28, the Provincial receipts from land revenue have decreased by Rs. 73 lacs; and from stamps and excise they have increased by Rs. 22 lacs and Rs. 67 lacs respectively. From the scheduled taxes Bombay is getting about Rs. 23 lacs a year, which is an addition to its resources; and Bombay has, of course, gained Rs. 56 lacs by the remission of contributions. This mean that Provincial revenues in Bombay have gone up by about Rs. 1.58 crores, of which the growth of its tax-revenue accounts for only about Rs. 92 lacs. These are the principal sources of revenue, and they have not shown the same buoyancy after 1921-22 as they did before that year; and it is not likely that their receipts will grow repidly in future. Land revenue, excise, and stamps yield more than 95 per cent of the total tax-revenue of Bombay, and as the incidence of these taxes per head of population is, leaving aside Burmas, the highest in India, they cannot be expected to provide much margin for development. The situation is certainly, therefore, disquieting in Bombay. Its scale expenditure is high, but it has been practically stationary in recent years. Its resources are also large, but they too have not been growing of late, and there is no reason to believe that they will pick up their rate of growth in the immediate future. With inexpansive resources and expanding expenditure, the Province cannot help feeling that its financial condition is acute; and the prospect of stagnation even at a high level of development is sure to cause a serious revulsion of sentiment. The insistence on Bombay that nothing short of a thorough revision of the Meston Settlement will meet the requirements of the case is, therefore, easily intelligible, and, viewed in the light of these facts, entitled to a sympathetic consideration.

Central Provinces

In the first year after the introduction of the Reforms the accounts of the Central Provinces showed a deficit, which was met out of its balances. In the following four years the Government secured an equilibrium of revenue and expenditure by imposing additional taxation and reducing expenditure. But the two Taxation Acts, passed by the first Council, expired on the 31st March 1926; and in 1926–27 the Province had again a revenue deficit of Rs. 67 lacs. With the remission of the Provincial contribution of Rs. 22 lacs, the position has again improved, though the margin between revenue and expenditure is very narrow, and any mishap is likely to upset the equilibrium. Revenue and expenditure have increased from Rs. 4.72 crores and Rs. 4.95 crores, respectively, in 1921–22 to Rs. 5.54 crores and Rs. 5.68 crores in 1928–29. The expenditure on general administration has increased by Rs. 17 lacs from 1921–22 to 1927–28, on law and justice by Rs, 1 lac, on police by Rs. 3 lacs, on education by Rs. 10 lacs, on medical services by Rs. 2 lacs and on other beneficent departments by Rs. 5 lacs. The scale of expenditure in the Province is low, though it compares favourably with that of Bihar and Orissa and the United Provinces. The Central Provinces has also to be considered a backward Province; and the need of supplementing its resources in order to provide funds for development must receive due attention in the general re-adjustments of the future.

Excise has been the most elastic source of revenue in the Central Provinces during this period, and its yield has increased from Rs. 1.05 crores in 1921–22 to Rs. 1.47 crores in 1927–28; and according to the statement of the Finance Member of the Province, made by him in his last Budget speech, a normal annual imcrement of Rs. 8 or 9 lacs in the Provincial revenues from this source may be expected. Income from land revenue has been actually decreasing from 1921–22 to 1927–28; and its yield was Rs. 2.50 crores in the latter year, as compared with Rs. 2.65 crores in the former. Revenue from forests has increased by Rs. 8 lacs and from stamps by Rs. 12 lacs; but irrigation revenue is a minus quantity in the finances of this Province. The bulk of its revenue is derived from land revenue and excise, and as the former is slow to expand, expand, excise is the only source of revenue which is capable of some expansion. If it is considered wrong to depend upon this 'tainted money' for carrying on and developing the administration of the Province, it must find new sources of revenue to keep pace with its expanding expenditure. What those new sources should be is the problem of the Central Provinces, as it is of the other Provinces and of the country as a whole.

Burma

The financial position of Burma is very peculiar. With a population slightly less than that of the Central Provinces, it stands first in point of area. Its total revenue and expenditue in proportion to its population are the highest in India, and its expenditure on different services, with one or two exceptions, is higher even than that of Bombay, and still it is contended on its behalf that Burma is far behind India proper in what its Government does for its people. The total revenue and expenditure have risen from Rs. 9.18 crores and Rs. 9.04 crores respectively, in 1921–22 to Rs. 10.73 crores and Rs. 11.78 crores in 1928–29. The Province has had deficits for seven years in succession since 1922–23, which have been met out of the huge opening balance of Rs. 5.72

crores. It has been spending very large amounts on buildings and communications, which have had to be constructed on account of the vastness of its area and its undeveloped condition. It has had at its disposal very large receipts realized before the Reforms from the system of rice control, which it has utilized subsequently for capital expenditure. The opening balance to the credit of this account amounted to Rs. 8.97 crores, which was drawn upon from 1923–24 to 1926–27 to the extent of over 6 crores till the end of 1926–27. This made it possible for the Government of Burma to do without borrowing till 1927–28 in spite of its heavy non-recurring capital expenditure. The expenditure on general administration increased from 1921–22 to 1927–28 by Rs. 24 lacs, on law and justice by Rs.32 lacs, on police by Rs. 2 lacs, on education by Rs. 53 lacs, on medical services and public health by Rs. 30 lacs, and on the other beneficent departments by Rs. 10 lacs. The recurring deficits, it is clear, are not due to the deficiency of revenues, but are an index of the enterprise of the Provincial Government in developing its administration. The case of Burma is not on all fours with that of the other Provinces on account of the fact that, recially and geographically, it is not a part of India proper, and the conditions here cannot be compared with those prevailing in other parts of the country. The demand for separation from India has, of late, been growing more and more insistent, and it is not easy to refute the arguments by which it is supported. Even if the new constitution does not satisfy this demand, the fact that the union of Burma and India is to be continued merely as a matter of expendiency or administrative convenience will necessitate a special treatment of the whole queation of financial re-adjustment between them. The Accountant-General and the Auditor-General have, for some years past, been taking a pessimistic view of Burma's finances; but if it does not embark upon very ambitious projects of expenditure, its financial position need not be viewed with any misgivings.

Land revenue receipts in 1927–28 were practically the same as those in 1921–22, the difference of 5 lacs being due to ordinary contingent veriations. Income from excise and stamps has gone up from 1921–22 to 1927–28 by about Rs. 24 and 20 lacs respectively. The increase of income from forests is not large; but if we take into account also the decrease of expenditure, the net increase amounts to about Rs. 21 lacs. Burma has also gained by the operation of Devolution Rule 15, but that is due to a circumstance which is purely fortuitous. Under this rule, the year 1920–21 is adopted as the basic year for the calculation of the Provincial share of income-tax receipts, and as till very recently there did not exist any properly organized machinery for the assessment of income-tax outside Rangoon City, the extension of the activities of the income-tax department has led to an increase of assessed income and therefore to a proportionate increase of the assignments to Burma under this rule. In 1927–28 Burma's assignment was Rs. 15.00 lacs, as compared with Rs. 3.85 lacs in 1921–22. The remission of the Provincial contibution has increased Burma's resources by Rs.64 lacs. In forests this Province has a valuable public estate which can be further developed. It is already getting more from this source than any three other Provinces put together, and with proper management it should be able to get much more. More than 67 per cent of its vast area is under forests, and though a very large part of it consists of inaccessible and undeveloped hill tracts, it cannot be assumed that the point of maximum revenue has been reached. Burma's complaint is that the Central Government is taking from it an unduly large share of its total revenues. With a population not more than one-twentieth of that of British India, it is contributing not less then one-tenth of the receipts of the Central Government, and as there can be no question of the locale and incidence of revenue collected in Burma being different, it is possible to argue that it has to pay very heavily for union with a country with which it has otherwise so very little in common. It is extremely difficult to allocate to Burma and the other Provinces their share of the Central expenditure; but as Burma is an organic unit in itself, and the separation from India will cause it no wrench, it is not likely to attach to the needs of the Central Government their due weight and importance. The need for special treatment emphasized in the preceding paragraph is reinforced by these considerations. The problem of federal finance in relation to Burma has a special aspect of its own. There is no strong desire for unity on either side; and it is not easy to devise an arrangement which will be accepted as equitable by the less willing partner. The position obviously needs careful handling.

Assam

Assam passed through two years of revenue deficits after the introduction of the Reforms, but since 1923-24 it has been having balanced budgets and realizing small surpluses. Its revenue has increased from Rs. 1.82 crores in 1921–22 to Rs. 2.78 crores in 1928–29, and its expenditure from Rs. 2.05 crores to 2.82 crores. The expenditure on general administration has increased from 1921–22 to 1927–28 by Rs. 3 lacs, on law and justice by Rs. 2 lacs, on police by 1 lac, on education by Rs. 5 lacs, on medical services by Rs, 8 lacs and on other beneficent departments by Rs. 2 lacs. Its scale of expenditure is one of the lowest in India, being only a little higher than that of Bihar and Orissa.

There has been an increase of receipts from 1921-22 to 1927-28 from all sources of revenue. The increase of income from land revenue amounts to Rs, 17 lacs and from excise to Rs 11 lacs. A very large proportion of its area, like that of Burma, is under forests; and it can be developed and made a source of growing revenues for the Provincial exchequer. The working of the Devolution Rule 15 has also specially favoured Assam, and its assignment under this rule has increased from Rs. 0.02 lacs in 1921–22 to 6.00 in 1927–28. This is due again to an accidental circumstance, and has not been accompanied by any marked expansion of assessable income. The income of tea companies in Assam forms the major portion of the assessed income in this Province; and as these companies were assessed to income-tax after 1920-21, it has been receiving large assignments under the rule. The revenues of Assam, in spite of an increase of 41.11 percent since 1921-22, are inadequate for its needs, and it requires much larger resources to attain a higher level of development. It has to be helped to come into line with the more advanced Provinces.

The Meston Settlement may now be reviewed as a whole. It has very few friends. Sir Basil Blackett has defended it against it adversaries on a number of occasions, and expressed the view that what is required is the amendment of the Meston Settlement, rather than a fresh deal. But this view is not shared by the Finance Members of the various Provinces, and they have declared themselves in favour of its revision and the redistribution of revenues. There is, as already stated, in the Provinces, a unanimity of opinion among officials and non-officials on this point, which is as significant as it is rare; and they are vying with each other in expressing their strong disapproval of the existing financial arrangements. The Finance Member of Bengal concluded his Budget speech of 1929 by referring to the manner in which the Government had put the case of Bengal before the Statutory Commission, and said: 'We presented a united front, and feel convinced that we impressed the members of the Commission that we have a strong case. We can only wait for the result of their deliberations and hope for the best.' This policy of presenting 'a united front' has also been followed by the other Provinces, and the Commission must have been impressed not only by the fact that some Provinces had a strong case for revision, but also that they were all dominated by purely Provincial considerations, and were apt in their zeal to make out a good case for themselves, to emphasize their rights more than their duties. Each Province has, of course, to speak for itself, and knows best the hardships which it has had to suffer under the present financial settlement; but the problem of federal finance cannot be solved without taking an all-India view of the matter, while at the same time the case of each Province is important, inasmuch as equity to all must be an essential feature of its solution.

Now let us see what is wrong with the Meston Settlement. The grievance that the Provincial contributions to the Central Government, fixed by the Meston Committee, were not equitable as between the different Provinces need not be considered. The abolition of the contributions being a settled fact, the grievance has now only a historical interest; and its only bearing on the present problem is that its redress has, in some cases, increased the inequalities in the allocation of resources. As that aspect of the question has already received sufficient attention, and is still to receive much more, it can be overlooked here. The contributions are a matter of the past now, and the other defects of the Settlement are of much greater practical importance.

There is another defect of the Settlement, which, in spite of the prominence which has been given to it by Bombay, is really a minor defect, and may be soon disposed of. The authors of the Reforms and the Meston Committee were, as will be easily remembered, against the provincialization of income-tax, and their view was strongly endorsed by the Joint Select Committee. But the latter assigned to the Provinces a share of the increase in the receipts of income-tax, due to the increase of the assessable income, to alleviate the disappointment of Bombay and Bengal. The actual results of the operation of Devolution Rule 15, in which this recommendation was inserted, show that, judged from the point of view of the Provinces, and especially of Bombay and Bengal it has been a failure. The only two Provinces which have received comparatively large amounts as their assignment under this rule are Burma and Assam ; but that, as already stated ,is due to their good luck on account of the changes of the income-tax law, and is not in accordance with the general intention of the rule. The failure of the rule is due to the adoption of the year 1920–21 as the basic year, and its results would have been different if a different datum line had been taken. The Government of Bombay have, as a matter of fact, advocated a change a in the datum line for the calculation of the Provincial share of income-tax receipts. The defect is there; but since the assignment of a share of the revenue from this source was never regarded as an integral part of the Meston Settlement, it is not necessary to dwell upon it at greater length. Its failure has been a source of disappointment to the industrial and commercial Provinces, but that cannot be urged as a reason for condemning the settlement itself.

This brings us to the three most importnat defects of the Meston Settlement. They have already been referred to again and again in the course of the arguments of this and the preceding chapter, but now have to be stated specifically. One defect, with regard to the existence of which there can be no difference of opinion, is that the revenues of the Provinces, with one or two exceptions, are utterly lacking in buoyancy. It is generally admitted that the functions assigned to the Provinces under the present constitution, and those with which they are likely to be charged under the new constitution, require that their resources should be capable of considerable expension in order to keep pace with their growing expenditure. The real trouble now is that, while the pressure of demand for increased expenditure falls on them, the most elastic and expending sources of revenue are reserved to the Central Government. Financially the Central Government has done well since the introduction of the Reforms. They have remitted the Provincial contributions of Rs. 9.83 crores, the cotton excise duty, reduced the salt-tax and the export duty on hides and tea and the import duty on cars (the total loss of revenue by the remission and reduction of taxation amounting to about Rs. 6 crores), reduced railway rates and fares, built up the Railway Depreciation and Reserve Funds, reduced the unproductive debt by Rs. 72 crores, financed heavy capital expenditure without having recourse to loans in several years, and made a liberal provision for the redemption of debt, both productive and unproductive. These are remarkable achievements, but they have been made possible more by the reduction of expenditure and better financial administration than by the growth of revenue. There has been increase of Rs. 9 crores in the receipts from customs, but the other important sources of revenue, *viz.* the income-tax and the salt-tax, have not shown any marked capacity for expansion. The salt revenue cannot grow rapidly without an enhancement of the rate; and the income-tax receipts have not been increasing on account of the trade depression, though they are now showing some signs of an upward movement. Since 1921-22 Provincial revenues as a whole increased more repidly than Central revenues, and there has been considerable growth of Provincial expenditure. But the outlook for the Provinces is gloomy when we look ahead, and take a forecast of their resources and requirements. They have to face the prospect of being called upon to meet the demands for increasing expenditure, which cannot possible be met without the re-allocation of resources. Their principal heads of revenue are all inelastic. In the permanently settled areas the yield of land revenue has been and will remain almost fixed. The conditions in other Provinces are repidly approximating to what we may call a state of quasi-permanent settlement. We have believed so long in the Permanent Settlement as the specific for our agricultural ills, that even though our enthusiasm for it has recently been on the wane, the habit of mind generated by long association of ideas still persists and is efficacious enough to become the cause of the increasing rigidity of what is and has to be the mainstay of Provincial finance.

It is extremely short-sighted to allow ourselves to move in the rut which we have made for ourselves. We shall thereby stereotype the anomalies and contradictions of our existing system of land taxation, and make the task of the fiscal reformers even more difficult in the future than it is to-day. The tendency which is at work is to be deplored, but one cannot expect that it will be revised without inviting the charge of being absolutely out of touch with the facts of the case. There is, therefore, no prospect of any change in this respect, and land revenue is and will remain an inelastic source of revenue. From 1921–22 income from excise duties has increased by about Rs. 2 crores; but though it may be possible to raise a larger revenue in those Provinces where the incidence of excise duties is low, their income on the whole is not likely to grow owing to the fact that excise rates have already been raised to a high level, and violation of the excise law has consequently increased. Prohibition will remain a distant ideal for years to come; and as the practical difficulties of enforcing it are more clearly appreciated, the people will learn to take a more matter–of–fact view of the question. But even so excise revenue is likely to decrease rather than increase, and restrictive measures will be applied with greater rigour. Excise is, therefore, to be looked upon as a liability and not an asset of our fiscal system, and it will give to the latter an inverted elasticity which will make the necessity of finding compensating factors more imperative than ever. Provincial revenue from stamps has increased by bout Rs. 2.5 crores, but that is mainly due to the revision of fees, judicial and non-judicial, and it is not possible to enhance them much further. Stamps revenue has been stationary since 1924–25, and its growth in the future will not import into Provincial revenues the elasticity which they need so urgently. Irrigation and forests will yield growing revenues in some Provinces; but receipts from these sources can grow only if large ontlay is incurred for capital expenditure, and even then it will take some time before its full benefits can be realized. The factors which led to the increase of Provincial revenues after 1921–22 seem to have spent their force in 1925–26 for Provincial revenues have not increased since that year. The present allocation of resources between the Central and Provincial Governments is open to serious criticism on the ground that the actual and potential sources of revenue allotted to the latter are inelastic and their receipts will be quite inadequate for thier requirements. Revenue from customs and incometax will expand with the recovery of trade, internal and external, and the expenditure of the Central Government will and should decrease unless there is another war and the conditions are abnormal. The Central Government will thus have a surplus which ought to be available for the development of the country. The Provinces, on the other hand, will need funds which they will not be able to get from their existing resources, and it is only a matter of putting two and two together to conclude that the Central Government ought to give and the Provincial Governments ought to receive the funds which are now at the disposal of the former. That in itself, however, will not do; and the necessity of imposing additional taxation cannot thereby be obviated, for the amount of money which the country needs for development is almost unlimited. But we have to make the most of our resources, and it is necessary that the Provinces should get some relief at the expense of the Central Government. The *modus operandi* of this transfer will have to be devised, and carefully considered. But what is to be done is clear, and the rest is a matter of detail.

Another defect of the Meston Settlement is that it leaves the Provinces with very unequal resources, and thus continues the disparity in thier financial strength which has existed since 1871–72. The inequalities are due to historical factors: but as the past cannot be wiped out at once, they have to be taken into account. The authors of the Reforms and the Meston Report knew that they were there, but expected that they would be smoothed out by the extinction of Provincial contributions and the growth of Provincial revenues. But that has not happened, and the disparity of revenue and expenditure is now even more striking than it was after the introduction of the Reforms. It was in 1897 that

Mr. Gokhale pointed out the existence of these inequalities, and said that it was high time that they should be rectified. But nothing was done then, and nothing has been done since to remove them. The advice, which was not taken thirty-three years ago, has now to be acted upon. It will not do to say, that if Provincial autonomy is to come and to be a reality, the Provinces must face the task of raising their own taxation. This consideration is important. and has determined the allocation of resources under the Reforms. But the inequalities are so glaring, and have such serious reactions on our whole political life, that it is not possible to proceed on the assumption that each Province must now cut its coat according to its cloth. The Government of India cannot disown responsibility for their existence. In the successive settlements till 1920–21, which were, as has been stated so often, based on needs, the Government of India either ignored or denied their existence, and allowed the factors, which aggravated them, to have free play. In 1921–22 they made an entirely new departure, and changed the basis of the financial settlement from needs to revenue with a view to ensure the fiscal independence of the Provinces, and relied upon their undemonstrated faith in the future for the rectification of inequalities. This was, to say the least, extremely unfair. For over fifty years the Government of India blundered on in the distribution of revenues which, as was pointed out again and again, formed one consolidated fund, and were to be applied to the purposes of the Government of India as a whole; and in 1920, finding that they had created a tangled problem for themselves, they sought to solve it by laying down the maxim of the fiscal independence of the Provinces, and leaving them to their own devices.

Provincial autonomy is and must remain the *sine quanon* of all political progress in India. Such independence as the Provinces have already achieved has to be conserved, and a larger measure of independence secured for them under the new constitution. But the Government of India cannot ignore the irreducible and stubborn facts, and assume that each Province can now rise to the level of others by self-help and enterprise, when all the realities point to the necessity of a well-considered and concerted action for the removal of these inequalities. Here again the problem is difficult, and has to be carefully thought out. Provincial autonomy is the foundation on which our whole political system is to rest. Nothing must be done to impair or weaken it, though the needs of co-ordination and national integrity are also paramount and have to be provided for. Financial autonomy is essential for political autonomy, and has to be duly ensured. The task of leavelling up has to be undertaken without undermining the position of the Provinces as self-governing units of the national Commonwealth. The misgivings of those who are keenly alive to the dangers of retarding the political progress of the country by making the Central Government again a predominant partner in its financial business are based on past experience, and have to be allayed. The problem is how the re-adjustments necessary for rectifying inequalities can be made without making the Central Government supreme in the administration of Provincial finances. Inequalities, due to the mistakes of the past, must be taken as a liability which has to be liquidated and made a charge on the national revenues; and this has to be done without placing the Provinces under the financial tutelage of the Government of India. The problem, to repeat ourselves once more, is difficult, but has to be faced. It cannot solve itself. The flux of time, to which so much is left, has already made it acute. It canno be shelved any longer.

Both these defects have arisen out of the third, which is still more fundamental. The doctrine of the 'clean cut', which has been the most important limiting factor in the whole settlement, was first laid down in the Joint Report, but has since then been so generally endorsed that it has become an article of faith with all who stand by the present constitution and its premises. This doctrine, as understood and applied in India, is a false doctrine, and must be discarded. In the allocation of resources, as pointed out already, the decisive factor was administrative convenience. Each Government was assigned the sources which it could administer efficiently and independently, and was to appropriate the yield of those sources for its own purposes. It was assumed that the sources so assigned would provide adequate revenues for the needs of the Governments concerned and satisfy the considerations of equity. It is not at all surprising that this anticipation has not come true, as there is nothing in the nature of things to ensure that the income of taxes, which each political authority can or ought to undetake to administer, will be adequate and no more than adequate for its requirements. On account of the broadening basis of the assessment and administration of taxes, it is becoming increasingly desirable to put the Central Government in charge of a number of direct and indirect taxes; and it is, of course, out of the question to reserve their entire income for the discharge of the functions for which the Central Government is made responsible. It is not at all possible to ensure a correspondence between the considerations of adequacy and administrative convenience.

It is because in the Meston Settlement this obvious fact was lost sight of that the Provinces were left with inelastic sources of revenue, and the disparity in their financial strength was so completely overlooked. It is important that the administrative responsibility of the several taxes should rest on the Government which is in a position to discharge it well; but it does not follow that is should use the proceeds of those taxes exclusively for its own needs, or depend upon them only for carrying on its administrative. Dr. Albert Hensel distinguishes between what he calls 'object sovereignty' and 'produce sovereignty' of taxes. By the former he means the exclusive right to impose a tax, and by the latter a similar right to utilize its income. The doctrine of the 'clean cut' takes it for granted that both these rights should be vested in the same authority, but their combination is neither necessary nor practicable. It is at variance with the facts of economic life, and disregards the vital needs of the body politic. In the new financial settlement it is necessary to shake off the obsession of 'securing a genuine and complete separation of resources'. Such a separation, as will be clear from the contents of the next chapter, does not exist anywhere in the world, and it is not possible to devise a settlement suited to our own special needs if we are to be bound by this doctrine of segregation of resources.

4

Industrial Development

Even before the dawn of civilisation in Western Europe, the birthplace of modern industrialism, the manufactures of India were in a flourishing condition. The skill of her craftsmen in the production of highly artistic and delicate cotton and silk fabrics, the working of metals and precious stones, and in all kinds of technical arts, has from ancient times evoked the admiration of the world. The Chinese travellers who visited India in the fourth and the sixth centuries, Bernier who visited India in the reign of Shahjahan, and Tavernier have left glowing descriptions of the marvellous products of Indian arts and industries.

Although insignificant in volume in comparison with modern figures, foreign trade in these manufactured goods played a not inconsiderable role in the economic life of India. To the dismay of foreign countries, the most significant feature of this trade was the one-sided importation of precious metals into India. Western Europe was brought into touch with Indian goods principally through the Crusades, and from that time onward a considerable traffic, sometimes wholly by land and sometimes by both land and water, developed to the eastern end of the Mediterranean. In the fifteenth century the Mediterranean contact was cut off by the Turks, and the European powers began a frantic competition to discover another route. This led, at the end of the century, to the discovery of the sea route to India by way of the Cape. For about a century after the arrival of the Europeans, trade was generally in the hands of the Portuguese and the Spanish. The merchants of England viewed their trade with envious eyes, and formed the East India Company; by the opening of the seventeenth century the Portuguese, the Dutch and the English were participating in the Indian treade. At first the enterprises of the British East India Company were merely voyages in which several merchants were associated. About

1657 the Company became a permanent corporation when "factories" were established and regular trading and warehousing begun.

The subsequent fate of the Indian handicraftsmen is too well-known: the political power won at Plassey was now deliberately employed to discourage the manufactures of India by the imposition of prohibitive import duties and other means; and this continued to be the settled policy of England towards India for fifty years and more. Meanwhile the industrial revolution had worked itself out in England, and the destruction of the Indian industries was complete. The inevitable happened, one industry after another succumbed, bringing destitution and desolation in its train. Throughout the nineteenth century the indigenous industries tended to decline, forcing more and more of the population into entire dependence on land.

After the assumption of direct rule by the Crown in 1858, the doctrine of *laissez-faire* was extended to India. The belief gained ground that India with her fertile soil and trying climate was more suited to the production of raw materials to be exchanged for the manufactured goods of English factories. As early as 1788 the East India Company began to take an interest in the expansion and improvement of cotton cultivation in India. Towards the beginning of the nineteenth century the Company resolved to revive the indigo industry and expert planters were brought out from the West Indies for the purpose, and the next fifty years saw its rapid expansion. The tea industry--the premier plantation industry of India–was likewise introduced and pioneered by the Government. The experimental tea garden started in 1835 was sold in 1839 to the Assam Tea Co., Ltd. Systematic cultivation of coffee was begun in India in 1830.

By the end of the eighteenth century modern factory industry had been well established in England and during the next quarter of a century was being further developed. By the middle of the nineteenth century England had become the workshop of the world. In India the outstanding industrial events of the nineteenth century were the decay and extinction of indigenous industries, and the rise of one or two modern industries. The earliest form of Indian enterprise was the application of steam to shipping. Gradually steam engines were also being employed in docks, in paper mills, in coining money, grinding flour and in the spinning and weaving of cotton, all in the neighbourhood of Calcutta and by Europeans. The early ventures did not flourish, and for good reasons. Machinery, spare parts and stores had to come by way of the Cape in sailing ships. The engineers, foremen and sometimes even the labourers had to be brought out from England. The regular mining of Indian coal did not commence until 1814: in 1854 there were 3 and in 1880 56 coal mines with a production of 1 million tons. The railway had not come into existence till 1853 when a short line was extended from Bombay; next year a line was opened from Howrah to the Raniganj coal-fields. The construction of this and other railways led to a rapid expansion of the coal industry and the two-million line of production was passed in 1890. By 1900 a yearly output of over 6 million tons was reached; imports had fallen to about 200,000 tons from 800,000 tons in 1880 and exports increased to nearly half a million tons.

With the development of collieries and expansion of railways some initial obstacles to the establishment of modern industries in India had been removed. Barring the ill-started Bowreah mills near Calcutta about the 1820's, the earliest cotton mills appear to have been built in 1854 in the Bombay Presidency by a Parsi gentleman. By the end of 1861, there were 9 cotton mills, and in 1880 there were 58. The first jute mill was started in Calcutta in 1855, and in 1868 there were 5 of them.

From these small beginnings India has now become an important industrial country. It is a truism that India is and must remain an agricultural country, but very few realise what great progress India has made in the industrial sphere. Within about 80 years over 2½ millions of persons have come to be employed in modern factories, mines and railways; India to-day ranks as one amongst the 8 leading industrial countries of the world and has a seat on the International Labour office.

In 1935 India had 9,261 large industrial establishments of all kinds employing 1,840,790 persons. The relative importance of the principal industries in India is indicated by the table of employment reproduced below :-

Industry		**Persons** ***employed***
Cotton (Spinning, weaving and other)	1935	516,000
Jute mills	1935	281,000
Cotton Spinning and baling	1935	180,000
Railway & Train way works	1935	116,000
Rice mills	1935	79,000
Sugar factories	1935	73,000
Tea Factories	1935	66,000

Printing and book-binding, etc.	1935	40,000
Jute Presses	1935	32,000

Industry		**Persons** *employed*
Matches	1935	21,000
Dockyards, shipbuilding and engineering	1935	21,000
Ordnance factories	1935	19,000
Bricks & tiles	1935	15,000
Oil mills	1935	15,000
Saw mills	1935	14,000
Rope works	1935	14,000
Cement, lme and potteries	1935	13,000
Tobacco	1935	12,000
Petroleum refineries	1935	11,000
Leather and shoe and tanneries	1935	8,000
Woollen mills	1935	8,000
Dyeing and bleaching and indigo	1935	8,000
Silk mills (including filatures)	1935	7,000
Glass works	1935	7,000
Paper mills	1935	7,000
Coach building and motor-car repairing	1935	7,000
Stone dressing	1935	6,000
Hosiery	1935	6,000
Flour mills	1935	6,000
Kerosin tinning and packing	1935	6,000
Rubber	1935	6,000

Some idea about our industrial development will also be conveyed by an enumeration of joint-stock companies. In 1933-34 the number of joint-stock companies at work of all classes incorporated in India was 9,434 with an aggregate paid-up capital of Rs. 300 crores, of which mills and presses accounted for Rs. 70 crores, plantations Rs. 16 crores, mines and quarrying Rs. 40 crores. The total number of companies incorported outside India, but which carry on work in India, was 916 with an aggregate paid-up capital of £818 million and debenture of £ 151 million. Of the paid up capital & debentures £ 191 million and £23 million, respectively, were invested in petroleum mining companies, £89 millon and £46 million in engineering, £69 million and £5 million in insurance and £57 million in iron, steel and shipbuilding.

The *Capital* index of business activity in India furnishes a very satisfactory standard for measuring industrial activity in this country. The pity is that it does not begin earlier than 1932–33. The recent progress of our industrial production will be best indicated by the table below calculated from the *Capital* index figures.

Industrial Production (Monthly average 1935-100)

	Cotton manu factures	*Jute Manu factures*	*Steel ingots*	*Pig iron*	*Cement*	*Paper*	*Coal*
Weights	9	6	5	8	5	3	7
1932-33	91.7	90.3	68.2	60.3	67.4	85.0	86.6
1932-33	85.2	90.6	83.4	76.2	73.1	92.4	87.2
1934-35	97.2	95.0	96.7	92.5	88.9	94.3	99.9
1935-36	104.6	101.1	101.9	106.2	101.4	101.7	100.8
1936-37	103.2	124.8	99.7	107.0	113.6	102.4	96.1
1937-38	112.8	129.0	106.8	112.6	130.3	107.5	111.9

In the five years from 1932–33 to 1937–38, the production of cotton piece-goods has advanced by 23 per cent, coal by 30 per cent, steel ingots by 56 per cent, pig iron by 86 per cent, paper by 25 per cent, cement by 94 per cent, and jute manufactures by 43 per cent. And these results were obtained notwithstanding the world's greatest economic depression.

We shall now attempt a brief description of some of the principal organised industries in India.

The Cotton Mill Industry

Its growth:–The cotton mill industry is by far the most important industry of India. The rise and growth of this industry will be indicated by the table below :–

Year (ending June 30)	*No. of mills*	*Spindles (1,000)*	*Looms (1,000)*
1851	1	29	
1876	47	1,100	9
1886	95	2,261	17
1896	155	3,932	37
1906	217	5,279	52

(ending Aug. 31)			
1916	266	6,839	110
1926	334	8,714	159
1935-36	379	9,857	200

The progress and relative stage of development of the industry will be still more explicit from the figures of consumption of piece-goods in India given below:–

Year	***Net imports-yards*** *(crores)*	***Net available mill pro duction-Yards*** *(crores)*	***Estimated hand-loom Production yards*** *(crores)*	***Net total available for consumption-Yards*** *(crores)*
1905-6	239	61	108	408
1912-17	295	113	104	512
1919-20	99	144	56	299
1929-30	190	229	140	559
1935-36	97	350	166	613

Roughly speaking, the relative position of the hand-loom is almost the same, but the comparative position of foreign imports and Indian mill production has been completely reversed. In 1905–6, imports constituted 50 per cent and mill production 15 per cent of consumption; to-day imports form only about 16 per cent and mill production 57 per cent.

During the earlier period of its history, the spinning section of the industry was more important than the weaving, and moe than half of the yarns produced used to be exported. In the present century, however, the foreces have been reversed; the export trade in yarns has been practically lost, due mainly to Japanese competition in the East, the expansion of the Chinese industry, and also partly due to increased domestic demand. In 1896 the number of spindles per loom was 106, in 1936 it was only 49. Another recent tendency has been the increasing spinning of yarns of finer counts, and growing importation of foreign cotton for the purpose. Our mills have widened the range of their products, and the improved designs and styles which they have introduced are selling at competitive rates. Dyed and printed voiles, poplins, white mulls, tussores, coloured Italian cloths and poonjees, formerly mainly imported, are being successfully produced in the country, and at this rate of progress the day is not far distant when Indian mills may be expected to meet domestic requirements both quantitatively and qualitatively.

The most outstanding event of the century, concerning the industry, has been the decline of imports of piece-goods from the United Kingdom, and the rise and phenomenal expansion of imports from Japan as is shown by the table below:–

Imports from the United Kingdom and Japan, and production in India, of cotton piece-goods (excluding fents) :-

(In million yards)

Year	*United Kingdom*	*Japan*	*Mill production in India*
1905-06	2,415	-----	------
1910-11	2,252	----	1,043
1911-12	2,379	1	1,136
1912-13	2,907	6	1,220
1914-15	2,354	16	1,136
1916-17	1,748	100	1,578
1918-19	851	238	1,451
1927-28	1,530	323	2,357
1929-30	1,236	562	2,419
1931-32	376	340	2,990
1932-33	586	579	3,170
1933-34	415	341	2,945
1934-35	552	374	3,397
1935-36	440	496	3,571

Between 1913-14 and 1935-36 the percentage share of Japan in the total quantities of piece-goods imported has increased from 0.3 per cent to 52.4 per cent, and that of the United Kingdom has fallen from 97.1 per cent to 46.4 per cent.

The above table also makes it clear that, in recent years, further inroad of Japanese piece-goods has been held in check. This result was, however, rendered possible only by the adoption of rather violent measures in the form of tariffs combined with bilateral trade agreements. In devising the scale of duty, it may be noted, a certain degree of preference has always been shown towards the United Kingdom.

The Mill industry versus the Indian cotton grower:– The making of cotton tariff in India is a delicate task of extreme complexity. India is the most important market for piece-goods from both Japan and the United Kingdom, and Japan is the biggest single market for Indian raw cotton. More than half of our exports of raw cotton, being nearly equal to the total consumption of indigenous cotton by Indian mills, goes to Japan alone. In protecting the Indian mill industry we can hardly afford to ignore Japan and thereby the interests of millons of poor Indian cultivators. At the same time, there can be little doubt that Japan will before long develop China as a cotton-growing country. The Manchukuo Government, over which her influence is paramount, has already inaugurated a scheme for bringing 750,000 acres of land under cotton cultivation within the mext twenty years. In the end the Japanese demand for our raw cotton is bound to contract, and if by that time further expansion of the Indian mill and hand-loom industries fails to absorb the surplus that cannot find an export outlet, where is the Indian cultivator to find an alternative market? At the same time, we are to avoid taking any step which may retard the development of the biggest industry of India towards its goal of self-sufficiency. It is in this background that we have to judge the negotiations that are, and that may be, carried on with Lancashire and Japan.

The Jute Mill Industry

Its growth:– The jute mill industry comes next to cotton in importance. The first jute mill in Dundee was established in 1838. In 1855 a beginning in spinning and weaving was made in Calcutta in earnest and a mill was erected with an output of 8 tons a day. The subsequent development of the Calcutta jute mill industry is indicated by the table below:–

Year	*Sacking looms*	*Hessian looms*	*Total*
1859	----	----	192
1877	2,948	910	3,858
1890	5,359	2,300	7,659
1910	13,421	18,334	31,755
1930	22,066	36,073	58,139
1935	22,693	37,704	60,397

In addition, a number of small and medium-sized mills have recently been started, and a few more are in course of erection. There are also mills in India outside Calcutta–4 in the Madras Presidency, 3 in Bihar, and 2 in the United Provinces. The total number of looms at present working in India will not be less than 66,000. It may be interesting to note that the number of looms in Dundee is only 8,500. The largest number of looms in any country outside India is in Germany where there are 11,000 looms. The total number of looms in all countries outside India is 48, 955.

This industry is by far the most important manufacturing export industry of India. The value of jute manufactures exported in 1928–29, the best year of prosperity, was Rs. 56.9 crores, being 17 per cent of our total exports, as against 2 per cent in cotton manufactures which occupy the second place amongst manufactured exports. The average value of exports in the period 1879–80 to 1883–84 was only Rs. 1.2 crores. Nearly two-thirds of the jute grown is now consumed by the Indian mills.

The problem of over-production:– Due to the economic depression, coupled with internal dissension amongst the mills themselves, of late the industry is passing through a period of extreme difficulties. The problem of over-production in this industry is almost as old as the industry itself and it was to meet such a situation that the Indian Jute Mills Association was brought into being in 1884. This Association has been of great value in regulating the output of mills and making profitable working possible; but with the increase in the number of mills outside the Association the conclusion of a satisfactory agreement for the control of production is proving difficult. On the admission of the Association itself and on the basis of 54 hours' working per week, 25 per cent of the machinery in the industry is redundant. The difficulties of the industry cannot be solved by restriction of output alone unaccompanied by rationalisation and diffusion of production on new lines.

The Iron and Steel Industry.

The rise of a modern iron and steel industry:– The earliest attempt to make iron by European processes was made about 1830 in the South Arcot district of Madras. The next attempt was made in Bengal in 1875 by the Bengal Iron Co. By about 1900 the average annual production of pig iron was 35,000 tons entirely from this company.

With the formation of the Tata Iron and Steel Co., and the

exploitation of the enormous quantities of extremely rich iron ore deposits in the Singhbhum and Manbhum districts and the feudatory states of Mayurbhang, Bonai and Keonghar, commenced a new era in the history of the Indian industy. The first pig iron was made by the Tata Co. in 1911, and the first steel in 1913. The Indian Iron & Steel Co. started manufacturing pig iron towards 1922. At the present rate of working–nearly 2½ million tons per year–the iron ore deposite are estimated to last 1,000 years. There are likewise abundant reserves of easily workable lime stones, manganese and fluxes and other refractory materials of excellent composition.

The recent development of the industry has been in no small measure due to the grant of fiscal protection in 1924 and its continuance in some form or other thereafter. The formation of the Bengal Steel Corporation last year marks an important step forward in the development of the industry. The Mysore Iron Works are already producing steel, though on a small scale. In addition there are a number of small re-rolling mills, roling from billets or scrap and confining themselves to a narrow range or products.

The statistical position of the industry is indicated below:–

Production (tons)

Year	Pig iron	Steel ingots	Finished steel goods
1913-14	218,000	------	------
1935-36	1,541,000	880,000	677,000

The position and efficiency of the industry:– The Indian industry has attained remarkable success; it produces practically all our requirements of pig iron, and exports about half a million tons every year. Further, our cost of production of pig iron is claimed to be the lowest in the world. The domestic production of steel is now 50 per cent greater than the total import. With the incorportion of the Bengal Steel Corporation and the projected extensions to the Tata factory, the time does not appear to be far off when India will become self-sufficient in the supply of steel as well. The Chairman of the Tata Co. is reported to have declared at the annual general meeting of shareholders for 1936 that by 1940 the company would require no protection.

The Cement Industry

Rapid expansion of the industry:– In spite of the large home market, and the presence of abundant raw materials, Portland cement was not manufactured in India until 1904, but the real beginning of the industry was made in 1912. Since then the industry has made phenomenal progress as is indicated by the table below :–

Year	*Sales of Indian cement in India* (tons)	*Imports into India* (tons)	*Totalconsumption in India* (tons)
1914	945	150,530	151,475
1916	38,672	80,543	119,215
1918	84,344	20,016	104,360
1925	360,549	68,200	428,749
1930	563,929	68,000	631,929
1935-36	886,267	42,900	929,167

Early attempts towards rationalisation:– In 1924 the industry was in parlous conditions and it applied for protection. The Tariff Board declined to recommend protection on the ground that the industry was suffering from internal competition due to over-production. It found that the Indian works were already capable of producing 600,000 tons whereas the annual consumption was only 390,000 tons. Following this report, the cement companies formed a pool known as the Indian Cement Manufacturers' Association. In the following year the Concrete Association of India was formed with the object of educating the public in the uses of cement and providing free technical aid and advice. In 1930 was formed the Cement Marketing Co. of India Ltd., to take over control of the sales and distribution of cement. In 1936 the Associated Cement Companies Ltd. was formed to merge 10 manufacturing companies. The merger is expected to control production and effect economics in working and distribution.

Recentexpansionandthedangerofover-production:–Thecement industry is one of the most vigorous and healthy industries of India. In a little over two decades a new industry has become firmly established. consumption has advanced from 150,475 tons to one million tons and at the same time price has been substantially reduced. Recently a number of new factories have been put up and a few more are in process of erection. In 1936-37 the manufacturing capacity of the associated companies was 1,465,000 tons. The capacity of the Dalmia group of companies (including the Rhotas factory) is estimated at another 575,000 tons, bringing the total Indian capacity to 2,040,000 tons, which is double the present consumption. Herein lies the danger, but as in the past, cheaper prices coupled with mutual co-operation, organised methods of selling and distribution, widnespread propaganda and education, may enable the industry to avoid the impending catastrophe.

The Sugar Mill Industry

Over-rapid expansion of the industry:– Till recently, Indian occupied the anomalous position of being the world's second largest grower of cane, and at the same time one of the biggest importers of manufactured sugar. Within five years of the passing of the sugar protection Act of 1932, this has changed, and India is now not only self-sufficient in her requirements of sugar but a potential exporter. In 1931-32 there had been 31 factories producing 158,581 tons of sugar. In 1936-37 the number increased to 153 with a production of 1,128,900 tons, while import of sugar fell from one million tons to below 23,000 tons only.

Attempted solutions:– Though the industry has shown remarkable growth, it has not prospered as well as it was expected to. Within five years the nightmare of overproduction is staring it in the face, and it is beset with a number of very difficult problems on the agricultural, manufacturing and marketing sides. The Imperial Council of Agricultural Research and other associated bodies are doing very valuable work on some of the problems. The Government of the United Provinces and Bihar have recently passed legislation of a far-reaching character to control and stabilise the industry.

The Coal Industry

Indian coal resources and their exploitation:– The regular mining of coal in India did not commence until 1814. In the absence of any modern industry the demand for coal was very limited at this early period. With the opening up of Raniganj with Calcutta by a railway in 1854 and the advent of the factory system the coal industry made very repid progress, as will be indicated by the figures of production given below:–

Year	*(Production (1,000 tons)*
1846	91
1880	1,019
1900	6,118

1920	17,962
1930	23,803
1935	23,000

The coal resources of India have been variously estimated at between 36 to 54 billion tons as against 189 billions for Great Britain. In 1936 the number of Joint-Stock Coal Companies at work was 217 with a paid-up capital of more than Rs. 10 crores. In addition there are a number of coal-fields owned and worked by the railways.

About 72 per cent of the total output of our coal comes from Bengal,Bihar and Orissa where the most valuable deposits of coal are found. The Raniganj and the Jharia are the two most important working coal-fields.

The problems of the industry:- Nearly 98 per cent of our production of coal is consumed in the country. The railways are the largest consumers, taking about one-third of the output, but they do not buy from the market all the coal they require as they have their own collieries. These railway collieries, often State owned, are offshoots of the high price of coal prevailing about 1921. The coal trade regards them as a menace and injustice to legitimate private enterprise.

We do not import any larger quantity of coal, neither do we export much. At one time our export trade was not quite insignificant, but the wagon shortage and Government control established during the post-war boom period gave it a death-blow.

The annal *per capita* consumption of coal in India is ridiculously low. Under the auspices of the Indian Soft Coke Committee constituted in 1929, a vigorous propaganda has been started for popularising coal with encouraging results.

Mining conditions are extremely favourable in India, the seams are thick and close to the surface, Till recently both above and under ground there was an extreme lack of mechanical equipment.

Existing mining methods are very wasteful. India possesses practically unlimited reserves of second-class coal but her reserves of good quality coking coal required for the iron and steel industry will be exhausted well before the reserves of good quality non-coking coal. Hence, to avoid a possible shortage of metallurgical coal, India will have to learn to utilise to the best advantage poorer-class coals and also, as far as practicable, adopt measures for the better conservation of coking coal.

The position of India as to the factors of industrial development:– "The abundance of raw materials, the high consuming markets and the cheapness of labour," says Dr. L. Nemenyi, "pre-destine India to become a highly industrialised country in the course of time." But, up to the outbreak of the last great war, the pace of industrial development in India had been very slow. The Industrial Commission mentioned various factors as being responsible for this retarded development. The natural conservativeness of the people, the inefficiency of labour, the absence of industrial and technical education, the lack of business enterprise, the shyness of capital for new undertakings, and the want of proper organisation for utilising such capital as is available are not deficiencies inherent in the Indian character, and will yield to better organisation, training and opportunity. In the words of the Indian Fiscal Commission, "education can be improved, banking facilities can be extended, technical assistance can be offered to industries." In the past the average Indian certainly showed a lack of interest in industrial development and left it to be done by the Europeans or the Parsees, but due to Swadeshi and other reasons a change has come over the spirit of the people.

Whatever detractors and interested critics might say, it is generally admitted that India does not lack in the other factors of industrial development. India is an agricultural country and must always remain so: it is natural that her leading industries are those engaged in working up agricultural products. Of the vagetable products used in manufacture, cotton, lines or jute, oil seeds, sugarcane and rubber are the most important all over the world.

Abundance and variety of raw mat~~r~~ials and minerals: Agricultural raw materials:– India is the second largest producer of cotton in the world. Nearly 50 per cent of the production is consumed locally; the rest is exported mainly to Japan, where, after being mixed up with American or Egyptian cotton, it has built up an industry which now threatens the most advanced European manufacturers. Indian cotton is short and coarse and will not spin yarn finer than 30 counts. In order to meet foreign competition, Indian mills find it necessary to import a certain amount of cotton mainly from Uganda and Egypt. In 1934–35, this import amounted to 4.6 lakhs of bales, being about a sixth of the total consumption of alll cottons by mills. The internal production of long staple (over one inch) cotton was 51,000 bales in 1934–35 and 85,000 bales in 1935–36. The importation of foreign cotton is to be deplored as India is one of the original homes of cotton and used to grow in earlier days cottons so fine as to produce the "Muslim." India suffers from no inherent defect of the soil or climate, but the cultivator has to be educated out of his indifference and conservativeness. The Sukker Barrage irrigation project opens up vast possibilities and the day may not be far off when India shall become independent of foreign supplies of long-stapled cotton.

Jute is the foundation of the second most important industry of India, and in its production India holds the world's monopoly. Though attempts have been made to grow it else where, they have not so far been attempted with any measure of commercial success. About two thirds of the crop are manufactured withing India and the rest is exported.

The sugar industry–an infant of five years only–vies with the jute industry for the second position in India's industrial ranking list. The deficiencies of Indian sugarcane and its cultivation are not inherent as is shown by the achievements of the Belapur and the Mysore Sugar Companies.

Our resources in forests are varied and vast in extent and value. They yield materials for various industrial purposes such as the manufacture of paper pulp, matches, tea chests, tool handles, etc. They also provide valuable tanning materials, certain kinds of essential oils, gums, waxes and resins. At the same time, it ought to be mentioned that a full exploitation of our forest wealth depends upon the development of transport facilities, extension of research and experimental works and the creation of a demand by systematic publicity and organisation.

In 1935–36 we exported 43,900 tons of raw hides and skins, though vagetable tanning materials of good quality are found in most parts of India. Before the war about double the quantity used to be exported. Here again, the problem is one of capital, enterprise and organisation.

In oil seeds, India holds the unique position of being the largest producer in the world. The total area under oil seeds generally averages round 14 million acres. Almost every variety of oil seeds is cultivated and a very large proportion of the crop is exported; much of the balance is crushed by small power plants or in country bullock mills. In 1930, including native states, there were in India 289 oil factories cmploying 14,269 persons. In 1935–36 the value of vegetable non-essential oils exported amounted to Rs. 36 lakhs, and the value of oil seeds exported Rs. 10 crores. In addition to domestic consumption, these oils constitute the basis of soaps and paints.

In 1935-36 India exported raw rubber valued at Rs. 88 lakhs and imported rubber goods worth Rs. 2 crores.

Minerals:- The mineral deposits of India are abundant and sufficient to maintain most of the 'key" industries. The iron ore deposits of Orissa constitute one of the richest in quality and quantity and exist in close proximity to good coking coal. Rich deposits of lead and zinc occur in the Shan States of, Burma. Copper is being successfully smelted in the Singbhum district and Burma.

The managanese ore deposits of India are probably the most extensive in the world. It is at present exported in the raw state in very large quantities. High grade chromium and bauxite deposits have been found and are being worked. South Burma is one of the richest sources of wolfram in the world. Tin is also found there and in other parts of Burma. In mica India holds the leading place in the world. The ingredients for the manufacture of good quality cement occur at many places. There are extensive deposits of medium quality coal and oil, though concentrated in limited areas which involves high cost of transportation. This drawback in power resources is likely to be mitigated in certain areas by the development of hydro-electricity.

The foregoing analysis shows that India is favourably placed in the supply of raw materials and mineral resources, Shortcomings there are, but in most cases these are neither inherent nor insuperable. Great improvements have already been made in several directions by the application of the methods of the West and still greater progress promises to be achieved if systematic and intensive attempts are made. In the case of our mineral resources, these are no reasons to think that the position of any country is superior to ours. Further geological surveys and extension of cheap methods of transport are likely to prove helpful.

Mere presence of raw materials is not, however, a sufficient justification for the establishment of manufacturing industries in a country. Sweden sends her iron ore to Germany: United States of America sends her cotton to Lancashire. But India has advantages in the form of an immense potential internal market and an unlimited supply of cheap labour. A full discussion of the labour position will take us too far afield. Suffice it to say that, given proper supervision and suitable plant, just as accurate work can be produced in India with Indian labour as in Europe. The experiences of the Tata Iron & Steel Co., Batas, Dunlops, Braithwaites and others lend strong support to this view. Moreover, in comparing efficiencies we must not foreget that Indian labour has to contend against a trying climate, less efficient management, backward factory equipment and a low standard of living. It is also necessary to remember that in India machinery is dearer and labour is cheap, while in Europe it is the reverse; hence the machine must be used to its utmost capacity even though a larger labour force has to be employed. It must, however, be admitted that India lacks the ready supply of skilled labour and scientific and techinical experts who can serve as managers, foremen and entrepreneurs.

Deficiencies in capital and enterprise:– In point of capital the problem is not so much one of amount as of its shyness for industrial employment. In spite of various official reports, nothing serious seems to have been done to produce a change for the better.

It is, however, in industial leadership that India is most deficient. In Europe factories were established by two groups; the master craftsmen and the merchants. In India, the master-craftsmen had not the capital nor the education or the ambition to embark upon large-scale factory industry. The merchants had no experience in handling labour, and they never cared to take any responsibility for the technical side of production. Moreover, the development of trade and communications gave them ample opportunities of engaging their money. No wonder, therefore, that the early enterprises were initiated by the Europeans and a handful of Parsees. Later on, others also have entered the field, but still the position is far from what it should be.

The Managing Agency system in relation to finance and management:– Any discussion of industrial leadership and finance would be incomplete without a reference to the Managing Agency system so prevalent in India. The great merit ofthis much-maligned system is that it has been the natural product of the special conditions of the country and was never made to order. Of all single factors, the contribution of the Managing Agents towards the industrial development of the country has been very considerable indeed. This system in India has done what the continental system of banking did for their industrial developments. They combine command over capital with enterprise, business ability and experience. In India the role of the entrepreneur has been played by these Managing Agents. The idea of a venture very often originates from them, they investigate and explore, they nourish the growth of new enterprises and take the responsibility of finding the fixed and working capital in good and bad times. The system has contributed greatly to induce the flow of capital into industry. In fact, capital moves more freely into a company floated and operated by a reputed firm of Managing Agents; and it is dificult to conceive of a more satisfactory form of industrial finance in the existing financial organisation and habits of the people. The system is a great economiser of overhead charged and should make possible considerable economies in the purchase of stores, sale of finished goods, maintenance of a highly technical staff, etc. It is also the most economical way by which scattered mills, mines, tea gardens, and miscellaneous mofussil industries can be linked up to the centres of Indian commerce, like Calcutta, Bombay, and through them to the channels of world trade. This, however, cannot be claimed of many firms of Indian Managing Agents. European firms, in spite of age, maintain their elasticity and responsiveness : but Indian firms generally confine their business to the family line and in the absence of infusion of new blood, stability and efficiency are bound to degenerate. Judged by foreign standards, the system may appear old-fashioned, but we must not overlook that in India business commonsense is undeveloped, the banking habit is a luxury of the few and the financial mechanism has been fashioned on English methods and tradition. The Managing Agency system is a peculiar Indian methods to cope with a peculiar Indian situation and that is its best recommendation. We must try to devise new and better methods, but units a practicable alternative has been evolved, our problem is one of mending and not ending; and it is this which the Indian Companies (Amendment) Act, 1936, has attempted.

II. The State in Relation To Industry

The policy of *laissez-faire* and its reaction upon public opinion:– In spite of the abundance of raw materials, the immense internal market, and other fairly satisfactory conditions, our industrial achievements in the nineteenth century had not been considerable; it in only during the present century, particularly after the last war, that any remarkable progress has been made. Among other factors, one most important influence contributing to this result has been the progressive policy of the state in relation to industries. About the close of the eighteenth century the industrial revolution was complete in England, and she had become the industrial leader of the world. She required markets for her manufactures, and quite naturally she adopted the policy of *laissez-faire*. After the assumption of direct rule by the Crown in 1858, the same policy was considered good for India even though conditions in this country were vastly different.

The consequences of this policy may well be gauged from the findings of the Famine commission of 1880. The Commission believed that a main cause of the disastrous consequences of Indian famines was the fact that, the great mass of the people directly depended upon agriculture, and that there was no other industry from which any considerable part of the population derived their support; and they pleaded for a diversity of occupations, through which the surplus population might be drawn to manufactures. But no action was taken by the Government. Meanwhile, the Indian National Congress had come into existence,and in 1887 it passed a resolution urging upon the Government the desirability of encouraging indigenous industries and providing technical education. Since 1905 an Indian Industrial Conference has met from year to year providing a forum for the expression of the growing spirit of economic nationalism which culminated in the Swadeshi movement of 1907-08. In 1887, mainly through private efforts, the Victoria Jubilee Technical Institute was started in Bombay, and in 1904 an association was established in Calcutta for the advancement of seientific and industrial education of Indians.

The contribution of the State during this period was, in the words of the Industrial Commission (Report, para. 105), "a very imperfect provision of technical and industrial education, and the collection and dissemination of commercial and industrial information," which practically amounted to the establishment of a Commercial Museum at Calcutta, an inquiry by the "reporter on economic products" into the industrial resources of India, the founding of the *Indian Art Journal* and a series of provincial monographs on Indian industries. It is interesting to notice that none of these concerned the organised industries, their position, prospects and possibilities. So, the conclusion is inevitable that up to the end of the nineteenth century the Government as whole did not take any part in the modern industrial development of the country, and that if any progress was made it was in spite of the indifference of the Government.

Slight modification of Government policy towards the end of the nineteenth and the early twentieth centuries:–Towards the end of the century, however, a few individual officers adopted a more forward policy. In Madras, Mr. A. Chatterton successfully developed the aluminium hollowware industry, improved the hand-loom, and introduced chrome tanning of leather. In 1905, Lord Curzon set up a separate Commerce and Industry Department of the Government of India. Several Provincial Governments also now began to evince a real interest in industrial development. In the United Provinces, after the Nainital Conference of 1907, a comprehensive scheme for technical education and encouragement of industries was adopted. Loans were given, an experimental sugar factory was set up and a pioneer oil mill was started, but with little technical success and considerable financial loss. In the other Provinces also a keen interest was being taken in the revival and preservation of cottage industries and the spread of technical and industrial education. With the object of promoting the developmet of new industries and the improvement of existing ones, the system of State Technical Scholarships, tenable abroad, was adopted in 1903.

The forward policy of some of the Provincial Governments received an unexpected check in 1910, when Lord Morley, the then Secretary of State for India, refused to sanction the creation of a separate Department of Industries in Madras on the ground that State pioneering of industries, creation of demonstration plants, direct financial assistance and other forms of direct aid were no function of the State, and the they would interfere with private enterprise. Lord Morley's despatch naturally had a paralysing influence upon the Provincial Governments and the Government of India, and much of what had been done had to be undone. The despatch of Lord Crewe in 1912 did not materially alter the position, though it allowed the creation of Provincial Departments of Industries.

How the last war stimulated Indian industries:– This was the position when India entered the war. The war at once demonstrated how dangerously India was dependent upon foreign countries for essential supplies; certain fromer imports were entirely cut off while others were reduced in volume, huge urgent purchases had to be made by the Government of India on war account, and whatever industries India had now entered upon a period of unprecedented prosperity. It was necessary to expand existing industries and to start new once, but how could it be done if importation of machinery, technical skill and supervision, stores and other materials was not possible? It was under this stress that the Munitions Board was established, and the Industrial Commission appointed in 1916. Factories were started under the direct management of the State and many more were encouraged to come into existence with State help and patronage in various forms. Unfortunately many of these war babies succumbed on the return of normal conditions after the war.

The Industrial Commission:– The Industrial Commission in their report in 1918, made far-reaching recommendations for the active participation by the State in the industrial development of the country and for setting up the necessary administrative machinery. The main activities of the State were to include (1) research, (2) industrial and technical education, (3) commercial and industrial intelligence, (4) direct assistance: technical and financial, and (5) purchase of stores. In compliance with their recommendations separate Provincial Departments of Industries with an Imperial Department for purposes of co-ordination, were set up. On the whole, these departments have not fulfilled expectations; a number of industries were pioneered, and loans and grants given, but the achievements were not encouraging. Better results were, however, obtained in the sphere of cottage and small-scale industries.

The Policy of Discriminating Protection:– For more than a generation the Indian public had been carrying on a persistent agitation in favour of a policy of protection as a means of industrial development, but the Government dictated and controlled as it was by the British Cabinet, had consistently refused the demand, and pursued a policy of free trade. Along with other factors, the last war brought a change in this attitude; it was now realised that an industrial India would contribute to Imperial strength. The Joint Select Committee of Parliament on the Government of India Bill laid down a convention which marks the beginning of a new era. This ultimately led to the appointment of the Indian Fiscal Commission, which found that the conditions of industrial development could not be attained without stimulus in the form of protective duties. The main recommendation of the Commission, that the adoption of a policy of discriminating protection would be in the best interests of India, was accepted by the Government in 1923, and forms the basis of our present fiscal policy.

Next to tariff policy perhaps the most far-reaching measure adopted for the furtherance of Indian industries was the introduction in 1931 of the Rupee Tender Rules. In the preamble of the Rules it was announced that the Government policy was to make purchases of stores in such a way as to stimulate the development of Indian industries to the utmost extent possible consistent with economy and efficiency.

Government interest in cottage and small industries:– The progressive policy of the Government is manifest in other ways also. During the period of depression the Central as well as the Provincial Governments have been taking keen interest in the revival of cottage and small industries with a view to tackling the problem of unemployment and standard of living. On the recommendation of the Tariff Board in 1932, the Government of India decided to spend a substantial sum over a period of five years in reviving the hand-loom industry. The Provincial Governments also have not been lagging behind: most of them have added to the grants from the centre im promoting schemes fo. .mprovements in marketing, providing technical guidance, the supply of materials at cheap rates, etc. The small man in the silk and other industries also has not failed to get a certain amount of attention. The Governments of the United Provinces and Bengal have gone so far as to establish Industrial Corporations under Government patronage and control with a view to lending money for small-scale industrial enterprise.

Industries under Provincial Autonomy

The new-born zeal of the Provincial Governments to promote industries:– The newly established autonomous Provincial Governments are extremely anxious to promote by all means in their power the development of industries within their respective Provinces. The Congress election manifesto which is the basis of the programme, not only in the Provinces where the Congress is in power, but to a varying degree in the other Provinces too, contains the following as to industrial policy:–

(a) Encouragement of Khadi and village industries.

(b) Protection of larger industries, subject to rights of producers of raw materials, workers, and safeguarding of village industries.

The promptness of the Governments of Bihar and the United Provinces in passing legislation for the better control of sugar factories, the appointment of a committee for investigating into the possibility of manufacturing power alcohol from molasses even before the publication of the report of the sugar Tariff Board, are only two out-standing instances of the new-born zeal of the Provincial Governments.

The Government of Bihar proposes to inaugurate shortly a grid electrification scheme for the expansion of tube-well irrigation on a wide scale and the promotion of industries. The idea is to generate electricity with coal distilled for the purpose. the estimated cost per K.W. of installed capacity of the Bihar scheme is expected to be lower than the cost of even the hydro-electric schemes of other Provinces.

The Government of Madras is trying to give a special impetus to hand-loom production by licensing the sale of mill cloth the introducing

Khaddar for police and other uniforms. The Bombay Government in addition to hand spinning and hand-weaving have approved several schemes for the promotion of industries. It has also established an Industrial Advisory Board to examine all new schemes and proposals relating to industrial development in the Province. The Orissa Government also is preparing an intensive scheme for the revival of cottage industries. Other Provincial Governments are not lagging for behind.

Attempts towards all-India planning:– A remarkable example of the new spirit is provided in the drive by Mr. V.V. Giri, the Madras Minister, to make India an industrially selfsufficient country. He has been making efforts to convene a conference of Ministers of Industries (as reported in the *Statesman* of June 8 and 9, 1938) from all the Congress Provinces, and from as many other non-Congress Provinces as possible, together with experts connected with basic industries, with a view to formulating a planned scheme for industrial expansion on an all-India basis.

One of the industries to be so examined will be the automobile industry. The possibilities of manufacture of locomotives for railways are also under consideration. The first scheme is likely to reach fruition soon, following talks between Mr. Giri and Sir M. Visweswaraiya at Bengalore. The proposal is to make a start with standard cars. Foreign technicians will be engaged initially with the object of training Indian for more responsible posts so as to finally make the concern Indian-owned and Indian-managed,

Another illustration of the same spirit is provided by Dr.Syed Mahmud, Minister, Education and Development Department, Bihar, who has invited the Industries Ministers of Provincial Governments to a conference to consider the question of development of key industries in India.For the proper development of these industries he considers the following measures essential : a list of important key industries deserving State recognition and encouragement should be drawn up; the industries should be fostered in areas which are economically most suitable; indiscriminate expansion should be controlled to keep pace with demand; and currency, tariff and railway freights being vital factors, these should be adjusted to aid the progress of these industries. All Provinces and States should, therefore, present a united demand to the Central Government for help. Once it is decided to "earmark" a particular industry for a selected Province or Provinces, all other provinces should combine to help in the disposal of products and to secure other facilities (*Statesman,* June 20. 1938, Dak Edn.).

The meeting of the Congress Working Committee, held in July 1938, adopted a resolution authorising the Congress President to convene, at an early date, a Conference of Provincial Ministers of Industries. In pursuance of this resolution, the Ministers met in Delhi, early in October, under the Chairmanship of the Congress President. They agreed that the time had come when definite decisions had to be taken with regard to the starting of major, medium and cottage industries with a regular programme. A Planning Committee was accordingly appointed and is expected to take about eight to ten months to submit its report. After this an All-India National Planning Commission will be appointed, which will include not only the experts who form the present Planning committee but also representatives of the Provinces and States willing to co-operate.

The project to make a preliminary industrial survey is both a necessary and a wise approach to the future planning of India's industrial development. It will ensure the ordered progress of industrial expansions, and help to eliminate the uneconomic competition to which many enterprises are still now exposed. The Planning Committee expects to have the co-operation of all the Provinces and some of the more important States. The Non-Congress Provinces also can by no means be said to be unmindful of the importance of developing their own industries. To the States it is an opportunity to develop their untapped resources for their own good and to find a place in the industrial structure of India. Unless the Provinces and States co-ordinate their efforts, success cannot be complete. Provincial jealousy, which has been already rearing its head in so many directions, which find no place in the evolution and working of the industrial plan.

The wisdom of the Provincial Governments themselves setting up an All-India Planning Commission may be doubted; but it cannot be helped so long as the Central Government is not democratised. It is felt that a scheme of industrial development supported by the Congress and Non-Congress Provinces and some of the States cannot fail to have a tramendous influence upon the Government of India.

As pointed out by the conference of Ministers, the ultimate object of industrial development is to solve the problem of "poverty and unemployment, of national defence and of economic regeneration in general." Hence cottage industries as well as middle-sized and large-scale industries must all find a place in such a scheme. Also there is no conflict of interest between industries and agriculture. For the soundness of our rural economy itself depends on the expansion of industries and the maintenance of a healthy balance between the two; also bacause the trend towards national self-sufficiency is now so well established that it might be regarded as a permanent feature of the economic structure of the future. It is no longer safe for us to depend to the same extent as before on fereign countries as outlets for our raw materials.

The solicitude of the Provincial Governments for labour:– In their anxiety to promote industries, the Provincial Governments can by no means be blamed of being oblivious of the interests of labour. In fact, it is being questioned if the pace of industrial reforms in some Provinces is not too fast. The acceptance of office by the Congress has coincided with the outbreak of labour unrest and strikes in all the important industrial centres. Further, the reports of the various Labour Euquiry Committees have made capitalists apprehensive about the future of industries in British India. These enquiry reports will serve a very useful purpose in exposing and removing long-standing injustices and inequities, but they must give a "fair deal" to the other party. If the capitalistic system is to survive at all, business activities must be conducted not for the benefit of any particular class but for the community as a whole. It is not unnatural that on the accession to political power of the wage-earning classes there should be a certain amount of effervescence, but the Provincial Governments would do well not to create any apprehension in the minds of the industrialists of any bias against them. Only by maintaining an impartial and judicious attitude will they be able to make their influence best felt and achieve the ends they have in view. The expansion and better organisation of industries which is so dear to the Provincial Governments cannot be brought about unless there is healthy co-operation between the employer and the employed. And to this end the time seems to be ripe for the establishment of an Industrial Council as suggested by the Whitley Commission. Indian labour is fully alive to its strength, and the use and potentialities of the strike; it, however, remains untrained in the art of negotiation and lacks the organisation and leadership so essential to the welfare of industry as a whole. The truth of this statement will be amply borne out even by a superficial examination of the history of any one of the large crop of major industrial disputes of the past and the present. It is urgently necessary for labour, and those who are interested in industrial development, and have the privilege and power to mould policy and practice, to realise that capital and labour are mutual trustees and that both are the trustees of consumers.

III. Conclusion

The extent of industrial development and the danger of over-production in certain lines:–The Indian Industrial commission, after a very searching inquiry, summed up the industrial position of India in the following words :–

"The industrial system is unevenly, and in most cases inadequately developed, and the capitalists of the country, with a few notable exceptions, have till now left to other nations the work and profit of manufacturing her valuable raw materials, or have allowed them to remain unutilised."

The Indian Fiscal Commission not only endorsed the findings of the Indian Industrial Commission, but went further to say that "the industrial development of India has not been commensurate with the size of the country, its population, and its natural resources." They summed up the then industrial position as follows:–

"We find in the cotton and jute mills two important industries of modern type, a considerable diffusion of mechanical engineering represented by the railway work shops and the private engineering works which are now springing up, the beginnings of a iron and steel industry, and a number of minor industries, none of which has yet reached a stage of being a serious economic factor in the country. In addition there is a large production of mineral oil, and there is the important industry of coal mining, on the future of which the industrial development of the country largely depends."

Since then, in a decade and a half, there has been phenomenal progress in certain industries. India now produces about 80 per cent of her requirements of cotton textiles,; in five years she has become self-sufficient in sugar; cement was produced for the first time in 1914 and now foreign cement has almost been eliminated; further, the consumption of cement has increased while its price has been substantially reduced. In the protected varieties of paper India is nearly self-contained; by 1940, when the projected steel works at Hirapur commence operation, India will hardly need any foreign steel. In matches she is already self-sufficient. India has two manufacturing export industries–jute and pig iron. The jute industry is in a serious plight partly on account of an undue expansion of productive capacity; and the foreign market for our surplus pig iron is extremely precarious and uncertain. The utmost that Indian industries can aim at, consistent with safety and stability, in their present stage of development is national self-sufficiency and that stage is being reached fast in some at least. In fact, over-production threatens three of our industries, *viz.*, jute, sugar and cement, and the immediate problem in them is one of consolidation and rationalisation rather than any further expansion of productive capacity.

In addition to these major industries, a wide variety of minor industries have also been started–some of which are fairly well established, but the majority are still struggling hard to take root in the industrial system of the country.

Drawbacks of our industrial developments:– Notwithstanding the substantial progress of recent years, the extent and stage of industrial development in India is far from satisfactory. Even after a century of industrialisation there are 9,261 large industrial establishments employing 1,840,792 persons, *i.e.*, only one in every two hundred of the population. The commodities produced by these factories meet only a fraction of the total requirements of the people and make a poor show by the side of the great volume and variety of goods imported from abroad. This is particularly regrettable in view of the abundance and wide range of raw materials which are available but exported and then received back as finished goods. Our major industries have very largely expanded their productive capacity, but most of them are of a basic and rudimentary character. The two foremost industries of India, *Viz.*, jute and cotton, are engaged in working up agricultural raw materials into simple manufactures: production of higher counts of yarn, the finest quality of piece-goods, jute canvas for shoes and other purposes, jute carpets and a variety of other goods in which jute is mixed up with other fibres or materials have not yet been seriously taken up in this country. We have a considerable iron and steel industry, but railway plant and rolling stock, machinery of all descriptions and many other types of metal manufactures are almost exclusively obtained by importation.

We are still engrossed with the problems of our coal, cotton, iron, steel and other basic industries, while the progressive countries of the would are trying to redress the balance of the old by developing the modern industries of electricity supply, the manufacture of radio and electrical equipment, aluminium, rayon, synthetic dyestuffs, foodstuffs, oil extraction from coal, air and motor transport, film production and cinema display. Although we are almost self-sufficient in the supply of cement, matches, sugar, pig-iron, and have lately made remarkable progress in the production of cotton piece-goods, steel and paper, we are still in the primitive stage of industrial development, and our dependence upon foreign countries for a thousand and one other manufactures is ridiculously sublime–particularly in the case of factory equipments, power plants, stores, replacement parts, etc. The chemical and engineering industries are universally recognised to be the starting point in modern industrial development, but in India we have hardly yet made a beginning in these directions.

There are a number of accessory industries, workshops, gins and presses, rice and timber mills, but complex industries requiring the employment of complicated machinery and processes, and involving technical guidance of an intricate and specialised character, and utilising by-products are absent. Certain recent innovations like the Bata Shoe Factory, the soap factories of Lever Brothers, the Dunlop Rubber Factory, the Western India Match Co., and the projected chemical works of the Alkali and Chemical Corporation are all monumental reproaches to the Indian.

Indian enterprises and capital are shy of developing on new, untried lines. We prefer to imitate rather than initiate. The potential productive capacity of the Cement Merger is greater than the present consumption, the production of the protected varieties of paper is nearly equal to its present consumption, and yet we have recently withnessed the flotation of a number of cement and paper companies.

We have no research departments attached to our industries. When a new and better process has been invented and tested to satisfaction if the West, we come forward to adopt it, but by that time it has probably gone out of date in its place of birth, and been replaced by a still better technique.

Judged by Western standards, our industrial achievements, however creditable in themselves, must be regarded as being extremely poor in quality and quantity. Even after 75 years of development, though there is no lack of raw materials and market, India is a baby in arms in industrial production. In fact industrialisation is only beginning in India and the present state of her industry can hardly be compared with that of England or Germany or America. It has not yet divorced the factory workers altogether from the land, nor produced the great agglomeration of wage-earners in cities so characteristic of industrial life. In consequence, industrial organisation is more difficult both for the employer and the worker, for the employer because he cannot count on a highly trained and largely permanent labour force wedded to industry, for the worker because collective action for improving his conditions of employment and stadard of living is much harder to organise. There is also lacking the same desire for higher standard as in the West. But this is not to be wondered at; in the early stages of industrial development, it is bound to exist, until people have tested the advantages of better living. The taste, however, comes repidly when it is encouraged. It is also true that peple in India cannot work with the same intensity as in temperate climates; the speed of production as well will never quite equal that of the West. There are many other features which distinguish Indian and Western conditions, at any rate in their present stages. But for all that it still seems that the general lines of development are at bottom the same.

The example of Japan:– Another eastern country, namely Japan, however, has done wonders in a shorter period and in far less favourable conditions. The immense quantity of goods she is pouring into the markets of the world, and particularly the low prices at which they are sold, are really shocking to her competitors. An important contributory cause of this was the depreciation of the yen by more than 40 per cent of its previous value, but another more permanent factor was the pressure of a large agricultural population with little room for expansion which kept down industrial wages and labour costs. The same situation exists in India, but with a different result. There is no reason why Indian industries should not approach the Japanese standard of efficiency, given capital, organisation, education and State aid.

Time is ripe for the appointment of an Industrial Commission:– To take stock of our industrial position as well as to suggest lines for future development, the time seems to us to be ripe for the appointment of an industrial Commission. Those industries which enjoy tariff protection may have their position examined periodically by the Tariff Board, but a Tariff Board inquires into an industry piece-meal cut off from its proper setting in the industrial system of the country. The task of such a Commission will be to take a comprehensive view of the whole system, to investigate into new lines which Indian industry can embark upon, to suggest measures for the consolidation and rationalisation of those industries in which over-production is threatened, to dovetail the policies and actions of the various Provincial Governments with each other and with those of the Central Government, to find the rightful place for handicrafts and minor industries in the Indian scheme of industrial organisation, to reconcile the contending interests of labour, capital and consumer and to investigate into other allied problems. The Commission will also go into the question of the advisability of attaching permanent Advisory Committees to Provincial and Central Departments of Industries.

During the last twenty years India has undergone rapid political and economic evolution. For good or evil, but as it seems to us quite inevitably, India is adopting the economic organisation of the West. The idea that a country should as far as possible produce what its people need is taking root in this country as well as Europe, despite all the teachings of Adam Smith and his disciples about the advantages of international division of labour. This tendency towards greater self-sufficiency is one of the outstanding features of economic development during the twentieth century. The spread of education, the advance of technique and the expansion of liquid capital produced conditions in which every country decided to develop its basis industries as far as raw materials, labour and a consuming home market were available. The last Great War gave a tremendous impetus in the same direction. It is useless to condemn it. Also it is necessary to realise that, as in many other matters, India can be no exception to this trend of world economic evolution, particularly because India possesses a superabundance of raw materials, vast domestic consuming markets and cheap labour. What we have to do is to reconstruct the economic system of the country on a basis in which nationalistic policies must somehow be incorporated.

It is in this light that the recent industrial policies and programmes of the Provincial Governments should be judged. To develop industries to the stage of self-sufficiency from a pin to a steamer has always been, and is, the cherished ambition of the average Indian. Provincial autonomy has given the chance, and quite naturally the various Governments are trying to bring about an industrial Millennium. After generations of governmental callousness, inactivity and open or veiled hostility, the present overflow of enthusiasm is not difficult to understand. But it must not be forgotten that State policy, though an important consideration, is not the only or the sole factor in industrial development. Subject to this qualification, the enthusiasm of the Provincial Governments is thrice welcome. There is unlimited scope for their activity in the fields of research, finance, marketing, etc., but in pursuing these aims care should be taken to avoid certain pitfalls. A healthy and vigorous industry cannot grow tied to the apron-strings of Government. The anxiety to promote industry may give rise to a sort of rivalry which may degenerate into extreme provincialism. Again, in encouraging small industries any conflict with big or organised industries should be avoided; in India there is enough room for both. Further there should be perfect understanding and co-ordination of the Provinces between themselves and with the Government of India. Development of industries may require not only the shelter of a protective tariff, but also the indirect support of a suitable exchange, currency, railway freight and kindred policies. The powers of the Provincial Governments in these spheres are after all limited, and they are helpless they can carry the Central Government along with themselves.

5

The Mineral Resources

In approaching the various problems concerning India's mineral industries one is faced with either of two difficulties. On the one hand there is the tradition that India is a land full to overflowing with valuable minerals, many of which have enriched her own people or merchants and others from other countries for centuries in the past. On the other hand we have the cry that the country is far too dependent upon other countries for commodities of all sorts and that every effort should be made to utilise to a greater extent the minerals already used in her industries, or exported, and also to search for and utilise to the fullest extent possible the hitherto undiscovered mineral resources and so render India as far as possible independent of other countries in the world.

The illusion of the traditional picture is the more difficult to dispel, at least among peoples of Western countries, who forget, or never properly realise, that India is not a country but a continent, with as many climates and varieties of geological and topographical structure as, say, the continent of Europe and with as many varieties (both actual and potential) of occupations and industries too.

A study of India's mineral resources and of the problems of its mineral industries must necessarily be largely statistical and comparative. The space at our disposal in insufficient for more than a mere cursory glance at the whole picture, attention being directed to specially interesting details here and there. In compiling the information that follows, an attempt has been made to bring into prominence those facts that speak for themselves. The student of economics should have no difficulty in seeing the directions in which further research is likely to repay the time spent on it.

The Geological Survey of India, the one important source of up-to-date information concerning the mineral resources of India, classifies the minerals of the country into two groups, namely:–

(a) those regarding which statistical information is more or less complete and reliable, and

(b) those regarding which the information is incomplete or almost lacking.

The student of economics requires information more readily accessible. Accordingly the minerals are here treated in alphabetical order.

Before attempting a systematic study of the minerals in alphabetical order, however, the following reference to their relative economic importance will be of value.

Relative Importance of Minerals

The minerals of greatest importance, measured in terms of annual value of output, are the following in the order given, the approximate sterling value of the output for 1933 (for minerals of annual output of £100,00. and over) being stated within brackets:–

Petroleum (£4,708,000), coal (£4,600,500), gold (£2,078,200), salt (£859,000), lead and lead ore (£851, 300), building materials (£800,000), tin ore (£533,100), silver (£497,200), copper ore (£392,250), mica (£307,650), zinc concentrates (£231,800), iron ore (£187,800), manganese ore (£123,150), nitre or saltpetre (£117,150), tungsten ore, nickel speiss, ilmenite, antimonial lead, chromite, clays, steatite, jadeite, refractory materials, magnesite, ruby sapphire and spinel, fuller's earth, monazite, gypsum, diamonds, ochre, barytes, zircon, beryl, felspar, bauxite, garnet, apatite, bismuth.

The order of economic value of a mineral varies, however, from year to year, on account of fluctuations, sometimes of such major importance as to cause food for serious thought for the economist and anxiety for both industry and government. If the above list is compared with the corresponding list for 1932 it will be found that the production of petroleum had increased in 1933 by barley 25 per cent, coal having lost first place partly on that account and partly on that acccount and partly on account of a 10 per cent fall in output.

The output of gold increased by 10 per cent. Not only so, but great quantities of hoarded glod exported in the last few years have raised the export figures to values totally out of proportion to the normal.

The output of gold more than doubled between 1932 and 1933 and that of antimonial lead almost trebled . The output of manganese fell by over 36 per cent – a matter of the greatest concern to the industry. The output of tin ore increased by over 50 per cent, and so on.

The economist who wishes to study teh mineral industries of India has an exceedingly interesting, but difficult and extensive, task before him, each important mineral requiring exhaustive consideration of statistics relating to a long period of years as well as of industrial and political events of peculiar significance and importance, especially those of very recent years.

In the list that follows there will be found a concise statement of the important sources of the various minerals, a note regarding annual output, and, as already stated, a brief reference to any specially interesting point that appears to be worthy of mention, such as disproportionate amounts of imports in the face of large resources, important uses, etc.

Industry's Shortcomings

The student of economics will be impressed, on consulting the literature, by the references to the shortcomings of suppliers of minerals and their derivatives in this country. Both European and Indian firms would appear to be blameworthy in this respect.

In spite of the spread of technical and scientific education in recent decades there frequently is a regrettable failure to apply scientific and even business principles in a practical manner and, whatever is to blame for it, whether climate or not, even imported talent frequently deteriorates in the same direction. A whole industry may suffer and almost collapse, as did the coal industry in the early post-war years, through causes traceable in large measure to this defect.

In the list that follows there occur many minerals that are extensively found throughout India but are at present little used. Their exploitation requires in many instances the highest degree of scientific training and technical experience. The student of Indian problems is cautioned against working up unjustifiable optimism or even undue enthusiasm over India's mineral resources. Mere possession of mineral wealth provides no short cut to industrial prosperitv

Effect of Railway Freights

There is one stumbling-block that has to be removed by the

heavy industries in India, and that is the crippling effects of railway freights. India is such a vast continent that great distances have to be traversed by mineral products before they can be used in manufacture. Coal is a striking example of this (see Coal) and of course the vast majority of mineral products require cheap coal for their conversion into marketable commodities or even for their transport to internal markets, quite apart from the export market. If the minerals in question are found at a great distance from the coalfields this same adverse effect operates. The difficulty is increased in India by the fact that most of the coal of the country is more or less localised. If there had been several important coalfields throughout the country the story would have been quite a different one.

This does not necessarily mean that railway freights are unfairly high in India. A case might be made out for such a contention, or as an alternative the economist might make out an excellent case for special discriminating freights on certain commodities, or on such commodities when conveyed to certain destinations, or in respect of certain minimum distances, which freights could not by themselves be considered but which , on account of possible improved internal trade and increased exports, might be more than justified.

Large Imports In Spite of Resources of Raw Materials

Undoubtedly the most interesting feature of India's mineral industries at the present day is the inability of the country to manufacture all of those domestic requirements for which she has the bulk of the raw materials. A glance at the figures regarding imports of manufactured articles made almost entirely from minerals gives point to this remark. An average quantity of well over Rs. 36,00,00,000 worth of such materials is annually imported Outstanding among these are machinery, mill-work plant, railway plant, rolling stock, cutlery and hardware. These alone account for Rs. 29,00,00,000. The predominance of imports of what are mainly iron and steel articles is striking.

Glass and glassware imports amount to over Rs. 2,50,00,000 and dyestuffs to over Rs. 2,00,00,000. It is doubtful whether India could for many years compete in the manufacture of the latter, but there sees little reason to doubt her ability to make most of her own glassware. Her iron and steel industry has for many years shown that time it is the only factor required to place it on a satisfactory footing in the matter of independence.

Of less importance in this study is the question of reserves, except perhaps in respect of deposits of petroleum. In spite of (perhaps partly because of) an army of experts, no one can authoritatively state what reserves there are of any mineral in the world, and estimates alter from decade to decade in such a manner as to render almost futile a close study of most of such figures. India's reserves of coal as at present calulated will probably last her for two or three hundred years. Her reserves of iron may be confidently expected to do the same. ***Quantities referred to below generally relate to annual production.***

Abrasives:– *Corundum or Emery* occurs throughout India. Certain varieties are well-known gemstones. Many artificial products are now on the market (*e.g.*, carborundum, hard steels, alundum, etc.) and little chance industry developing. Occurrences: Salem (Madras); Hunsur (Mysore); Pipra Rewa State). 10 tons to 60 tons (Rs. 1,000 to Rs. 5,000). *Garnet* another important abrasive: Ajmer; Tinnevelly (Madras); locality between Afghanistan and Chitral. Up to 1,000 tons (480 in 1928) from Tinnevelly.

Alum and Aluminous Sulphates:– (Does not include aluminiu, for which see Bauxite.) No workable deposits. Former manufacture of alum from pyritic shales almost extinct. Almost entire output fro Mianwali (Punjab): 6,000 cwts. (Rs. 1,00,000), 1922; 478 cwts. (Rs. 8,000), 1928; none since. 60,000 cwts (Rs. 4,00,000) ann. imports alum and similar compounds. Used in tanning, dyeing , water softening and pharmacy. Import duty 25 per cent advalorum or Re 1/6 per ton (whichever is the higher).

Aluminium:–See BAUXITE.

Ammonium Sulphate:–See COAL.

Antimony:– Formerly mined various localities but only now from amherst dist., Burma. 500 tons (Rs. 10,500), 1927; 370 tons (Rs. 10,300), 1928; 3 tons (Rs. 60), 1930; none since. Antimonial lead (contains lead, antimony and silver) exported by Burma Corpn. to U.S. Over 1,000 tons (Rs. 3,20,500), 1926; almost 1,500 tons (Rs. 2,40,000), 1933.

Antimony largely used in form of alloys, *e.g.*, type metal. Compounds used in pharmacy; manufacture of pigments, matches, fireworks, etc. Antimonial lead used for lead plate accumulators.

Arsenic:–Extensive deposits orpiment and realgar Chitral. Arseno-pyrite near Darjeeling and Bhutna valley (Kashmir). Orpiment in Kumaon. Av. ann. export arsenic 6 tons (Rs. 5,000) Ann. import 80 tons (Rs. 1,00,000) of which 10 tons re-exported. Arsennic compounds important in many industries. Orpiment and realgar are important natural pigments. Ann. imports up to 9,000 cwts. (Rs. 2,15,500).

Asbestos:– Good long-fibre deposits rare but occasionally found, and valuable. 20 tons (Rs. 1,876 from Bhandra dist. (C.P.) recently; 40–150 tons per ann. from Seraikela State (B. and O.), 90 tons (Rs. 9,000), 1932. Cuddapah and Ajmer-Merwara also important. Production for India nearly 320 tons (Rs. 16,160), 1929; 33 tons (Rs. 1,190), 1930.

Asbestos extensively used as lining for electric furnaces, fireproofing purposes and as heat insulator.

Barytes:– Alwar State (Rajputana); Betamcherla, Anantapur and Cuddapah (Madras). 2,303 tons (Rs. 31,341), 1924; 5,651 tons (Rs. 41,517), 1932. Mineral of rapidly increasing importance, used in point industry, as filler for paper, India rubber etc., and in pharmacy. Large ann. imports: 9,400 cwts. (Rs. 40,000), to nearly 1,700 tons (Rs. 1,37,000).

Basic Slag:–See Iron And Steel and Phosphates.

Bauxite:– Only source of metal aluminium at present but in spite of extensive good quality deposits no present production of metal. Aluminium manufactured by elaborate electro-chemical process requiring enormous amounts cheap electric current. Reliable supplies mineral cryolite also essential. Production nearly 4,500 tons (Rs. 8,300), 1932. Approx. 70 per cent of world's ann. requirements bauxite (1,500,000) used for production aluminium; remainder for manufacture of abrasives, chemicals, refractories, cements, etc. Enormous potential industry even for latter substances awaits development in India. Nearly 70 tons aluminium imported 1933.

Bismuth:–Small quantity bismuth minerals obtained as by-product during treatment wholfram and tin deposits Burma. (See Tin.)

Borax:–No occurrences known in India. Ann. imports from Ladakh and Tibet, and other countries (over1,000, tons 1933), increasing.

Building Materials:– Complete statistics not available. Large variety natural rocks used locally all over India. Transport expense generally limits use to localities of occurrence. At Calcutta, Bombay, Madras, etc., foreign stones, *eg.*, Italian marbel, Scotch, granite, extensively used for flooring and ornamental purposes, though similar material available in India. Enormous quantities of the following used: igneous rocks of Charnockite series of Madras; gneissose granites of Mysore; slates and limestones of Central India. C.P. and U.P.; Gondwana sandstones of Bengal, Bihar and C.P.; coralline limestones of Narbada valley; numulitic limestones of north-west; Porbandar stone of Kathiawar and innumerable ornamental stones.

In addition large quantity materials mined and quarried for manufacture of cement (q.v) and bricks. (See CLAY.) In spite of large qauantity available, enormous quantities annually imported: Rs. 1,1,00,000 building materials, including bricks, tiles, asphalt, cement, etc. See CEMENT.

Annual production over 1 million tons granite and gneiss (Rs. 20,000,000) for building and road metal. Bulk of this in Rangoon for railway development and town reclamation work. About 400,000, tons (Rs. 10,50,000) sandstone annually quarried in B. and O., Burma, Rajputana, etc. Limestone extensively used for building, manufacture of cement and as flux in iron and steel works. 2,750,000 tons (Rs. 48,00,000) to over 3,000,000 tons (Rs. 52,00,000) limestone quarried annually (includes 20,000 tons to 300,000 tons dolomite). Some hard forms laterite used for building and road metal. Statistics unreliable but annual production probably from 300,000 tons (Rs. 3,50,000) to 700,000 tons (RS. 6,85,000). Slate also important material found Kangra dist.; Gutgaon dist. (S. of Delhi); Kharakhpur hills (Monghyr dist., B. and O.). Annual production: 12,000 tons to 19,000 tons (Rs. 1,80,000). Used also for electrical switchboards . Stone for road metal is not liable to import duty. Other stones and marble subject to 15 per cent *ad valorem.*

Cement:- Nearly Rs. 7,00,00,000 industry firmly established since Great War. Annual production. Portland Cement under 100,000 tons before 1920 ; now well over 500,000 tons. But annual imports over Rs. 50,00,000. Importduty formerly Rs. 9 per ton (Portland cement) or 15 per cent *ad valorem* (other cements including white Portland cement) now Rs. 18/4 and 30 per cent respectively (20 per cent *ad valorem* if from U.K.). Some Indian limestones fortunately contain all chemical elements, and those in nearly correct proportions, cecessary to make high grade Portland cement, without other ingredients. Others require addition clayey material and even gypsum during processes involved. Complete list localities of manufacture impossible in space available. Following specially important: Katni (C.P.); Dwarka (Kathiawar); Japla (Daltonganj); Banmor (Gwalior); and Shahabad (Hyderabad State). Chemical composition all cement making materials exteremely important. Rapid setting cements, containing high proportion alumina, manufactured (not in India) from bauxite and limestone. Possibility considerable extension cement industry in India on account of great natural resources of both those minerals.

Chromite:- Source of metal chromium and its compounds; also arefractory. Foundin Baluchistan, Mysore, Singhbhum, Andaman Islands amdSalem (Madras). Annual production 35,000 tons to 60,000 tons, falling recently; 15,500 tons (Rs. 2,23,000), 1933. Except for small quantities used for manufacture of firbricks, bulk is exported. Compounds used in chemical industries and for tanning and chromium plating.

Clays:- Statistics of clay and allied industries are valuable index of industrial life of a country. Reliable Indian statistics not available, partly owing to widespread village industry. Large quantities fireclay for manufacture of firebriks, and other refractory materials obtained in B. and O. especially the coalfields. China clay for manufacture of fine pottery and earthenware obtained in B. and O.; Jubbulpore (C.P.); Burma; Mysore; Madras and Delhi. Fuller's earth mined Mysore; Rajputana; C.P. Recent annual output by organised industry over 200,000 tons clay (Rs. 2,50,000), plus 25,000 tons China clay (over Rs. 1,00,000). Annuals imports, however, over 26,000 tons China clay (Rs. 20,00,000) mainly from Cornwall, England. Well over Rs. 1,00,00,000 manufactures: pottery, earthenware, China, etc., and clay imported annually. Clay other than China clay subject to import duty of 25 per cent *ad valorem.*

Important field for manufacture of glazed pottery, incl. sanitary ware, insulators, scientific apparatus, etc.

Coal :- Vast reserves of coal, estimated at over 50,000,000,000 of tons, including coal suitable for manufacture of good quality metallurgical, (*i.e.* "hard") coke. Mostly relatively high ash but comparing favourably with coals from S. Afr., Japan and U.S. Bengal and B. and O. coalfields' output over shadows all others but adjoining C.P. field is of increasing importance. Recent annual production over 22,000,000 tons, of which over 90 per cent from Bengal and B. and O. Over 1,600,000 tons converted into hard coke. From 12,000 to 21,000 tons coke imported.

Hyderabad production about 3 per cent of total; coal friable and rather poor quality. Assam and Punjab coals sometimes of very low ash but much sulphur. Bengal, B. and O. and C. P. coals have little sulphur. Much very friable lignite in Kashmir and Bikaner.

A recent development is the soft coke industry to provide comparatively smokeless domestic fuel–and effort to utilise low-grade coal and discourage waste of cow dung (fertiliser). Industry growing partly owing to intensive sales propaganda, partly to research into scientific methods of manufacture, both financed by Indian Soft Coke Committee. Coal distcessllation by-product industry relatively less important than in more highly industrialised countries, partly due to competitive price of imported ammonium sulphate, of which nearly 35,000 tons imported 1933, whereas only 10,000 tons made. Important industry is the production of coal tar for road-making, manufacture of paints, phenols, etc.

Recently much competition from coal imported from Britain, S. Afr., Portug. E. Afr., Australia, and Japan S. Afr. and Jap. coals competing mainly on account of price cutting, but partly due to heavy inland freights, which inevitably hamper industry , raising price per ton from a few rupees to Rs. 15 or Rs 20. Industry suffered after Great War largely due to improper attention to maintain quality. Between 1924 and 1925 export trade almost disappeared. Confidence restored and imports risen since establishment of Coal Grading Board (1925), and exports rose to over 2,000,000 tons, but world depressicn caused exports to fall to under 500,000 tons (Rs.41,00,000), 1933. Exports mainly to Ceylon (200,000 tons), Hong Kong, U.K., Straits Settlements and Philippine is Coal, coke and patent fuel liable to import duty of 10 as. per ton. Coal tar and pitch to an import duty of 25 per cent *ad valorem*.

Many intersting problems, economic and otherwise, worth investigation. Great difficulties in way of scientific development of industry, research, etc., which require funds that financial state of industry does not at present appear to justify. Co-operation in matter of pumping, selling, etc., which might greatly help industry apparently impossible of achievement without intervention of Govt. Inland market would appear to offer some hope of expansion but not in near future. In this connection note large imports of fuel oil which is replacing coal or being used where coal might be used if conditions other wise favourable. (See Petroleum.)

Cobalt:– Occurs Khetri, etc. (Rajputana). (Also rich deposits Nepal.) Cobalt and nickel present in small quant. in manganese ores. 3 per cent to 4 per cent cobalt in nickel speiss from Burma. (See Nickel.) Khetri ores used for production of blue enamel.

Copper:– After several decades of alternating slight prosperity and complete disaster industry now established and progressing by careful and capable exploiting of natural resources. Occurrences: Singhbhum (B. and O.) and surrounding country; and to a less extent various places in South India, Rajputana and along outer Himalayas. Also occurs in Burma Corp'n. mines, and much copper matte obtained during treatment of ores. (See LEAD.) Only important deposits worked are those of Indian Copper Corp'n. near Ghatsila (Singhbhum). Annual production of ore, containing about 3 per cent copper, 30,000 tons 1928; 76,800 tons, 1929; over 200,000 tons (Rs. 22,13,000) 1933. Copper matte from Burma, 10,000tons (Rs.20,00,000) to 12,500tons (Rs.30,00,000). Almost unlimited field for utilisation of copper in India, especially for bazaar and other requirements in brass for domestic utensils, brass and bronze castings for engineering purposes, etc., and for electrical purposes. No electrolytic copper (essential for last mentioned made in India but when made in future, imports of electrolytic copper will presumably disappear and nickel present in Singhbhum ores may be recovered.

Diamonds:- Indian output insignificant. Found mainly in three areas: dists. of Guddapah, Anantapur, Bellart, Karnul, Kistna and Godaveri; Mahanadi Valle, *e.g.*, Sambalpur and Chunda; country around Panna *e.g.*, States of Panna, Charkhari, Bijawar, Ajaigarh, Hothi,Pathar, Kachhar, Baraunda and Chobepu. Accurate statistics not available. Recently 200 carats (Rs. 36,000) to over 1,250 carats (Rs. 63,695), 1933.

Dolomite:-See Refractories.

Fireclay:- See Clays.

Fluor Spar:- Useful flux, and source of element fluorine and of fluorides. Small quantities found extensively, *e.g.*, Barla (Kishangarh State); Sleemanabad (Jubbulpore); Drug (Rewa State). Barla deposits most important. High cost of freight prevents working at present. Bengal and B. and O. annually import 500 tons 2,000 tons for iron and steel industries.

Gemstones and Semi-Precious Stones:- Difficult to apply proper perspective to this group of minerals. Statistics not available owing to widespread nature of industry, methods of leasing mining rights, etc. Practically any pretty stone may be regarded as precious. DIAMOND and RUBY, SAPHIRE and SPINEL treated separately (the last thee under "RUBY"). Only very brief notes follow as volume of trade does not justify more. Agate, carnelian, cat's eye, etc., rock crystal, rose quartz, amethyst, etc., opal;, found in rivers draining Deccan trap. Rajpipla specially famous for agates. Amber found at Myitkyina and Upper Chindwin (Upper Burma). Beryl, aquamarine, etc., found in chief mica districts in B. and O.; Nellore; Ajmer-Merwara; Scardu (Kashmir), etc. Beryl is also source of metal beryllium. (See RARE MINERALS.) Garnet rarely good enough to be precious. Large quantities mined for abrasive (q.v.)., Tourmaline found in Ruby Mine dist.,Upper Burma.

Glass-Making Materials:- Glass-making is a rapidly growing industry in India. Good quality sand is a most important raw material.

Occurrences: Mangal Hat and Patraghatta (Rajmahal Hills); Loghra and Borgorh (near Allahabad); Sankhada and the river at Pedhamli (Baroda); Jubbulpore (C.P.); and many other places. Some usable deposits are sands, some sandstones, some quartzite rock, etc. Another important ingredient is soda, as soda ash or salt cake. Bulk of soda ash is imported. Lime is also used. (See CEMENT and BUILDING MATERIALS). Saltpetre (which supplies potash) is sometimes important. (see SALTPETRE.) Enormous quantities glass and glassware imported, *e.g.*, over Rs. 2,50,00,000 per annum. Japan, Czechoslovakia, Germany, U.K., Belgium are most important sources. Bangles and beads account for Rs. 1,00,00,000 to Rs,1,40,00,000 of imports; bottles and sheet and plate glass for Rs.30,00,000. Extent of potential industry may be gauged from above figures. Minor but important ingredients for making special coloured or optical glasses are also found in India. Note that for making the articles from them, a very high degree of technical skill and many years' experience are required.

Gold:– Out of 20,000,000 oz. gold produced in the world annually India produces about one-third of a million ounces (about 2 per cent of total), and is eighth among world's producers. Over 99 per cent of India's gold comes from Kolar gold field (Mysore). Small quantities from Madras, Kashmir, Punjab, U.P., and Singhbhum (B.and O.) Annual production, 330,500 oz., 1931;339, 700 oz., 1932; 336,100 oz. (Rs. 2,76,40,000), 1933. Kolar field noted for great depths reached in mines (over 7,400 ft.) with high temperatures (up to 130^{0}F.) and great danger due to rock- bursts. An important associated industry is production of electric power (for the mines) at the Cauvery Falls, over 92 miles away.

Graphite:– Occurrence sporadic throughout India, *e.g.* Vizagapatam hill-tracts, Orissa Feudatory States, Chota Nagpur (Bihar), Goorg, Godaveri Dist., Upper Burma, Travancore, Sikkim. Travancore deposits (Morgan Crucible Company), formerly most important; up to 13,000 tons–from 1898 to 1912, total 35,000 tons. No Travancore output since. Small output (1,318), 1916, mainly Rajputana and from 16 tons up to 252 tons in various years up to 1921, mainly from Orissa. Cost of transport militates against success of industry at present. Improved rail facilities may remedy this soon, but quality of most Indian graphite hitherto discovered (except from Sikkim) rather poor.

Uses:– Manufacture of crucibles (Ceylon graphite most extensively used), foundry facings, lubricants, stove polish, electric motor brushes, boiler scale preventatives, etc. Price has varied in past years up to £100 per ton, but as little as £4 per ton is common for amorphous (*i.e.*

non-crystalline varietes).

Much graphite imported as (*a*) graphite and (*b*) crucibles. Over £15,000 of (*a*) and £ 17,000 of (*b*)annually recently, the former partly from Ceylon and partly U.K., the latter from U.K.

Gypsum:– Found in Bikaner, Jodhpur and Jaisalmer (Rajputana); Jhelum (Punjab); Baroda and Kashmir, and in smaller quantities throughout India. Annual production 35,000 tons to 60,000 tons, falling to 33,000 tons (Rs. 66,000), 1933. Used as fertiliser, for manufacture of Plaster of Paris and in small quantities in cement industry. Many other uses known.

Ilmenite:– Ore of iron containing titanium oxide. Monazite sands of Travancore, formerly used for extraction thorium oxide (see Monazite), now treated for ilmenite present Greatly used for manufacture of white paints. Annual production, Travancore, 640 tons (Rs. 16,500), 25,307 tons (Rs. 5,00,000), 1928; 50,052 tons (Rs. 7,00,000), 1932, but declined to 43,384 tons, 1933. Present value approx. £1 per ton.

Iron and Steel:– India second in British Empire in production of iron ore. Important deposits those of Singhbhum, Keonjhar State, Bonai State, Mayurbhanj State (B. and O.); Central Provinces and Mysore (Singhbhum deposits among most important in the world; contain from 60 per cent to 69 per cent of iron.) Annual production steadily rose from under 500,000 tons, 1914, to nearly 2,000,000 tons (1928), falling again to 1,760, 500 tons (Rs. 39,20,000), 1932, and 1,230,000 tons (Rs.25,00,000), 1933. Over 88 per cent production is from B.and O. Small quantity ore mined in Burma used only as flux in lead smelting.

Annual production of metal, approx. 1,000,000 tons pig iron, of which from 250,000 tons to 370,000 tons exported (about 50 per cent to Japan). Annual production of steel from pig-iron, from 430,000 tons to 500,000 tons. In spite of large resources, nearly Rs. 50,00,00,000 pig iron, ingot steel and manuf. iron and steel goods imported.

In recent years industry protected by bounties on rails and fish-plates wholly manufactured in India as well as on iron and steel railway wagons. Whole question of protection of iron and steel industry much under discussion in recent years. Certain tariffs still exist on certain classes imported steels. 232,671 tons manufactured steel articles were imported in 1933.

Methods of production of pig-iron and steel in India quite equal to those employed elsewhere in world. Apparently little or no production basic slag in spite possibilities. (See PHOSPHATES.) Further important to note that (except for ferro-manganese) no ferro-alloys (for special alloy steels) produced in India, though tungsten, molybdenum, chromium are all available, 1,432 tons ferro-alloys imported in 1933.

Lead:– Practically only source of supply in India is Burma Corp'n's Bawdin mine in Burma, one of the greatest lead zinc-silver mines in the world. Bawdin ores contain zinc, lead, silver and copper. Reserves calculated at over 4,000,000 tons, with over 25 per cent lead. Small Quantity of lead occurs also in Southern Shan States and Yamethin dist., Burma, and at Panjori, Jaipur State.

Annual production 300,000 to 450,000 tons lead ore, 454,791 tons in 1933. Over 72,000 tons lead (over Rs.1,00,00,000) extracted in 1933, of which 65,045 tons exported. (See also ANTIMONY.)

Limestone:– See CEMENT and BUILDING MATERIALS.

Magnesite:– Important refractory. (See REFRACTORIES and BUILDING MATERIALS.) Also used as boiler lagging material, for manufacture of sulphite paper pulp and fireresisting paint.

Manganese:– One of the most important mineral products of India, an essential in iron and steel industry. Largely used for manufacture of ferro-manganese (necessary for conversion pig-iron into steel). Georgia, in Russia, before the Great War was world's chief producer. India has twice displaced Russia, producing from 33 per cent to 37 per cent of world's total output. Sources: Balaghat, Bhandara, Chhindwara, Nagpur, (C.P.); Sandur State and other areas (Madras); Keonjhar, Singhbhum, Bonai State (B. and O.); and certain districts in Madras. Annual production fallen from 1,130,000 tons (1927) to just over 218,000 tons (£123,000), 1933, due to depression. Chief competitor Russia, owing to very low selling price. Large production of high grade manganese ore now possible form S. Afr.

As regards manganese content India's ores are the best. As regards low silica content her ores stand next to those of Brazil. High phosphorus content of ores gives India low position. Present depression in India's manganese industry provides economist with mass of problems that appear almost impossiblc to solve. Depression mainly due both increased production by and competition from Russia and discoveries of new deposits in other countries, with consequent fall in exports.

Mercury:– See QUICKSILVER.

Mica:– India long noted for excellence of mica. Produces from

75 per cent to 85 per cent of the world's production. Important sources: Gaya and Hazaribagh dists. of B. and O.; Nellore; Nilgiri dists. of Madras; Ajmer-Merwara and Jaipur State (Rajputana). Annual production; 30,000 cwts. up to over 86,000 cwts.; 32, 713 cwts. (Rs.14,35,401), 1932; 41, 075 cwts. (Rs. 16,82,045), 1933. Industry suffers from great fluctuations and effects of extensive loss through thefts from mines. Chief importers: U.K., U.S., Germany and France. Mica largely used for insulating purposes in electrical industry and as heat insulater and resister. Some use as dry lubricant. Large quantities of artificial sheet mica (micanite) now made from small pieces, affecting trade in large sheets. World trade affected by increased production by S.Afr. in recent years.Interesting fact: recently as much as 4,000 cwts. mica imported by India, but imports now negligible. There would appear to be field for manufacture of mica and micanite articles in India.

Mineral Waters:– Mineral waters of undoubted medicinal value exist all over India, but no trade.Possible that by judicious advertising on large scale the mineral waters of certain districts, including radio-active waters of Tuwa, might have some commercial value.

Monazita:– Mixed phosphates of cerium, lanthanum and other "rare earth" metals, as well as thorium oxide, the latter essential for manufacture of incandescent gas mantles. Important sources: Travancore. Annual production formerly as high as 2,000 tons (£ 60,000), practically nil 1925. Declining trade mainly due to increased use of electricity. 90 tons (£ 890), 1931; 654 tons (£6,150), 1932. Recent production partly due to demand for ilmenite (q.v.) which also occurs along with onazite.

Nickel:– No very important ores of nickel yet found in India. Occurrences noted in Khatri and other places in Rajputana; Kolar goldfield ; South Travancore and in the copper ores of Singhbhum. Also occurs in Burma Corpn. mines and there is steadily rising production of nickel speiss, *e.g.*, 1,000 tons in 1928 to 3,150 tons in 1930; 3,350 tons Rs.10,28,500), 1933. Speiss contains 25 per cent nickel, and copper, with small quantities cobalt (3-4%) and silver. Considerable quantities nickel imported, especially for manufacture of 2-anna and 4-anna pieces. Annual imports over 2,000 tons nickel for manufacture of coinage. Burma Speiss not treated in India. Nickel occurring in copper ores of Singhbhumm not at present recovered but possibly production of eletrolytic copper may render the nickel available.

Oil:– See PETROLEUM.

Paints:– (Not artists' colours.) Various ores of iron, particularly the ochres, used from time imemorial as paints. Large quantities of ochre and similar highly, coloured earths suitable for manufacture of Paints in India, *e.g.,* Jubbulpore; Panna State; Singhbhum and Puri (B.and O.); Hanamkonda (Hyderabad State): Myingyan (Burma). In the working of manganese ores quantities of ochres could be made available. Black slate has been used. Recent production of ochre: 1,000 tons up to over 6,000 tons; 6,237 tons (Rs. 33,110), 1932; 11,630 tons (Rs. 60,895), 1933. C.P. and C.I. are main producers. (See also Arsenic (orpiment and realgar), BARYTES, COAL, ILMENITE.)

Petroleum:– India produces less than 1 per cent of world's petroleum, standing 11th or 12th in order of importance. Annual production just under 300,000,000 gallons (Rs. 8,46,00,000, or over £6,250,000), but insufficient for India's requirements. From 170,000,000 to 230,000,000 gallons (Rs. 8,40,00,000 to Rs. 10,44,00,000) imported. Occurrences: Burma, Assam, Punjab and Baluchistan. Burma heads list, with annual production of over 5/6 of total, Assam next and Punjab last. India's petroleum industry highly organised and resources very carefully and efficiently exploited. Owing to almost certain future exhaustion world's supplies petroleum other methods of obtaining petroleum, or substitutes, will be necessary. Known deposits may be further exploited by mining methods, and shale oil further considered. There are also unlimited vegetable and animal sources of oils and alcohols, though the latter not likely for any years to assume importance.

In 1933:–

68,818,733	gals. petrol	produced;	2,379,708	gals.	imported
139,354,915	gals. kerosene	,,	57,778,363	gals.	,,
17, 699,739	gals. fuel oils	,,	104,968,758	gals.	,,
9,623,817	gals.other oils	,,	19,833,481	gals.	,,

The following import duties levied on petroleum products:–

Mineral oil for lamps and kerosene: Rs. 3/9 per gal. (there is an excise duty on kerosene of British Indian manufacture of Rs.2/9/9 per gal.). Heavy mineral oil: Rs. 15/10 per ton up to 12½ per cent *ad valorem.* Lubricating oils: Rs. 2/6 per gal. (6 pies if from U.K.). Other mineral oils: 25 per cent *ad valorem.*

Phosphates:– Apatite (calcium phosphate) is valuable source of phosphorus for fertilising (bone ash is same chemical substance.) Occurs Singhbhum, Hazaribagh and Giridih (B. and O.); Raniganj (Bengal); Trichinopoly, Nellore and Vizagapatam; Narukot State (Bombay); Jhelum (Punjab); Mussoories (U.P.); etc. etc. Some of these, especially Singhbhum, have been worked but no record of important trade. Note, however, large exports of bone and bone-meal, *viz.,* up to 75 per cent of total manures exports of which up to 120,000 tons recorded. Basic slag is additional source of phosphorus but not produced in India. Possibly addition of Indian apatite to blast furnace charge would give valuable supply of phosphate.

Potash:– See Saltpetre.

Potash Minerals other than Salpetre:– No recorded source in India. 109, 716 cwts. imported in 1933.

Quicksilver (Mercury):– No recorded sources. 239,090 lbs. imported in 1933.

Rare Minerals:– Expression includes the following or their compounds: beryllium, cerium and other "rare earth" metals, columbium, gadolinium, iridium, molybdenum, niobium, osmium, platinum, radium, tantalum, titanium, uranium, yttrium, etc. Occurrences of minerals containing the above reported throughout India. Some by no means rare but their uses unfamiliar or still in experimental stage. Only beryllium, molybdenum, "rare earth" metals, and tantalum noted here.

Bryllium. Indian beryl is very high grade (see also Precious Stones) Jaipur State, Ajmer-Merwara (Rajputana); Koderma dist. (B. and O.); Nellore and Krishangarh. Uses for beryllium metal have been found in metallurgy. No production statistics.

Molybdenum. Sulphide of molybdenum, a valuable metal used in manufacture of important alloy steels. Occurrences: Wagon region (Tavoy); Chota Nagpur (B. and O.); Cherrapunji (Assam); Kunaveram, and Palni, Madura (Madras); Kishangarh (Rajputana). Only output that from Tavoy : 7½ cwts. (Rs. 1,400), 1923, none since. See also reference to ferro-alloys under IRON AND STEEL.

"*Rare earth" metals.* Occur in many minerals found in India, e.g., at Sankara mica mine, Nellore: Yedur, Bangalore; and Tavoy specially in the mineral monazite at Travancore. (See reference under MONAZITE.) "Rare earth" metals used for manufacture special alloys used as: "flints" in automatic lighters. No Indian production statistics.

Tantalum. Tantalum and columbium occur, associated with iron and manganese, and rarer metals such as uranium and the preceding. Occurrences: Gaya, Koderma and Moghyr dists. (B.and O.); Madura, Nellore, Salem and Trichinopoly (Madras); various districts. Maysore and near Machil (Kashmir). Tantalum formerly used for manufacture of electric lamp filaments (now replaced by Tungsten, q.v.). Now mainly used in construction of radio and X-ray valves and neon lamps. No output reported.

Refractory Materials:– Large variety mineral substances used for furnace linings, fire-bricks, etc. Commonest is *fireclay*. (See Clay) High grade *siliceous* rock used for manufacture of silicia bricks and other specially resistant articles. *Kyanite* and *sillimanite* increasingly used in recent years, especially in ceramic industries. Occur throughout B. and O. Smaller quantities in Ajmer, Merwara and Mysore. 14,000 tons (Rs, 35,000), 1932; up to 19,300 tons (Rs. 1,07,000), 1933. *Zirconium oxide* or zirconia (obtained from ziron, another important refractory). Occurs along with *ilmenite* (q.v.) in the *monazite* sands (q.v.) Travancore. Production approx. 500 tons, up to 1,465 tons (£8,129), 1927; 490 tons (£3,805), 1932; 603 tons (£3,018), 1933. *Magnesite* and associated mineral *dolomite* (double carbonate of lime and magnesia) important material for manufacture of blast furnace, linings (especially for treatment of phosphatic ores). Former extensively quarried in India, both for Indian use and for export, especially to U.S. Sources: Chalk Hills in Southern India. Very high grade obtained. Annual production from approx. 10,000 tons (1926) to 15,200 tons (Rs. 29,000), 1933. (See also Asbestos, Bauxite, Chromite, Clays, Graphite, Steatite.)

Ruby, Sapphire and Spinel:– These occur together in the Mogok Stone Tract of Upper Burma. Statistics of one important company available but no record of individual workers' output. Nearly 150,000 carats (Rs. 4,67,000), 1926. Output fallen and company ceased operations, 1931. Industry formerly chief mineral source of revenue in Burma. Kashmir another important area: 1,434,285 carats sapphire and corundum (Rs. 92,000), 1933.

Salt:– Salt industry, India's fourth most important mineral industry. Production always well over 1,000,000 tons. Occurrences: Desert region, Rajputana; Salt Range, Punjab; Kohat (N.W.F.) ; Madras; Bombay, and Aden. Salt manufactured from sea water, *e.g.*, Bombay, Madras , Aden and Burma; from sub-soil and lake brine, e.g., Rajputana and Burma; and from rock salt, by quarrying, *e.g.*, Salt Range, Punjab. Bombay is largest producer. Climatic conditions do not give promise productions in Bengal. Annual consumption, 13½ lbs. per head of population, incl. salt used in agriculture and industry. Annual production excluding Aden salt: 1,712,400 tons (Rs. 1,14,25,000), 1923. Imports fell from 553,000 (Rs. 82,32,500), 1932, to 400,000 tons (Rs. 51,18,000), 1933. About 2/3 of production recovered from sea-water; rock salt accounts for about 1/8. Important source of revenue to Central Govt. Excise duty on salt

Rs. 1/4 (1923) per maund, Rs. 2/8 (1924), reduced again to Rs. 1/4, but raised later: Rs. 1/9 per ton (plus temporary additional duty of as. 2½), equiv. to Rs. 42/8 (plus Rs. 4.4) per ton, 1935. No duty on salt imported for manufacturing purposes and for fish curing.

Salpetre:– Crude saltpetre manufactured throughout India by primitive methods, decomposition of cow dung and subsequent treatment of soil with wood ashes. Bihar section of Gangetic plain specially noted. Punjab and U.P. also important. Statistics not now recorded but nearly 190,000 cwts. (Rs. 15,60,000) exported, 1933. Some used in teagardens in India and for manufacture of gun-powder, especially in coalfields and other mining areas. Small quantity imported by sea and more from Nepal, *e.g.,* nearly 4,000 cwts. per annum in recent years.

Soda:– Soda, like sulphuric acid, an essential in many important industries (*e.g.,* soap-making, glass-making, etc. etc.) and India deficient in deposits. Alkaline soil-surface deposits at Champaran, Muzzafarpur and Saran State (B. and O.); Benares, Azamgarh, Janupur, Ghazipur, etc. (U.P.); Lower Lake, Berar; Khairpur State, Sind; Sambhar Lake (Rajputana). Approx. 750 tons soda compounds from Khairpur State in recent years. Rs. 1,50,000 to Rs. 1,75,000 compounds exported annually from Karachi. From 50,000 tons to 75,000 tons soda compounds imported annually.

Establishment of a soda industry in India is a pressing necessity for development of many other industries on an economic basis.

Steatite:– Mineral of varied uses, *e.g.,* potstone (for making dishes, pots, etc.) soapstone (for carvings), and (the hardes form) for gas burners. Also used in manufacture of lead pencils, and one variety is talc. Manufacture of domestic articles is largely a village industry, and no records are available. Bricks made of steatite also used for furnace linings. Occurrences: Idar State (Bombay); Jaipur State (Rajputana); marble rocks, Jubbulpur, Gowari and Lalpur, south side Narbada river; Pakokku hill tracts, Burma; Maddavan and Betamcherla, and Salem (Madras) . Production variable–from 3,000 tons (Rs. 71,000) to 17,000 tons (Rs. 1,83,000), 1933.

Sulphur, Sulphuric Acid and Sulphates:– Enormous quantity sulphur essential in industry but India possesses practically no supplies of natural sulphur. Sulphur formerly mined at Barren Island, Bay of Bengal , and Kalat State, Eastern Baluchistan. Supplies of sulphur would be of great value to India. Other possible sources of sulphur are metallic sulphides, *e.g.,* iron pyrites, copper pyrites, zinc concentrates, etc., and sulphates such as gypsum, barytes, etc. Important industry is manufacture of sulphuric acid which in turn is essential in other heavy chemical industries. Many plants for manufacture of sulphuric acid started in recent years in India but sulphur practically all imported. Annual import 10,000 tons to 25,000 tons; 28,200 1933. This does not include ammonium sulphate, of which 1,640 tons imported, 1933. Sulphur imported mainly from Sicily, Japan and Germany. During treatment of copper and zinc ores much sulphur dioxide, equivalant to upwards of 3,000 tons of sulphur at present which could be converted into sulphuric acid, escapes into air. (See also ALUM, ALUMINOUS SULPHATES, ETC., and ZINC.) Sulphur is not liable to import duty.

Tar:– See COAL.

Tin:– Practically the only sources of tin is cassiterite (tinstone) deposits of Burma. Ore is mined and treated to obtain concentrates for export (not for smelting). Formerly some smelting to obtain tin took place. Annual production tin ore risen rapidly since Great War: 4,500 tons (Rs.45,10,000), 1932; 5,000 tons (Rs.71,00,000), 1933. Large quantities block tin imported annually; from 2,000 tons to 3,000 tons ; 2,500 tons (Rs.47,50,000), 1932; 2,080 tons (Rs. 53,00,000), 1933. Practically no workable deposits of tin ore in India proper.

Tungsten:– Tungsten ore, wolfram, occurs along with tin ore, q.v. Important district, Tavoy; Southern Shan States also. Tinstone and wolfram deposits carefully treated to obtain tin concentrates and wolfram concentrates separately. Annual production 2,023 tons (Rs. 7,04,000) , 1932; 2,147 tons (Rs. 10,84,639), 1933. Tungsten metal specially valuable for manufacture of high-speed tool steel. Tungsten compounds also used in chemical industries, dyeing, fireproofing, and in anufacture of electric lamp filaments.

Zinc:– Only deposits those of Burma Corp'n. at Bawdwin Mine. Zinc concentrates produced at Namtu. Annual production of concentrates has risen rapidly from 20,000 tons to about 60,000 tons; 61,432 tons (Rs. 30,83,000), 1933. Zinc metal not smelted in India, though much zinc required for manufacture of brass. (See Copper.) Copper and zinc smelting in India could provide sulphur dioxide gas for manufacture of sulphuric acid.

6

The Federal Finance

Federalism is only a method adopted for the attainment of an ideal and Federal Finance is a nacessary corollary to it. It is true that in most federations in history,the primary incentive has been the sentimental impulse to unite on the part of peoples having some form of racial, cultural or regional affinity, but this impulse had in all cases essentially a political and economic background. It was either to gain strength by pooling their resources for aggressive or protective purposes or to gain economic advantages by way of economies of administration and facilities of trade. The essential factor, therefore, in the creation of the desire to federate is that there should be a reasonable prospect of the federating units gaining definite material advantages both individually and collectively. In order to gain these advantages and to make the Federation effective and useful, a number of sovereign states voluntarily entrust some of their administrative activities to be conducted by joint organisation, and provide adequate sources of revenue to enable this joint body successfully to carry out its responsibilities.

The extent to which this division of power and functions between the federating units and the Centre is agreed upon amongst the constituent elements has differed from case to case. A vital Question is whether the residue of sovereignty lies with the centre or the constituent elements. Where the centripetal forces are stronger that the centrifugal ones it lies with the former and vice versa. The British Commonwealth of Nations, comprising as it does, of practically independent dominions, is a good example of a Federation where the tendency is for power to recede from the Centre, while in the present German Republic the forces are acting in the contrary direction. There are thus no hard and fast rules governing the form of a Federation. It depends entirely on expediency, the special conditions of the case, and the express or implied will of the federating elements. The only common characteristic of Federations is that Federalism necessarily implies a division of the sovereign powers and functions between the Federal Authority and the federating units. As every activity of government requires the means to conduct it , the power to levy taxes and incur expenditure, is of necessity exercised by the Federal Authority, though this power is limited to the extent of its Federal responsibility. This function of the Federal Authority is now a days commonly expressed by the term "Federal Finance," as opposed to "Unitary Finance," applicable to the financial transactions of countries having a centralised form of government.

By a successive process of scientific reasoning and research the economists of various countries have evolved certain basic principles and laws which comprise the modern science of Public Finance, and these principle are equally applicable both to Federal and Unitary Finance. It is a commonplace that the government of a country is responsible for the performance of certain functions and duties which involve expenditure and necessitate the exercise on the part of the government power to raise revenue. In organised communities these processes are conducted through the medium of money, and the raising of revenue is usually done by the imposition of various taxes and less frequently by exacting actual services from the nationals. In the words of Dr. Hugh Dalton: "Most of the operations of public finance resolve themselves into a series of transfers of purchasing power. These transfers are made by taxation or otherwise, from certain individuals to public authority, and back again from these authorities by way of public expenditure, to other individuals," and thus these transactions bring about a maximum of welfare by the transference of consumable resources from the rich to the poor. There are, however, of some forms of expenditure that involve a net loss to the country and may result either in a dead loss as in the case of indemnity payments or in partial loss as in case of payments to foreigners for services which could be performed by the nationals on a lesser scale of remuneration. It is only too evident that one of the main objects of a sound financial policy should be on the one hand to minimise this loss as much as possible and on the other to promote the welfare of the people at large by the transference of purchasing power from one class of people to the other.

This latter principle when applied to Federal Finance is, however, beset with some difficulties. As opposed to Unitary Finance, here an additional factor, the regional, has to be taken into consideration. The process of equalisation has to be carried out not only as amongst the various classes of people, but also as between the Federating States *inter se.* Yet another difficulty is that in Federations there is always the chance of the financial transactions of individual States, counteracting those of the Federal Government resulting in an inequality of burdens and benefits. To safeguard against these difficulties, the activities of the Federal Government should be so regulated as to supply any possible deficiency in a particular State without encroaching as far as possible upon the freedom of action of the Federating State. This purpose may be achieved in many ways, for example by devising an intelligent system of taxation, the richer States may be made to benefit tthe poorer ones or the Federal Government may grant special subsidies to the latter to enable them to carry out beneficent projects. Moreover the fiscal policy of the Federation may be so devised that production is encouraged in the less productive States, and the flow of wealth from the richer States to the poorer ones is facilitated.

Another point to be remembered in this conection is that the constituent units within their own spheres of activities should be free from interference by the Federal Authorities and allowed to develop their resources without a feeling of cramp or injustice. The method of special subsidies should be resorted to only in very special cases, for its overdoing may lead to lethargy and lack of initiative among the States. Further, the sources of revenue and power to impose taxes should be so distributed between the Federal and State Government that it would not only be adequate for the proper discharge of functions allotted to each, but would also allow of considerable expansion in times of emergency. On the other hand, in allotting sources of revenue care has to be taken as to whether a certain source can be better administered by the Federal or the State Government. For example, there is little likelihood of fraud or evasion if local authorities administered taxes on real property or income because, from the very nature of things, a State Government is in a better position to assess and control them than the Federal Government. It follows, therefore, that the most suitable sources of revenue for the Federal Government would be those which can be administered without a great deal of detailed and expert information and permit of little chances of fraud or evasion. Taxes on consumable goods, for instance customs and excise, would thus readily occur to one as the more fitting to the requirements of a Federal Government. And, of course, the concept of economy in the cost of administration has always to be remembered in the transactions of public finance.

Keeping these broad and cardinal principles in view, we should turnprinciplesinview, weshouldturnourattentiontothespecialconditions of India and see how a system of Federal finance can be evolved that would bring about the maximum of benefit to the Indian people as a whole. It is evident that if an All-India Federation comes into existence at all, it will be only with the free consent of the Indian States that are at present independent entities in perpetual alliance with the British Crown, and their agreement to any proposed scheme of administrative or financial adjustment will be the deciding factor. The nature of the Federation will depend on the extent to which the States are prepared to relegate their sovereign functions to the Federal Authority, and consequently power to raise revenue will be delineated in proportion to the sphere of Federal activities thus agreed upon. The Princes do not appear agreeable to make considerable surrenders of their sovereign rights and privileges, and therefore a system of finance, which implies the economic allegiance of the States to an outside body, has to be ruled out of consideration. In an Indian Federation, therefore, the system of clear demarcation of Federal Authority and taxing power with full independence of action, of the constituent units in regard to residuary matters will of necessity have to prevail. It also follows that if any semblance of uniformity of relationship between the Federal Government and constituentt elements is maintained, the sphere of Federal activity will have to be restricted to a minimum consistent with the idea of Indian unity and the rights and privileges of the Princes.

It is obvious, therefore, that the mainstay of Federal finance in India will be a number of clearly defined indirect taxes that are capable of expansion and the imposition of which does not materially affect the sovereignty of States. Taxes like customs and excise on salt and petrol, for example, would evidently satisfy these requirements. So long as such taxes provide sufficient funds for the efficient discharge of Federal functions subject to the legitimate claims of the States for a share in these taxes being duly satisfied, there would be hardly any necessity for interference in the financial independence of the States. The Federal taxes by nature of their elasticity would make it possible for the Federal Government to meet minor emergencies and only in case of serious emergency, such as war, recourse may be had to direct

Federal levies or taxes, although even then, in deference to the sensibility of the Princes on this point, such levies may be realised in the form of contributions from the States.

The activities of the Federal Government in regard to the equalisationof the welfare of the constituent peoples will need, at least in the early stages of Federation, great caution and judicious discretion. Most of the States, for reasons described in previous chapters, and several British Indian provinces, e.g. the North-West Frontier Province, are comparatively less developed than other Provinces, and the usefulness of the Federation will lie to a great extent in removing these inequalities. The Federal Government may incur expenditure in such a way that the poorer provinces and States get greater transfers of purchasing power. But this is again beset with difficulties. It may not be always possible to procure goods and services of a high standard from these units, and at best this method alone may not fully rectify the position . The Federal Government in India may, therefore, fine it necessary to impose some levies on the richer of the British Indian Provinces and distribute the money so realised among the poorer Federal units to make up their deficits or enable them to develop their resources. The leads us to two fundamental questions.

What would be the just measure of a Federal levy on a rich unit, and what should be the equitable basis of granting subventions to the poorer ones? The first guiding principle that would occur to anyone in this connection, is that in order to avoid causes of interstatal jealousy and sense of injustice these transactions should not be based on arbitrary decisions. The classic formula, "from everyone according to his capacity and to everyone according to his nees" can with profit be applied in these cases. The Federal Government will have to keep correct and up-to-date data to determine the average *per capita* incomes and minimum standards of living in various Federal units. Far from solving the problem, this willl only serve in a rough manner which of the units are poorer than the others. How much of its revenues a unit can forego will depend primarily on the amount of its average budget surplus after providing for normal administrative responsibilities, and ultimately on the excess of the total taxable capacity of the people of the unit concerned over and above the actual tax burden.

With regard to the question of granting subventions to needy States the same principles would apply inversely, though in these cases several other matters will have to be considered. The mere fact of the index numbers of a certain federating unit showing comparative of its *porative of its* nationals would not be enough to call for a Federal subvention, for, *a prime facie* case would only be established when it is known that the State in question, in spite of imposing a high rate of taxation, is unable to raise to the average its cost of administration. It will be the proof of the fact either that the extensive territory and a sparse population necessitate greater *per capita* expenditure on administration or that, though it has a large population, the proportion of poor people to rich is larger as compared with other States. This particular activity of the Federal Government, however, will have to be administered with the greatest caution and should be designed specially to guard against the promotion of parasitism among the federating units.

The financial relations between the Federal Government and the constituent units will thus consist in effect only in payments being made by the Federal Government to each unit or payments in the opposite direction. For the incidence of the Federal indirect taxes will fall on the people of the federating units. But so far as the Indian States are concerned a settlement will at the outset have to be arrived at with regard to their financial claims, based on their treaties and engagements.

It would be wrong to ask the Indian States to waive their just claims merely because they show their willingness to enter the Federation. It has been suggested that these claims may be adjusted from Federal surpluses. But this is not so simple as it seems. In the first place the Federal Government for a long time to come may not have any surpluses at all and secondly, granted that there would be surpluses available, it would be very difficult, in view of the lack of sufficient data, to make an equitable distribution among the States.Under these conditions the best course would be to surrender the items of revenue in dispute at their very source so far as it is practicable. For example, the claim of the Indian States with regard to sea customs can be amicably settled if the duties on goods in bond intended for the States is collected at the sea ports and reimbursed to the States. By a judicious application of this principle the majority of such clmais would be satisfied, and in the case of other claims that cannot be so settled recoures may be had to direct payments.

Another important problem, to be considered in connection with the question of the States' entry into an All-India Federation, is that of the Public Debt of the Government of India. On March, 1935, the interest bearing obligations of the Government of India amounted to Rs. 1,235.74 crores, comprising Rs. 722.38 crores in India and Rs. 513.36 crores or £385.02 million in England. Of this total , the amount of Rs.

981.03 crores was covered by interest yielding assets, and a sum of Rs. 51.52 crores was held in cash, bullion and securities on treasury account. The balance of total interest bearing obligations not covered by the above assets was thus Rs. 203.19 crores.

These obligations include debts incurred on behalf of several Provincial Governments, the debenture stock of various railways taken over on the transfer of the lines to Government, and the capital value of liabilities undergoing redemption by way of terminable annuities. These debts are chargeable to the revenue of British India which in effect means that their burden lies on the people of the British Indian Provinces. The Indian States naturally object to join as partners in a concern which is not slovent. It has been urged that in Federation these debts will continue to be charged to the revenues of British India, but this position is not quite distinct in its implications. In case of Federation, the Federal Government will step into the shoes of the present Central Government of India and will control sources of revenue towards which the people of British India and the Indian States will equally contribute. So long as payments for debt services are made from Federal revenues it will be next to impossible to let the burden of debt fall only on the British Indian people and not to effect the interests of the Indian States. The whole suggestion is, in fact, a platitude designed to lead the Princes into a situation which is highly injurious to their interests.

The natural solution would be to commence the Federation with an entirely clean sheet. It is the people of the British Indian Provinces that are responsible for the pre-Federation debts of the Central Government, and a considerable proportion of these includes debts actually incurred on their behalf. The position, so far as the incidence of the burden is concerned, will in no way change if this public debt is distributed amongst the Provinces. It will remove a serious obstacle to the Princes' entry into Federation and will give the Federal Government a free start at the outset. An equitable basis of distribution of the debt among the Provinces may be found by a just application of the principle of "Capacity" and to enable the Provinces to meet their obligations, adequate sources of revenue may be transferred to them.

In a previous chapter we have shown how the Government of India have in the past persistently followed a policy by which the Indian States were made to suffer for the benefit of British India, and it is a moot question to ask how far this policy, highly injurious and unfair as it was to some of the staunchest supporters of the British rule in India, helped to improve conditions in British India. An examination of those conditions and their causes will enable us to see whether this policy was really beneficial toBritish India in particular and the Indian Empire in general.

A hundred years of British rule gave India a much needed peace by protecting her from external aggression and internal disorder and by developing modern means of transport and communications and constructing vast systems of irrigation, very nearly succeeded in stamping out the terrible scourges of rapine and plunder, famine and pestilence from which India periodiacally suffered from time immemorial. On the other hand and the same rule exposed India to promiscuous foreign exploitation, so that while some conditions contributed to the increase in India's population, other causes checked India's efforts to increase its national dividend in the same proportion.

It has been estimated that the average income of a British Indian citizen is about Rs. 44 or a little over £ 3¼ a year as compared to the English *per capita* income of over £ 50. The Indian Banking Enquiry Comittee(1931) discussing agricultural incomes in India, said: "The income of the agricultural population per head when separately assessed will be much smaller. From the reports of the Provincial Committees and other published statistical information, the ιotal gross value of the annual agricultural produce whould work to about Rs. 1200 crores on the basis of the 1928 price levels. On this basis and taking into consideration the probable income from certain subsidiary occupations estimated at 20 per cent., of the agricultural income, and ignoring the rise in population in the last decade and the fall in prices since 1928, the average income of an agriculturist in British India does not work out at a higher figure than about Rs. 42 or a little over £3 a year. Thus the general poverty of the agricultural classes is a matter which is beyond dispute." This extremely low income is further reduced by Rs. 7 if we make allowance for taxes, so that the actual income per head is 1.6 annas or amount 1¾ d. per day. Evidently this income is not sufficient even to procure the minimum of food necessary to nourish a human being, much less to provide clothes or house room on the very lowest scale. It is not surprising then to find the large majority of India's population to be underfed and underclothed, and of whom nearly one-fourth have never had a full meal in their life or a house worth the name to sleep in. The years of plenty followed by long or short periods of famine and plague that were a characteristic feature of the India of pre-British times have now given place to an era of constant and universal misery unparalleled in any country in modern times. The causes that have led to this situation are manifold, and it would be useful to examine them here cursorily.

The first thing that strikes one in this connection is India's low standard of productivity. In view of its huge population and vast potential resources the productivity is surprisingly low as compared with other countries. In the year before the war India's gross produce, according to a liberal estimate, was Rs. 1573 crores, or a little over £ 1,000 million, while the figure for Great Britain for the same year was supposed to be £2,000 million. So far as agricultural produce is concerned the yield per acre in India of staple products like wheat, rice and cotton is much lower than in most countries, although natural conditions are proverbially favourable for agriculture. Evidently the economic efficiency of the people is very low. The condition of semi- starvation which has continued during the last hundred years under foreign exploitation has been undermining the physique of the people, and with the continuance of those conditions the process of deterioration goes on at and accelerated pace from generation to generation. At the same time the existing low level of national income combined with the potential drain on India's resources do not allow for any surpluses that could be utilised for adequate industrial expansion or general improvement in methods of agriculture on which such a large proportion of the population depends.

The direct drain on India's resources may be estimated to be well over £100 million a year. This comes about in a variety of ways. One item is the administrative expenditure in England chargeable to Indian revenues, which in the year 1932-33 amounted to £ 26,244,000 and included interest on public debt incurred in England, some military charges and furlough and pensions payments to the European employees of the Government of India. Next there is the profit on foreign capital invested in India, the amount of which it is not easy to estimate. The authors of "The Wealth of India" guessed that in the year 1914-1915 the foreign capital invested in joint stock companies, exchange banks, insurance companies, navigation and general trading companies, was £568 million. Since then the foreign investments have increased in volume and the above estimate does not take into account foreign capital invested in central and provincial loans floated in India, the interest of which is not included in the Home charges and the innumerable private firms, plantations and other holdings in landed property scattered all over India. We may, therefore, safely assume the amount of foreign capital invested in India apart from that guaranteed by the Secretary of State, to be in the vicinity of £ 1,000 million, and putting the yield at 5 per cent., a very low figure for business enterprises in India, the profit on this capital would be £ 50 million. Another source of drainage is the payment for services of foreigners who get paid "on the average in salaries more than five to one what the natives are paid, " and who send the greater portion of their incomes to be used and spent in a foreign country. The amount thus lost to India was estimated in 1873 by Mr. J.M. Maclean, a witness before the committee of the House of Commons on E.I. Finance to be no less than £ 20 million. To-day, when the number of foreign employees in Government and other institutions is larger and the scales of allowances in many cases higher, the sum of £25 millions would be a very modest estimate.

It would, therefore, not be far from the truth to say that of the total production available for distribution the sum of over £ 100 millions is irretrievably lost to India. It has been argued that most of this expenditure consists of payments made for actual services rendered, and as such cannot be considered as a direct loss to India. But the fallacy of the argument becomes apparent when it is remembered that the employing of every non-Indian throws at least one Indian out of employment and that the cost is much less if the same services are performed by Indians. Similarly, the activities of the Government of India in regard to floating of external loans, force Indian capital, owned by people who would invest only in gilt edged securities, to lie idle or be invested in less profitable manner. This aspect of the question, however, we will discuss in another connection at a later stage.

But these are only the evident and direct losses that can be noticed and measured in terms of money. As a consequence of its connection with England, India suffers many indirect losses. Under the auspices of theBritish Government a number of handicaps have been imposed by the foreign vested interests on India's efforts to solve its own problems in so far as they effect such interests. It was, for instance, to benefit Lancashire that the unpopular excise duty on cotton manufactures was imposed, and various restrictions were placed on India's developing a mercantile marine in order to protect British shipping interests. It is primarily to safeguard the foreign invester and promote trade with England that India is forced to have its currency linked with pound sterling, in spite of the fact that the whole country is united in its demand for monitary independence, and expert opinion considers the subordination of the rupee to sterling as highly injurious to the best interests of the country.

Thus the dissentient member of the Royal Commission on Indian Currency and Finance (1926), criticising the currency policy of the Government of India, mentioned the various ways in which India incurred material loss. He remarked that:

"*(a)* It has involved the circulation of a very large number of token coins in India which could not be converted into international money, and, indeed, have proved to be a source of embarrassment to the Government in periods of weak exchange . This led to the unparalleled difficulties of the Government of India in 1918 , and necessitated the purchase of large quantities of silver at abnormally high prices involving a correspondingly heavy loss on the Indian Exchequer.

(b) It has locked up the Gold Reserves in a form which admittedly involves difficulties in realising them.

(c) It has been the cause of grave misunderstandings between the Government of India and the public of India, misunderstandings for which the Government cannot possibly be blamed, and which can only be regarded as natural, and inevitable under the circumstances, on the part of the people of India. The policy of secrecy adopted has aroused serious distrust in their minds of the system as a whole. This distrust having continued over a period of a quarter of a century cannot be removed without wholehearted measures. It is true that the policy adopted had earned for India a certain amount of interest on her reserves. It is stated that, up to March 31, 1925, the net profit on investments has been £17,962,466 in interest and discount, after allowing for losses due to depreciation in value. The loss on sale of Reverse Bills in India exceeds Rs. 22 crores. Besides this, one has also to take into account the effect produced on the public mind by the inability of the Government to realise at critical junctures the securities in which the Reserves have been locked up."

The average Indian is therefore forced to conclude that the miserable plight India finds itself in, is the unfortunate outcome of its liason with England. It is well known that the territories now comprising British India were acquired in the first instance by a British trading concern whose primary aim was profit and, although by force of events the East India Company found itself the ruler of vast territories in the

East, it remained essentially a business concern, for all its wars were fought and territories acquired and administered purely with the object of material gain. The act of governing was reduced to a particular form of commercial activity, and there are numerous instances in the history of the Company's rule in India in support of this assertion. For example, in the war between the Rohillas and the Nawab Vizier of Oudh, the Company placed part of its military strength at the disposal of the latter in consideration of a sum of money, and at a later date the Himalayan portion of the conquered Sikh kingdom of the Punjab was sold in full sovereignty to the highest available bidder, partly to meet the cost of the last war and also to get rid of a difficult and sparsely populated province the administration of which did not for the time being promise any profit.

With the taking over of the Indian administration by the Crown in 1858 the outlook somewhat altered, but in stepping into the shoes of the defunct East India Company the Government of India under the Crown also inherited certain traditions, which were kept alive by the services, the composition of which was not materially affected by the change of constitution. In the home country India continued to be looked upon as the "brightest jewel in the Crown of England," not because it was a great and ancient country, but because of all the dependencies of England, India contributed to the greatest extent to its national income. In giving India its wonderful systems of railways and irrigation England also incidentally found new ways for investing its surplus capital, and by giving the country peace without power it placed the nation at the mercy of foreign exploiters.

In a previous chapter we discussed how by the Government of India's policy of interference and penetration into their affairs, the Indian States were made to suffer, but British India as we have seen did not appreciably gain thereby. That policy was dictated by the sole motive of bringing the Indian States, like British India, under the sphere of effective British exploitation. The first step in the direction was taken when the States agreed, in most cases under pressure, to accept British Indian currency and step by step the way was made easier by extending the scope to further fields such as railways, post and telegraph, customs, salt, opium and a numeber of other things.

But although the rights of the States were thus flagrantly violated, sometimes on the pretext of public expediency, and more often under the undefinable principle of paramountcy, there was still one important obstacle that did not allow the foreign exploiter, working under the patronage of the Government of India, absolute freedom of action in States, as in the case of British India. This was that the States were internally autonomous principlities and the writ of His majesty did not run in their territories. Their treaties, which defined their rights and which were entered into when the British power was still weak in India, were now a hindrance in the path of the furtherance of British interests and though the new formula of paramountcy cold in effect render these treaties mere "scraps of paper," the form of treating them as "inviolate and inviolable" had still to be kept up.

A way, however, was found out of the difficulty. Indian agitation for Home Rule had gathered an intensity that could no longer be ignored without risk of grave consequences, and so long as the economic subservience of India to England was maintained and the coercive authority retained in British hands not much harm would be done to British interests, if popular demands were met by giving India a limited form of self-government. Popular sentiment all over India was strongly in favour of an All-India Federation, and if the States could be induced to join in, they would not only from a group in the legislature on whom the British Government could rely for support to their policy , but their very act of joining the Federation would bring them under effective subordination of the Federal Authority, to the further prejudice of their independence and internal sovereignty, which as we have shown in a previous chapter had already been encroached upon. How far our conjecture is true, we shall see in the following chapters in our examination of the British Government's proposals for Indian Reforms.

To continue our narrative, we have seen what india's present plight is and have discussed briefly some of the causes that have led to that said plight. There is little likelihood of any betterment in the welfare of the Indian masses as long as those causes are not radically removed and so long as the condition of the average Indian citizen is not improved, the grant of a constitution that gives India only a semblance of self-gevernment, without power to tackle its own problems, will be of little practical use. To make it worth while such constitution should give India real economic independence, that is to way, it should give India complete and unrestricted power to improve by all measures possible the economic efficiency of the people, to stop the drain on India's potential resources and abolish all handicaps imposed by vested interests in the development of its resources. Drastic ailments need drastic remedies and in the herculean task of ameliorating the lot of its 352 million citizens, living on the margin of starvation, a number of radical steps would be necessary. From the study of the problems involved, it would be evident that a constitution that withholds from India the following powers is not intended to be in the best interests of the country.

(1) India should be free to adopt whatever monetary policy it cosiders most advantageous to itself.

(2) The export of capital and precious metal should be regulated.

(3) The Indian Legislature should have the power of imposing restrictions on persons other than Indian citizens to work for remuneration or do business for profit in India. This would probably affect recruitment abroad for Indian public services and may necessitate tackling the question of buying over by Indian nationals of external businesses and investments in India.

(4) A greater proportion of public revenues should be made available for nation building activities by making all round economies in administration by all means possible.

(5) The export and import of commodities should be controlled in such a way that would enable India to expand its industries to the fullest extent and give not only employment to more and more workers, but also increase national income and stop drainage of wealth.

These are some of the fundamental remedies that suggest themselves readily to one, but they need not be resorted to indiscriminately and can only be considered as the possible and temporary means to an end, i.e. the welfare of the Indian masses. Most of the modern nations are to-day having recourse to methods similar to those mentioned above, and it would be inequitable that India, which is the poorest of all, in its average per head income, should not be able to conserve its resources and improve the welfare of its people. If Federation brings about real fiscal and economic independence, the States would be well advised to join it, for in parting with a portion of their sovereignty, they will be joining a partnership that would be beneficial to them as well as to India as a whole. But in case such independence is not in sight, the loss in sovereignty consequent upon their entry into the proposed qualified Federation will only mean the continuance of the disabilities under which they are suffering and possibly a further deterioration in the wellbeing of their peoples.

This leads us of necessity to examine critically the scheme of Federal Finance as it evolves from the plan of proposed Reforms, to see whether in the light of the scientific principles it can be considered satisfactory. The main questions that naturally arise in this connection may be summarised as follows:

(1) Is the general plan of Federal Finance under the proposed Reforms scheme workable?

(2) Is the scheme based on sound principle of public finance and those of equity implying an equitable distribution of burdens and resources among the component units?

(3) Does the plan take into account the special view of the States and provide adequate safeguards to their treaty rights? And finally:

(4) Does the proposed plan provide real remedies for India's difficulties?

In the following chapters we will take up these questions one by one and as answers to these questions may fundamentally affect our conclusions it would be advisable to subject them to more than a mere cursory examination.

The essence of success of any scheme of Public Finance lies in its being well balanced and the primary task of a Finance Minister is to make as nearly as possible correct estimates of income and expenditure and adjust them in such a way as to provide for the maximum of economy and efficiency in administration together with the greatest wellbeing of the people. The gift of prophecy being unatttainable, the task of estimating what the revenue and expenditure are likely to be during a fixed period in future is a very difficult one. Such forecasts have to be based primarily on the needs of the administration, and an appreciation of the economic conditions that may reasonably be expected to prevail in the country during that period. Unforeseen causes may falsify the forecasts, but good finance consists in giving due consideration to factors that can be humanly foreseen. The first test of the work ability of the proposed scheme, therefore, is whether the forecasts in the scheme of Federal Finance with regard to the financial position of the Federal Government and the Provinces are reasonable. This would bring us to compare the existing financial position with the forecasts on the basis of which the Government of India Bill was drawn, viz., the forecasts of the Federal Finance Committee (1932) and the recommendations of the Joint Committee on Indian Constitutional Reform (1934).

The following table compares the Federal Finance Committee's forecast of the Central revenue and expenditure with the actual figures for 1934-35 and the budget estimate for 1935-36.

Revenue.	Percy Committees Forecast.		Revised Figures for 1934-35		Budget estimate for 1935-36	
Customs.	51.20		51.17		51.84	
Collection	.90		1.09		1.15	
Net.		50.30		50.08		50.69
Salt	6.70		8.55		8.73	
Expenditure	1.15		1.16		1.18	
Net.		5.55		7.39		7.55
Opium	.78		..		..	
Manufacture	.73		..		..	
Net.		5		.36		.25
Railway (net).		5.00		..		..
Currency and Mint (net).		3.80		.55		.74
Miscellaneous (net).				3.52		1.83
Ordinary	1.66					
Reparations	.30					
Total.	1.96					
States Contributions		.74		.74		.74
Income Tax	18.00		17.25		16.40	
Collection	.80		.85		.92	
Net.		17.20		16.40		15.48
Total		84.60		79.04		77.28

Expenditure.	Percy Committee's forecast.	Revised figure for 1934-35.	Budget estimatte for 1935-36
Debt Services Interest	11.25	10.28	10.39
Sinking Fund	6.50	3.00	3.00
Military Budget (net)	47.00	44.34	44.98
Civil Administration	.6.85	9.37	9.11
Pensions and Superannuation Allowances	2.65	3.41	3.50
Civil Works	1.60	1.23	.94
Frontier Watch and Ward and Subventions to N.W.F.P.	2.70	2.10	2.06
Miscellaneour	1.55	5.18	3.24
	80.10	78.91	77.22

The above comparison reveals in a striking manner how far removed the Percy Committee's forecast is from the real state of affairs. On the revenue side the Committee have admitted that in making their revenue forecasts they "have not taken into account the special surcharges on Customs, Income Tax and Salt as at present in force." An examination of the above figures will show that, their calculations have been entirely falsified by subsequent events. With the surcharges still in force, the Customs Revenue for 1934–35 was actually less than the committees forecast by Rs. 22 lakhs and the inconsiderable excess in the budget estimate for 1935–36 of Rs. 67 lakhs over the previous year's gross receipts was based chiefly on the expected betterment of receipts from excises on motor spirit, sugar and matches. The total net receipts under Income Tax, including super tax and taxes on low incomes for 1934-35 were 16.40 crores, i.e. 80 lakhs less than the Committee's forecast, while the estimate for 1935-36, with only a partial (one-third) reduction in the rates of surcharges and taxes on low incomes was only Rs. 15.48 crores. The salt revenue alone shows a considerable excess over the Committee's forecast, but this was due mostly to large issues of salt in 1934 in anticipation of an increase in salt duty, while the estimates for 1935–36 were based on the assumption that the demand would continue at the same or a higher level.

In the event of surcharges on income and tax on low incomes being removed, the loss of revenue under Income Tax receipts would be Rs. 5.09 crores, reducing the revenue estimates for the year 1935-36 to Rs. 12.75 crores instead of Rs. 15.48 crores, and so far as customs are concerned the removal of emergency charges would very largely reduce revenue under that head. Since 1931, import duties have been increased all round. For instance, the duty on machinery and printing material has been increased from 2½ to 10 per cent, on iron and steel railway material from 10 to 15 5/8 per cent., on spirits and liqueurs from 15 per cent. to nearly 22½ per cent., on tobacco, cigarettes and cigars from 75 to 112 ½ per cent., and on cotton fabrics from 15 to 25 per cent., and heavy excise duties on motor spirit, sugar and matches have been imposed. The removal of these emergency duties will reduce revenue under customs by at least 20 per cent., or in other words the estimate for 1935–36 would be about 40.55 crores instead of 50.69 crores. The reduction of salt duty from 25 anas a maund to 20 annas would mean a further loss of 1.62 crores on an estimated consumption of 52 million maunds.

Under the proposed scheme railways would come under the

Federal Railway Authority entailing entire separation of railway finance from Federal Finance, and although stipulation has been made in the Government of India Act for the apportionment to Federation of a proportion of the surpluses, there is little liklihood of there being any surpluses at all for some time to come. During the financial years 1933–34 and 1934–35, railway receipts, iess working expenses, amounted to 32.87 and 32.38 crores while interests and miscellaneous charges for the same years were 32.87 and 32.38 crores respectively, so that there were no surpluses at all. The Committee's estimated surplus of 5.00 crores can only be obtained if gross traffic receipts from railways reached a figure of 113 crores. The maximum amount so far realised has been 103¾ crores in 1928-29 which included 5 crores on account of the railways in Burma, so that in order to obtain a surplus of 5 crores the traffic receipts of Indian railways, excluding those of Burma, have to exceed the best figures so far attained by about 14 crores. This is not a reasonable probability.

On the other hand in making their forecasts the Percy Committee "have assumed that Burma will be separated from India and have estimated the results of this change on such materials" as were available, while the figures for 1934-35 and 1935-36 given above comprise the total Central revenues of British India including Burma. In the opinion of the Joint Select Committee, the separation of Burma would involve a loss of revenue to India which may be "as much as 3 crores per annum, less the yield of any revenue duties on imports from Burma which may be introduced from the date of separation." Assuming that Burma was separated and the emergency surcharges were removed, the budget estimates for 1935-36 would be reduced to the extent of loss:–

due to separation of Burma.	3.00 crores
removal of surcharges on Incomes	.73 crores
removal of surcharges on Customs	10.14 crores
removal of surcharges on Salt	1.62 crores
Total	17.49 crores

So that the actual revenues for that years would be 59.79 crores. The Committee's forecast of Federal revenue thus exceeds the estimates for 1935-36 by 24.81 crores on the basis of the separation of Burma and the withdrawal of emergency surcharges, and even if these surcharges were retained the position would still be worse by 10.32 crores after accounting for loss due to separation of Burma. The Joint Select Committee, on whose recommendations the Government of India

Bill was based, generally endorsed the Federal Finance Committee's scheme and suggested that the Provinces should share to the extent of 50 per cent. in the proceeds of the taxes on income. If this is taken into consideration the revenue position would be further adversely affected by about 7 to 8 crores and by an additional 1 crores due to a"freshfactor"thecostoffinancialadjustmentswiththeStates,asproposed under the scheme.

On the expenditure side the actual position in 1934-35 was 1.19 crores better than the Percy Committee's forecast, and the estimates for 1935-36 were better by 2.78 crores, the principal differences being a reduction in debt charges due partly to redemption of loans bearing high rates of interest, and partial transfer to railway account of charges for the reduction and avoidance of debt, retrenchments in the Military budget and some other items on the one hand along with an under-estimation in the Committee's forecasts of expenditure under Civil Administration and Pensions and other charges. These forecasts, however, do not take into account the additional expenditure that would be involved under the proposed constitutional changes. Apart from the loss of 3 crores to Indian revenues consequent upon the separation of Burma, there would be, in the opinion of the Joint Select Committee, an additional expenditure of ¾ crores "attributable to the establishment of the Federation" and chargeable to Federal revenue, "by reason (*interalia*) of an increase in the size of the Legislatures and electorates or the establishment of the Federal Court."

The separation of Sind would involve an initail deficit in Sind of about ¾ crores "and will have to be met by subventions from the Federal revenues," although the Joint Select Committee hoped "the this will gradually diminish and be ultimately extinguished over a period of some 15 years by the end of which time it is believed that the agricultural developments connected with the Sukhar Barrage scheme will be complete." It is interesting to note that the Committee in this connection took some pains to prove that except for 10 lakhs, the cost of new overhead charges, there would be "no additional burden imposed upon the taxpayer of India as a whole," basing their argument on the fact the "if Sind were not constituted a separate Province this deficit would fall, to be met from Bombay revenues, except for a small sum of Rs. 10 lakhs" for the overhead charges. The Committee apparently overlooked the fact that the Central Government derived a sum of over 14 crores from emergency surcharges which are admittedly hard on the taxpayer, and the Government are pledged to remove them as soon as circumstances permit. The effect of relief given to Bombay by the separation of Sind will not be felt at all by the taxpayer in Bombay where the financial position does not promise the possibility of a reduction in provincial taxation in the near future. On the other hand the additional charge of ¾ crores will reduce to that extent the chances of relief in the Federal taxation. The total cost of the separation of Sind should therefore be regarded as an additional burden on the taxpayers of India as a whole. Considerations similar to those of Sind arise in the case of Orissa, which will require a subvention of something like 30 lakhs per annum. It follows, therefore, that the net burden on the taxpayer consequent upon the inauguration of Federation will be increased by about 1.80 crores due to the creation of these new provinces.

Basing our calculation on the revised budgetary figures for 1934-35, when the position was better than that forecasted for 1935-36 , we find that in the event of the separation of Burma, the Federal revenue with the retention of surcharges and the States' contributions would be Rs. 76.04 crores, while the expenditure with the additional cost of the separation of Sind and Orissa and other Federal overhead charges would be Rs. 80.71 crores, entailing a deficit of 4.67 crores. If, as suggested in the proposed scheme, the surcharges on incomes were removed, the receipts from taxes on income shared between the Federation and the Provinces on a fifty-fifty basis, the suggested financial adjustments with the States enforced and the emergency duties on salt and imports removed, the total revenue that the Federal Government can rely upon would not be more than Rs. 53.14 crores, implying a deficit of about 27 crores, on the Committee's estimated Federal expenditure of Rs. 80.10 crores. This investigation there fore forces on us the general conclusion that the estimates of revenue and expenditure on which the proposed plan is based are not only too optimistic but are in all reasonable probability unattainable under the conditions obtainable in India.

Having examined this aspect of the problem we should now see how far the general scheme of distribution of resources between the Federation and its component units would in practice help in the satisfactory discharge of their respective duties. The first question in this connection is whether the plan provides the Federal Government and the units witth adequate resources to perform their duties and allows for elasticity to meet unforeseen emergencies. So far as the Federal Government is concerned, it is clear that it should have adequate resources for the discharge of its functions. These functions are, under the proposed scheme, defence, foreign and political affairs, monetary policy and responsibility for loan and pensions charges, together with certain important functions, especially medical and agricultural research works, commercial intelligence and trade representation. We have seen in the foregoing paragraphs that in the event of Federation coming into being, and other factore remaining the same, there would be huge deficit of about 27.00 crores if the Federal Finance Committee's plan was adopted, and one of 4.67 crores on the basis of actual budget figures for 1934–35 and 1935–36 with the retention of emergency surcharges. There appears, therefore, no reasonable prospect of presenting a balanced Federal Budget, unless

(1) the deficit is met by additional taxation, or

(2) further sources of revenue are appropriated by the Federal Government at the expense of the Provinces, or

(3) large scale reductions and retrenchments are made in Federal expenditure.

The difficulties in the way of further increase in taxation are great in India. All authorities are, in fact, agreed on the point that the burden of taxation, is already heavy. The match excise duty, on the imposition of which the Federal Finance Committee so much relied for balancing the Federal budget, and which, in the first year of its imposition, realised a revenue of 1.15 crores, has been included in the estimates for 1934-35 and 1935-36. So are the new excises on motor spirit, kerosene, silver and sugar included in those estimates. With regard to tobacco excise the Federal Finance Committee were themselves doubtful of its success and admitted that the duty in the near future could not be relied on to yield a substantial revenue. The only resouce thus left to the Federal Government is an increase in salt tax and it is doubtful whether, in view of the political implications involved, any popular Government would take that responsibility without risk of widespread disaffection. As it is, the excises on matches and kerosene have been extremely unpopular since their imposition, as they affect the poorest in a community whose average income hardly justifies the imposition of these "poor man's taxes". The suggestion to levy a Corporation tax or super tax on the income or capital of companies is not without its difficulties. In the first place it will have a restricted and uneven incidence on general business profits, for the reason that only a small proportion of the business of the country is carried on by registered companies and secondly, all the States may not agree to the tax, realised from companies subject to their laws, being appropriated by the Federal fisc. The possibility of allocating to the Federal Government a special super tax on high incomes is worth consideration in this connection.

As regards appropriation of provincial sources of revenue, the mere suggestion is out of place. In the first place it is clear that in the contemplated Federation, the sphere of the Federal Government will be practically limited to services like defence and foreign relations which, by their very nature, cannot be controlled by Provincial Government, while responsibility for all the nation building and beneficent activities like education, public health and agriculture etc., on which the social advancement and economic wellbeing of the people depends, will rest with the Provinces. It follows, therefore, that the Federal expenditure will have to be kept in check so as not to starve those services for which the Provincial Government would be responsible. The Joint Select Committee admitted that "The provinces have rarely had means adequate for a full development of their social needs, while the Centre, with taxation at a normal level, has no greater margin than is requisite in view of the vital necessity for maintaining unimpaired both the efficiency of the defence services and the credit of the Government of India." On the other hand "there are a few Provinces where the available sources of revenue are never likely to be sufficient to meet any reasonable standard of expenditure" and will require substantial subventions from the Federal exchequer. Under these conditions when the provincial finances generally are already highly strained and their nation building activities are being starved, it is impossible to rely on any help from the Provinces.

The two ways as seen above being closed, the only thing left is to explore the possibility of reducing Central expenditure. The military budget promises greater scope because of the size of the amount involved. The Government of India hold that reductions in the military budget have already reached a limit where further reductions would be impossible without seriously affecting the size and the efficiency of the army. While placing budget proposals for 1935–36 before the Assembly, the Finance Member warned the members "that the large reduction in defence expenditure in recent years had been secured to some extent by emergency measures of a temporary character, and that the figure of Rs. 44.38 crores could not be regarded as representing a new permanent level of defence expenditure." The expenditure under this head is, therefore, expected to increase rather than decrease in the near future. Expenditure under civil heads has been reduced from 20.00 crores in 1930-31 to16.82 crores in the estimates for 1935–36, an increase of 59 lakhs over the actual figure for the previous year, and it is held that the expenditure has been reduced to such a low level that it can hardly be permanently maintained.

At this stage it may be argued that the foregoing conclusions have been based on facts and figures pertaining to a period of abnormal economic depression, and that in the event of general economic recovery the budgetary position would necessarily improve. In estimating the effect of such a reaction a number of other factors have also to be reckoned with. A glance at the revenue figures of the past five years would show that the average revenue of the Government of India has been little affected by the depression. This is chiefly because drastic emergency measures have been taken to meet the Government's needs, and it would be a mistake to regard the average level of revenue for the past few years as a permanent one. In the special economic conditions available in India it would take not only a general and very substantial economic revival, but also a long time before any appreciable results can be felt on the revenues so as to make the position secure.

The precariousness of India's economic position may be realised from the present condition of its foreign trade. In order to meet its normal external payments, ranging from Rs. 60 to 70 crores annually, its balance of trade should be favourable to that extent. In the year 1932-33 exports of merchandise totalled Rs. 135.66 crores, while the imports were 132.27 crores, leaving a balance of trade in merchandise of Rs. 3.39 crores. On the other hand the transfers of funds on Government and private account during that year amounted to nearly 69 crores and the excess demand had to be met by export of treasure, mainly gold, to the value of Rs. 64.92 crores. Taking into consideration the condition of the world market for India's produce it is not probable that there will be a marked increase in exports, and if, in the year under review, no gold was forthcoming for export, the natural reaction would have been towards a reduction in imports to the extent of about 57 crores, and thus would have reduced the customs revenue by about one-third . Up to the year 1931, India used to absorb gold and silver, to the value of about 38 crores annually to satisfy the well know needs of the people, and if this psychological factor comes into operation again, even to the extent of with-holding from export gold remaining in the country, the effect on customs revenues, shipping and other trades would be very serious. It is obvious then that the prospects of an increase in revenue from economic recovery are far removed, and in forecasting the budgetary position of the Federation no reliance can be placed on this factor.

Having examined the scheme so far, we should now see what chances there are for the Federal machine to run smoothly on the lines suggested. A close examination of the proposed plan of Federal Finance would show that it provides ample ground for the clash of interests between the Federal Government and constituent units to an extent that might endanger the successful working of the constitution. In the legislative field, a fertile source of clashes may be found, to quote a few instances, in the powers of both the Federal and Provincial legislatures to make laws with respect to any of the matters enumerated in "the Concurrent Legislative List," which contains subjects like marriage and divorce, successions, health insurance, factories, labour and trade unions regarding which the policy, in view of the peculiar conditions in India, may differ from Province to Province, and another source may be found in the powers of the Governor General and H.M.'S Government to interfere in strictly Provincial affairs.

In the financial sphere also the prospect does not seem very promising. The Government of India Act allocates succession duties, stamp duties and taxes on income to the Federal Government, subject to the provison that the latter may distribute the proceeds among the Provinces as may be prescribed. The Provinces have come to consider the above mentioned taxes as properly belonging to them, and the public in the Provinces will feel that income which is reasonable theirs is being kept from them. The proportion of the above taxes which the Federal Government may, if at all, grant them will vary from year to year according to the needs of the Federal Government and the result will be that the finances of the Provinces will be working under the handicap of a very doubtful factor. With the inadequate resources at their disposal and the popular demand for more expenditure on beneficent services, the Provincial Governments will find it impossible to defend unpopular measures of economy or taxation. The Provincial Legislatures as well as the representatives of the Provinces in the Federal legislature will combine in their efforts to prove the impossibility of continued appropriation by the Federal Government of the proceeds of those taxes, and by restoring to obstructionist tactics may bring about a state of deadlock that may endanger the Federation itself.

At the same time the coming in of the States. on conditions suggested, will further intensify the strain on public opinion. The States have made their position abundantly clear that by joining the Federation they are not prepared to lower a position which has already been made worse by unjustified encroachments on their rights. Under the principle of *status quo* as put forward in the proposed scheme every State would join, on its own terms, a Federation that can only be considered solvent if the Provinces bear many of the burdens which the States would refuse to bear. This would give rise to a feeling of inequality of burdens among the Provinces on the one hand and on the other a state of constant uneasiness among the States which would look with the greatest discontent on the efforts, which the Provinces would naturally be prompted to make under those conditions, to equalise the apparent burden, although the real burden on the States, as we shall see later, would be actually heavier than that which they might be justly asked to bear.

Moreover, the Government of India Act leaves the position unsatisfactorily vague about the residuary powers of taxation. The Percy Committee, having attempted to give exhaustive lists of heads of taxation for Federal and Provincial Governments, admit that they are not exhaustive and that "the taxes included in all four lists overlap at various points." They go on to say: "We doubt the possibility of drawing up a complete and comprehensive list of taxes not included in the first three lists (Federal), and the definition of the taxes in all the lists, so as to avoid litigation resulting from a conflict of jurisdiction, must in any case be a matter of legal draftsmanship." The Joint Select Committee have simply avoided the question as to who, the Federal Government or the units, should have the power toimpose taxes hitherto uncontemplated, and the Government of India Act is equally silent about it. The possibility of overlapping jurisdiction which the authors of the plan themselves admit, and uncertainty with regard to residuary powers of taxations will both provide prolific bases for embarrassing disputes between the Federal Government and the federating units.

It may be seen that in drawing up the Federal plan the authors of the scheme have failed to grasp the peculiar conditions under which the Federation is to be set up in India. Most Federations in history with only a few exceptions, like Canada and some of the South American States have been the outcome of centripetal forces, where a number of States joined together and relinquished part of their sovereignty to attain a common cause. So far as British India is concerned, it is still in the process of breaking down its unitary for of Government under strong centrifugal forces and striving to preserve its varied cultures and races in autonomous entities, while past experience has shown that public opinion in the Provinces is not sympathetic towards the Central Government. The danger of clashes occurring in Federations that are born of centripetal or other natural forces is well known in history and in the case of India, where those consolidating forces are wanting, the danger would be still greater. Common sense demands that the constitution should be drawn up in such a way as to avoid as far as possible conflict of interests between the centre and the constituend units: yet, as we have seen, the whole scheme is arranged in a way that makes such conflicts inevitable.

Thus our examination of the plan of Federal Finance as contemplated by the Government of India Act forces us to conclude that it is based on forecasts drawn in an atmosphere of complete unreality and cannot be relied upon, that it is not sufficiently elastic to help both the Centre and the units in the satisfactory discharge of their respective functions and that it does not eliminate causes for clash of interests and embarrassing disputes in future and that on the whole the plan of Federal Finance is fundamentally defective and in all probability unworkable.

The activities of a Government with regard to Public Finance consist in the raising and spending of revenue–the amount raised depending on what it is required to spend. The question how far Government expenditure should be carried has been explained by the well-known precept that it should provide the maximum of satisfaction with the least sacrifice on the part of the citizens. But this precept of itself does not carry us far in solving the problem unless account is taken of the inter-actions of a number of other factors.

Part of the Government expenditure arising from past contracts may be irrevocable and has to be met if the credit of the country is to be maintained. Such expenditure of the Government of India comprises its debt obligations and charges of the character of pensions and furlough payments which are definitely the first charge on the Government revenues. A closer investigation of the problem, however, would show that in the case of India the position is not so simple as it appears at the first glance. The above assertion is based on the assumption that contracts are entered into in the best interests of the country, and are of nature as to safeguard against undue wastage and drain on the country's resources. So far as the Public debt of India is concerned, a scrutiny of the past transactions of the Government of India would show that the position has been far from satisfactory. The total amount of loans in India outstanding on March 31, 1923, rose from Rs. 339.83 crores to Rs. 438.28 crores on March 31, 1935, and the amount of loans raised in England during the same period rose from £222.92 million to £ 323.57 million so that while the Indian Public debt in India increased by nearly 30 per cent., that in England increased by 45 per cent. In other words the financial policy of the Government of India during the period under review withheld from the people of India the opportunity of profitably investing capital to the extent of over £100 millions, and increased the foreign indebtedness of the country to that amount with proportionate increase in recurring loss of interest on capital, although it was possible to get loans in India at the same rate of interest as in England.

The Government of India Act, stipulates that on the establishment of Provincial autonomy "all powers vested in the Secretary of State in Council of borrowing on the security of the revenues of India shall cease," but this has been qualified by certain provisos that adversely effect the force of this stipulation. One provision is that during the transitional period that may transpire between the commencement of Provincial autonomy and the establishment of Federation, the Secretary of State may, under Parliamentary regulations, contract sterling loans. Past experience has shown that the Government of India have persistently been partial to the promotion of sterling stock entailing a direct loss to India and the success of the stipulation contained in Sec. 161, will very largely depend on how the borrowing powers of the Secretary of State are utilised during the transitional period.

Similarly with regard to pension charges, the question of the payment of tax on superannuation and other incomes earned by a large number of residents outside India, but chargeable to Indian revenues, has been decided in an inequitable manner. Under the proposed arrangements the whole of the tax on such incomes will not be realised by the Indian Government and would go principally to the British Exchequer instead. Considering that these payments are a definite charge on her revenue, the tax should in equity belong to India and be leviable at the source.

It is, however, not impossible to tackle this problem in an equitable manner, once the principle of India's legitimate share in this class of tax is admitted. The scale of taxes on income in England is higher than in India and, in all probability, will remain so for a long time. Residents in the United Kingdom earning this type of income may continue to pay income tax at the present rate into the British Exchequer, but the amount of tax that they would have paid under the Indian system should be remitted to the Indian revenues, or alternatively the Indian portion of the tax may be deducted at the source. Another, and probably the more practical, method would be to apply the Rules of Dominion Income Tax Relief on such incomes. Under these rules, relief from the United Kingdom Income Tax is granted where income which has borne, Dominion Income Tax has also borne, or is liable to bear, United Kingdom Income Tax. The rate at which such relief is calculated is either the Dominion rate of Tax or one half of the appropriate rate of the United Kingdom Tax, whichever is lower.

We may realise thus, that India's "irrevocable" obligations have accumulated to their present proportions under a Policy that was not always governed by the principle of maximum economic advantage to India and that the Government of India Act withholds from the people power to minimise the burden of these obligations which, as we have seen, are not incapable of being controlled.

Another type of expenditure that is subject to control and is not irrevocable may be of such a nature as not to allow for considerable economies due to special conditions of the country. In India expenditure on defence, judiciary and police may be considered as belonging to this class. These services are of an admittedly essential nature and reduction in expenditure cannot be carried too far, especially in the case of judiciary and police without jeopardising the peace and tranquility of the country. The point is whether it is possible to reduce expenditure on these services in the light of the above remarks.

Expenditure on defence particularly needs such examination. In the financial year 1932-33, the sum of Rs. 50.37 crores was spent on defence out of the total gross receipts for the Central and Provincial Governments of Rs. 210 crores. i.e.,24 per cent. of gross revenue went towards the defence of India. In the United Kingdom for the same year the expenditure on Army, Navy and Air Force amounted to £103 million,* out of a total revenue of £745 millions, so that it bore a proportion of 14 per cent. to the latter. It is evident that the burden for the upkeep of defence services was comparatively heavier in India than in the United Kingdom, and when it is borne in mind that in 1932–33, the British Army comprising a total strength of 467,000 men* cost £ 35.88 million while the Indian Army numbering only 254,354 * entailed a cost of over £37 millions,§ the conclusion forces itself on one's mind that there must be tremendous extravagance in the conduct of the Army department in India.

Central heads and Rs. 84.34 crores for all the Provincial heads of revenue in British India.

* The expenditure was distributed as follows :

Navy	£50.01	Million
Army	£35.88	"
Air Force	£17.10	,,
Total	£ 102.99	

*The establishment of the British Army in 1932 comprised:

The Regular Army	189,000
Army Reserve	124,500
Supplementary Reserve	17,500
Territorial Army	136,000
Total strength of effectives	467,000

* The strength of the Indian Army, excluding non-combatants, in 1933 was

Commissioned Officers (British and Indian)	10,988
British, other ranks	57,903
Indian, other ranks	142,256
Indian Reservists	43,207
	254,354

§ The sum of Rs. 50.37 crores converted into sterling at the rate of 13 rupees to the £ equals £378 million, and deducting from this £400,000, the cost of the Royal Indian Marine and India's subsidy to the British Navy and £80,000 the cost of India's Air Force, the expenditure on the Indian Army comes to about £37.32 million.

This conclusion gains further strength when it is remembered that the Indian soldier costs much less than a British soldier, that more than three-quarters of the strength of the Army consists of Indian soldiers, and that the equipment of the British Army cannot be considered as inferior to that of the Indian Army. Taking the above comparisons into consideration, and other things being equal, it should be possible to bring down expenditure on the Army roughly by about 10 to 15 crores.

Other expenditure not coming under the above categories may be classed as optional. Some items under this class may be very important such as education and public health, but their nature is such that large reductions in budget allowances would not effect the country's credit or its peace and tranquility, although such action may withhold from the public some very urgent amenities of life. On the other hand such expenditure is capable of being indefinitely expanded and therefore in distrubuting resources among different uses the precept of "the greatest good of the greatest number" would provide a useful principle for guidance. It has been maintained that the financial policy of the Government of India was not always guided by this principle; but, to limit our remarks to the scheme of proposed reforms, we may profitably quote one relevant instance.

Under the Government of India Act, the special functions of the Governor-General include among others the control and management of the ecclesiastical affairs, and its cost, that may extend to Rs. 42 lakhs a year, will be among the first charges upon the revenues of the Federation. Every rupee out of these 42 lakhs may be regarded as made up of parts contributed by the Indian tax-payers of all classes and denominations, and should in equity be spent for the benefit of the majority of them. But this expenditure can at best provide satisfaction to less than 2 per cent. of the population. The Act, by making statuary provision for the maintenance of the department at public expense, forces upon India an expenditure which does not promise the greatest good of the people. In the United Kingdom, where the majority profess the Christian faith, the tax-payer has for a long time ceased to pay for the cost of this kind of service and in India, where the Christian population is less than 2 per cent. and the real burden of the taxation is much heavier, this expenditure on the part of the Government is much more unreasonable. Such expenditure should, more properly be met, as in England and other advanced countries, by voluntary contributions . In fact, statutary provision in this respect, is not only iniquitous, but actually harmful as it would perpetuate the feeling that the Government of India forces the public to bear burdens that are not in its interests.

With regard to the aggregate cost of administration, Prof. Pigou postulates that "expenditure should be pushed in all directions up to the point at which the satisfaction obtained from the last shilling expended is equal to the satisfaction lost in respect of the last shilling called up on Government service," From this it follows that expenditure should be so controlled that it expands proportionately with an increase in the aggregate income of the community, that the development of new sources of profitable investments such as Government monopolies make it possible to raise more revenue and that the expenditure is "larger the less even is the distribution of income among the citizens and the more progressive is the revenue scheme" that the Government decide to employ.

The average income of the Indian community being extremely low and the marginal sacrifice involved in the payment of poor man's taxes like duties on salt, matches, kerosince oil and cotton fabrics, already excessive, it will take a very substantial increase in the general scale of incomes, and this seems far from right under the existing conditions, before it may be possible to expand expenditure considerably on this basis. Further opportunities for the development of Government monopolies, also are very restricted and railways and irrigation works on the whole are earning incomes only to the extent of meeting their working expenses and interest on capital. The last assumption in the previous paragraph promises some help as the inequalities of incomes in India are well known. An intelligent scheme of progressive taxation may affect transference of purchasing power from the richer few to the collective purse and eventually to the needy, directly by way of actual services like education and medical aid, or indirectly by way of reducing the incidence of taxation on the poorer sections.

Experience has shown that though the Government of India has very often utilised the above principle in raising more revenue, it has not at the same time provided relief to the poor. In fact there have been instances in which, when relief was possible, it was given actually to the richer sections of the community. In 1931, a number of surcharges on income tax and super tax, tax on low incomes and cuts in pay of higher Government servants were imposed, to meet heavy deficits in the Budget, and heavy duties on matches , kerosine oil and sugar, were later imposed in addition to an increase in duty on salt and other exports and imports. The Budget forecasts for 1935–35, made it possible to dispose of a surplus of Rs. 1.42 crores and the Finance Member of the Government of India, in placing the budget before the Legislative Assembly, laid down the principle that "relief must come first in restoring emergency cuts in pay, and secondly in taking off the surcharge on income tax" and proposed an all round reduction by one-third on surcharges on income tax and super tax as well as on taxes on low incomes.

The Legislative Assembly did not approve of this proposal, but decided to remove tax on low incomes altogether, to retain surcharges on higher incomes and to give relief to the poor by reducing duties on some necessaries of life. This attitude, however, did not meet with the approval of the Government of India and the Governor-General in the exercise of his overriding powers, sanctioned the enforcement of the Bill as proposed by the Finance Member, so that not only was a popular opinion rejected, but an inequitous scheme of taxation was arbitrarily maintained. What happened in March, 1935, may happen again when the proposed Federation comes into being. The Government of India Act empowers the Governor-General under certain circumstances to enact Legislatve Acts in his own discretion if it appears to him that such action is essential to enable him "satisfactorily to discharge his functions," and provides no remedy against the assumption of dictatorial powers by the Governor-General in face of consistent and repeated wishes of the Legislature.

With regard to the principles governing the raising of revenue, we need not here enter into details of essential considerations that should regulate a just scheme of taxation. These properly belong to the theory and principles of Public Finance and form such an important feature of the scientific investigations of modern times. So far as broad principles are concerned, we may do no better than quote Prof. Pigou who says that, "There is general agreement that all of a Government's activity should be regulated with a view to promoting in the highest possible degree, the welfare of its citizens. This is the touchstone by which the whole of its legal system–and its tax laws are, of course, a part of its legal system-must be judged. The day in which the welfare of one category of citizens could plausibly be ranked above that of another is past. Nobody would venture to claim now that a smaller amount of welfare accruing, say, to a noble an should be preferred to a larger amount that might be made to accrue to a peasant. So fa: as political theory is concerned, maximum aggregate welfare is everywhere accepted as the right goal of government; and when as of course often happens, actual Government pursue a different goal, their practice may be more or less plausibly explained away, but is never openly defended. In the special field of taxation this general principle is identical with the principle of least sacrifice. Its validity appears to be given directly in intuition."

Some aspects of the question have already been touched upon in connection with our study of the policy of public expenditure, but we may consider here usefully one or two other points, with reference to the Government of India's policy of raising revenue, that require some attention. We have seen that their financial policy was not always governed by the principle of "maximum aggregate welfare" of the people while in the field of taxation the principle of "least sacrifice" has very often been overlooked and the Government of India Bill promises little hope of these inequalities being rectified. Since 1931, several indirect taxes have been imposed on a number of necessaries of life in disregard of the wellbeing of the people and the anticipated increase in public expenditure in view of the proposed Federation, gave the Government of India an excuse for imposing further duties like those on matches, sugar and kerosine oil. The position thus is that while the burden on the poorest sections of the community has been constantly increasing, that on the richer section has not been proportionately adjusted.

The case of Bengal is an instance in point. That Province has for some years been experiencing heavy budget deficits and has, consequently, been demanding some kind of special treatment with regard to the distribution of resources between the Province and the Central Government. A case has been made out for that Province for the allocation of a substantial share of Income Tax imposed on incomes earned in Bengal, the whole of which under the existing arrangements is appropriated by the Central Government. The principle of subventions, which is one of the principal methods for securing equalisation of conditions between federating units, may with benefit be resorted to only when it has been established that the unit demanding such relief in spite of having exhausted all its resources of revenue, common to other units, is yet unable to meet its normal requirements.

A scrutiny of the revenue figures for Bengal, which comprises the most fertile part of India, would show that receipts under "land revenue are remarkably low as compared with other Provinces, the average land revenue per million acres of cultivated land being lower only in two Provinces, viz., Bihar and Orissa and the Central Provinces and Berar. So far as the Provinces of Bihar and Orissa are concerned, the reasons for low revenue with respect to the northern part are similar to those of Bengal, while with regard to the southern part, the average is reduced by inclusion in the total cultivated area of vast tracts of very poor land in Chhota Nagpur and Orissa. Land in the Central Provinces and Berar has a much lower productivity than other Provinces due to the thinness of soil and difficulty of irrigation. The reason for this low land revenue in Bengal and Bihar is to be found in its land revenue system. Under the Zamindari system of U.P., Punjab and other Provinces, land revenue represents 35 to 50 per cent. of the rent derived by the landlords from their tenants and, by reason of its being subject to revision periodically, has been enhancing with the rise in the price of agricultural produce. The system in Bengal and Bihar, however, which was introduced by the British at the close of the eighteenth century, with the intention of converting large farmers of revenue in Bengal into landlords occupying a position similar to that of land owners in

England, is not so elastic. Under this system the amount of revenue was fixed in perpetuity, so that, while the general level of prices has gone up many fold since 1795, the land revenue has remained the same. Bengal is at present a country of big landed proprietors, whose huge incomes do not bear the burden of taxation to the same extent as similar incomes in other Provinces. The total rental in Bengal has been estimated at about Rs. 16 crores, and if temporary settlement was introduced, the land revenue, even at the minimum scale of 35 per cent. of the rental, would be Rs. 7 crores instead of the present amount of a little over Rs. 3 crores.

So long as this inequality of burdens exists, the taxpayer in other Provinces may not approve of the payment of huge subventions to Bengal without a feeling of injustice. A revision of land revenue assessment to equalise the burden is the evident remedy, but in view of the Governments's pledge it may not be possible to tackle the problem in this manner. As an illustration, let us imagine that an estate in Bengal had, in 1795, a rental value of Rs. 1,000 and land revenue on it was assessed at Rs. 400 per annum on a 40/60 basis and that, in 1935, its rental had increased to Rs. 3,000 the land revenue remaining the same. Under normal conditions the revenue would have been proportionately increased to Rs. 1,200 and thus the unearned portion of the land owner's income would apparently be equal to Rs. 800, to which the Government may lay its claim. This pre-supposes that the property remained in the same hands throughout, for if it was sold at a later date, the capital value would have been determined on the basis of the current rate of interest, on the total net income of Rs. 2,600.

The difficulties in the way of reassessment of land revenue in Bengal and Bihar are therefore great, and the problem has to be tackled on different lines altogether. In British India, agricultural incomes are exempt from Income Tax for the reason that such incomes already pay a high rate of duty by way of land revenue. There is some justice in the application of this principal in areas where land revenue is subject to periodical assessment, but in permanently settled areas it does not retain the same strength. Most of the land in these areas is divided among big hereditary magnates, whose present huge incomes are quite out of all proportion to their real tax burden, and it would be only fair that they should bear that burden to a greater extent than they do now. In this connection the question of taxing larger agricultural incomes, somewhat on the lines of the present super tax, may be usefully considered. Such a tax will not only remedy the financial difficulties of Bengal and Bihar to great extent, but would also enable the Federal Government to give help, if at all, to Provinces which really need it.

Yet the Joint Select Committee, have ignored the fact that a subvention from Federal revenues can be justified, not by reason of a deficit bugdet, but only if a Province, having exhausted its sources of taxation in common with other Provinces, is unable to meet its normal demands and have advocated a "special treatment" of Bengal in its claim for a share in jute export duty, on the argument that a Province is justified in claiming a share of the proceeds from duty on a commodity that it produces. This line of resoning is a dangerous one, for once the principle has been acceded to in one case it may be difficult not to entertain the claims of other Provinces, all of which produce some commodities that are exported and are subject to duties, and if the Provinces manage to show deficits over a number of years, it may entail a wholesale re-shuffling and re-adjustment of Federal Finances. In fact, Assam has already put forward a similar claim to a share in the proceeds of the exise duty, now a Central head of revenue, on petroleum produced in that Province, although in this case the claim for relief may be more justified than that of Bengal. So far as Bengal is concerned the treatment recommended by the Joint Select Committee and acceded to is, as we have seen, decidedly "special" but not equitable.The taxation policy of the Government of India has very often ignored the principle of "equal sacrifice among similar and similarly situated persons" and the scheme of proposed Reforms does not give hope of any betterment in the equalisation of the tax burdens.

The next point to be considered is whether the scheme provides adequate resources to the Federating units to enable them successfully to carry on their nation building activities. The Joing Select Committee, commenting on the existing system of finance in British India, said that "from the point of view of expenditure, the essentials of the positions are (and no change in this respect is to be expected) that the Provinces have an almost inexhaustible field for the development of social services" and that they "have rarely had means adequate for a full development of their social needs." The Committee seem to have arrived at no constructive plan to remedy the position beyond that of suggesting that there was "little or no prospect of the possibility of fixing a higher percentage than 50 per cent." of the Income Tax proceeds to be shared by the Provinces, and the Government of India Act has recognised the principle of distribution between the Federal Government and the Units, of receipts from Income tax, salt, excise, export duties and certain succession and stamp duties. We have seen how unreal are the forecasts on which the scheme is based and so long as the general plan of administration and finance remains in its present form or altered according to the proposed scheme, it is very doubtful whether at any future date, that can reasonably be foreseen, it would be possible for the Centre to forego a substantial portion of revenue under these heads.

The social needs of the Provinces may be realised from a comparison of the amounts spent in 1933-34 in different Provinces on Education and Public Health given in the following table:–

Province	Population 1931	Gross Revenue 1933-34in lakhs of Rs.	Amount Spent On Education and Pub. Health	Per Capita Expenditure of Educ. and Pub. Health Rs.
Bombay	21,930,601	18,73.72	2,54.32	1.2 ans.
Madras	46,750,107	22,46.66	3,73.16	13 ans.
U.Province	48,408,763	11,23.6	2,44.60	8 ans.
Bengal	50,114,002	12,02.78	2,18.77	7 ans.
Punjab	23,580,852	12,38.46	2,22.12	15 ans.
Bihar and Orissa	37,677,576	5,95.02	1,18.90	5 ans.
Central Provinces	15,507,723	5,80.29	67.52	7 ans.
Assam	8,622,251	2,48.59	49.65	9 ans.
Total for British India incl. Burma	271,526,933	2,09,55.2	17,88.4	10 ans.

It will be evident how inadequate is the expenditure on these essential nation building services. As compared to this, the budget grant for these two services in the United Kingdom for the year 1933-34, was over £73 million * out of the total state receipts of £744,791,000 so that the former figure bore a proportion of nearly 10 per cent. to the latter and gave an expenditure approximately of £1 15s. per head of the population on these services. In British India, on the other hand, expenditure in 1933-34, on Public Health and Education was about 8 per cent. of the total receipts while the cost per head of population was less than a shilling. The effect of this very low expenditure on the population in general was further reduced because of the discriminatory manner in which these services were rendered. For example in 1933-34 , in the Province of Bengal, 11 per cent. of the

total expenditure on Education was incurred for the benefit of one-thousand of the population.†

* The actual figures for 1933-34 were:

	£	£
Board of Education	42,061,901	
Museums	325,473	
Scientific investigation	197,573	
Grants to Universities and Colleges	1,890,000	
Public Education and Museums in Scotland	6,730,025	
		51,204,972
Ministry of Health	19,200,445	
Dept. of Health for Scotland	2,832,265	
		22,032,710
	Total	£ 73,237,682

† Education of Europeans has been treated as a reserved subject since the inauguration of the Montagu-Chelmsford Reforms and is outside the legislative control of the Provincial Councils. In 1933-34 expenditure on general education in Bengal was Rs. 1,15,75,000 while expenditure on European education was Rs. 12,54, 000. Out of a total population of over 50 million in Bengal the number of Europeans and Anglo-Indians according to the 1931 census was 50,587. The benefit derived by these communities was thus more than a hundred times that derived by an average Bengali from the Government's activities with respect to Education.

This invidious distinction is given statutory sanction by the Government of India Act which provides that unless a Provincial Assembly resolves otherwise, by a clear majority of three-fourths, all grants for the benefit of the Anglo-Indians and European communities in aid of Education shall, after the inauguration of Federation, not be "less in amount than the average of the grants made for its or their benefit in the ten financial years ending on the 31st day of March, 1933." *

As compared with British India, the position in the Indian States is a good deal better. In the following table the proportion of expenditure on Education and Public Health is shown with regard to a number of States taken indiscriminately from different parts of India.

1. State	2. Population	3. Gross Revenue	4. Expenditure on Education and Public Health	5. Per cent. of 4 to 3	6. Per Capita Expenditure on Educ. and Oub. Health
Jodhpur (1932-33)	2,125,982	1,40,15,921	10,97,000	8%	Re. 0 8 ans
Wankaner. (1030-31)	44,280	8,26,427	49,66	6%	" 1 2 "
Baroda (1932-33)	2,500,000	2,70,10,000	43,05,000	16%	" 1 11 "
Indore (1929)	1,151,578	1,36,06,200	12,15,791	12½%	" 1 1 "
Bhopal (1932-33)	692,448	48,13,000	5,64,000	12%	" 0 9 "
Sangli (1932-33)	258,442	15,48175	1,98,398	12%	" 0 12 "
Cochin (1932-33)	1,205,016	1,05,57,328	20,52,465	19%	" 1 10 "
Mysore (1933-34)	6,557,302	3,42,87,244	61,31,400	18%	" 0 15 "
Travancore (1933-34)	5,095,973	2,34,82,00	57,30,000	24%	" 1 1"

It may be noted that, under existing disabilities, about 30 per cent. of the legitimate revenues of the States go to increase the revenues of British India, and yet the former manage to spend more on beneficent services than the latter. The natural conclusions that may be derived from the position are, firstly, that the attitude of the States' Governments is more sympathetic towards the social services than that of the British Indian Governments and the invidious distinctions that are a feature of British Indian administration are not found in the States, and secondly, that there is not so much administrative waste in theStates as in British India, which fact enables them to find comparatively larger funds for their nation building activities.

So far as sources of revenue are concerned, we have seen that under the proposed scheme they are totally inadequate for the expanding needs of the Provinces and the chances of help from Federal Revenues are very doubtful. The door for the stoppage of administrative waste also in closed to them. The chief waste is through the proverbially high scale of salaries paid to public servants in India, and the Government of India Act reserves all matters concerning conditions of service for the higher services to the Secretary of State. Even the strength of these services has to be prescribed by the Secretary of State so that it will be beyond the power of the Provincial Assemblies to reduce the scale of pay in case of future employees or the cadre of the services in order to release more funds for the beneficent activities.

Thus our examination of the scheme of Reforms as contained in the Government of India Act, shows:

(1) That the provisions of the Act with regard to the promotion of public loans are not in the best interests in India.

(2) That it does not provide a remedy for the loss incurred by the Indian Exchequer from taxes on incomes received abroad but charged to Indian revenues.

(3) That there is a large wastage in the conduct of the Army Department in India and the Act withholds from the Legislature power to control the military expenditure.

(4) That the Act forces on India certain types of expenditure that are not for the greatest good of the greatest number.

(5) That the scheme of public expenditure is too rigid to allow for an increase or decrease in aggregate expenditure with a rise or fall in the average income of the community.

(6) That the scheme of taxation is inequitable as it does not promise any relief to the poorer sections of the community, but advocates imposition of further burdens on them, without providing for an equitable transference of purchasing power from the richer sections.

(7) That it advocates unfair principles of subsidising the Provinces from Federal Revenues, whereby purchasing power will be transferred to Provinces that do not deserve it by reason of the fact that there is great unevenness of incomes in the Provinces and where the incomes are at the same time concentrated in the hands of a few.

(8) That the scheme does not provide adequate resources for the Provinces generally for carrying on their nation building activities.

(9) That the Act perpetuates invidious distinctions and is partial to certain categories of citizens.

(10) That it witholds power from Provincial Legislatures to stop wastage and extravagance in the conduct of the administrations of the Provinces.

And that on the whole the scheme ignores the generally accepted principles of public finance and provides for an inequitable distribution of burdens and resources between the Federation and the units and also as between different sections of the community.

7

Labour Problem

A Large part of the cotton industry is in the hands of Indian firms and individual proprietors. The British firms that have no Indian representatives on the directorate are few. The jute mills are almost entirely in the hands of Europeans, principally Scots.

There is diversity in the composition of the external management in cotton mills. In the majority of cases there are boards of directors to whom the managers at the mills are directly responsible, and agencies to which the commercial side of the business is entrusted. Occasionally the latter firms not only attend to the commercial side, but under the name of managing agents, or of secretaries and treasurers, intervene between the baord of directors and the manager. Sometimes, where this is not the case, there is a secretary at the mill as well as a manager. A large number of enterprises, however, are in private ownership. The exact line between this and the former is difficult to draw, as joint proprietors or partners may denote something not very different from a small board of directors. The large number of ginning factories are in private ownership.

In the jute industry, on the other hand, mills, with only two or three exceptions, while under the control of boards of directors, are run by managing agents. It is noticeable that the same groups of names of directors occur again and again in different mills, with perhaps in the case of each separate mill one name or two added. Thus in 1920, in the directorate of thirty-six mills, there are three names commonly, but not always, found together, of which one occurs fourteen times and the other two eleven times each. There are only two or three jute mills owned and run by Indians; occasionally an Indian name is found on the directorate of a mill otherwise managed by Europeans.

A similar tendency to gather control of industry within a small circle is found when the names of managing firms are examined. In the same year one firm acted as managing agent for nine jute mills, four tea gardens, one oil factory, and one fire-brick and pottery factory, and other firms for nine jute mills, two saw mills, two sugar factories, for a fire-clay and silica works, for a graphite company, for a mica works, and for a lac factory. In the mills so run the resident manager is responsible to the managing agents, and they to the directors.

Both in the cotton industry and in the jute, the manager is assisted by a varying number of assistant managers, each of whom is responsible for a department. Sometimes the general manager, besides having control of the working of the mill, is also departmental manager over one department. Under this group of managers there are the babus, or clerks, who check work done and pay wages, and the large and important body of control composed of the foremen and forewomen, of whom it will often be more convenient to write under the names used in India, because these vary in different localities and so suggest the place to which reference is being made. It is impossible to get the full content of the Indian terms into a word that is familiarly used for a clearly defined position in British industry.

In the cotton mills of Bombay the words used are jobber for the man, and naikin for the woman. In cotton mills in other districts these words alternate with mukadam and mukadamin. In ginning factories contractor jobber or mukadam is used. In jute mills, where there are seldom, if ever, forewomen, in spite of the large numbers of Maggies employed, the word for the men in charge of the various groups of workers is sirdar.

Though the titles are different, the powers and privileges are similar, with this modification, that the Calcutta sirdar has probably more influence than is usually wielded elsewhere, because in so many cases the managers and assistant managers under whom they work are Europeans. Even if they have acquired a certain knowledge of Bengali and Hindustani, there are still four or five other languages which it would be necessary for them to know in order to be able to talk freely with all their workers. The necessary frequency of furloughs and the early age at which many European managers retire add to the strength of the body of sirdars as a wall of separation between the management and the workers. Men who on their first arrival are eager to understand, and if it might be to secure better conditions for those whose work they direct, grow accustomed to accept as inevitable things they cannot change, and if later on they find themselves in positions of authority they may retain their kindly feelings towards the labourer, but only in rare cases are they inclined to agitate on behalf of the latter. They occupy a position strictly hemmed in on both sides.

It is impossible to generalize about their relationships with the workers. Some of those whose outward manner is most domineering yet retain considerable human touch with individuals and groups, especially with women and children. In many cases groups of workers gather round to assist in answering the questions a manager may put to the overseers in translating for a visitor, and there is a hubbub of many answers all shouted together, and a vision of gesticulations and laughter. This same eagerness to be in whatever is going on makes it quite impossible to get photographs of workers within mills even when the machinery is stopped for that purpose. The machines are left and the immediate foreground is a mass of laughing faces and pushing figures, till at last, in despair of getting any quiet moment, the stop is pressed and the film is sacrificed! In some mills the relationship between the manager and the little children is a delightfully personal one. Sometimes friendliness accompanies a coercive manner. The same man who gripped a lad under his chin, and threw him aside with a look as of utter amazement that anyone should dare to be in his way, laughed and chaffed with other workers, especially with groups of women, and is famed for his power of managing labour. Another, who seemed to be on specially good relations with his workers throughout the three mills for which he was manager, was consistently courteous to all. More than once, as he led the way through the compounds, little girls ran up to him and slipped a hand into his for a few steps and then fell back again. He had made a study of one branch of Eastern culture, and had spent his leisure in trying to understand something of the history of the people. One manager had the habit of giving each baby a small coin. In watching the reception it got, it was noticeable how soon the sense of the desirability of money was roused in the children. The gift seemed to be only for those who were still closely dependent on their mothers, and who, if they could walk at all, had only just reached that stage of development. Yet only one showed indifference to the pice. His little face, dulled in expression, probably by fever, showed entire indifference, as he grasped his drinking vessel tighter and paid no attention to the offered gift. In strong contrast to him, a tiny girl began to stretch out her hand, then , realizing that it was already full of fragments of sugar cane, and that somehow things would not work that way, spread the fingers wide, scattering the fibres on all sides, and grasped the coin. She had already showed a very clear perception of how to attain a desired end. When the manager, who had lifted her on his arm, tried to set her back on the iron ledge on which she had been sitting, her little body stiffened itself straight, in graphic protest, and it was only when her attention was distracted by the coin that she consented to be set down again. With all the kindliness, it is rather sad to think of the creation of so early a knowledge of the possibilities of money and, from another point of view, still more tragic to think that so small a sum should create the evident eagerness on the part of the mothers that their chidren should not be overlooked.

Whether the manager be European or Indian, his position, unless the mill be a small one, is very onerous. The hours, regulated for the workers, and the weekly holiday they enjoy, are not necessarily shared by him. Where a day-shift system is in operation, he and his assistant are responsible for the whole time covered by the double relay of workers, and when repairs have to be undertaken in holiday time it is often at his own risk that he is absent. As one put it: "If an accident happened (during repair work) and I was not there, I would be dismissed." In many areas, too, it is exceptionally difficult for a manager to get an annual holiday, as the season at which it is most needed coincides with the time when labour is scarcest in the mills.

It is not difficult to realize the kind of pressure that is brought to bear on the manager to increase output and to reduce expenditure. In his effort to secure these ends he is confronted with the sirdar or jobber.

The importance of the latter in the whole conduct of mill operations and the vital difference between his position and functions, and those of a British foreman, can scarcely be too strongly emphasized. He stands between the employer and the employed. In many cases he is still an absolute wall of partition, and greatly delays reforms that might otherwise be brought about. From the manager's point of view, it is only through him that workers can be secured. If the employer or the manager went to his mill gates, or to the coolie labour bazar, and asked for workers, he would be received with laughter. At present he must have this body of men to engage his labour and to control it in the mills. The smooth running of the departments and the regular output depends on them, and to a considerable extent their remaining in the mills depends on the manager's non-interference.

From the worker's point of view, the presence of the sirdar is even more inevitable than from the employer's. Long-established custom gives him his pre-eminence. For it is not only in modern industry that he is found. Wherever there is group employment there is a leader chosen who negotiates for the group. At the railway station a glance round the circle of coolies who have carried and stowed away the traveller's luggage is at once answered, not only by the stepping forward of the one who claims to be head, but also by the looks and gesture of the others who fall back. The same occurs in the case of rickshaw runners. At the end of the ride three fall back, either in fact, or in attitude, and the fourth stands out. He is sirdar on a small scale. He receives the payment for all and engages for all for future work.

The story is told of a group of workers in Calcutta engaged to cut a plot of grass. Two hours passed and the workers were still seen sitting on the grass. The reply to the inquiry why they had not begun to work, was that they were choosing a sirdar. Even for this temporary and casual piece of work the need of leader was felt, and the choosing of him was a weighty matter. The sirdar stands, in his crude way, both for the interests of the employer and for those of the labourer. It is his part to see that an adequate amount of work is done and to minimize as far as possible the fluctuations in the supply of labour. From the worker's point of view, he is necessary, not only as a protector of his rights against vague, unknown powers, but also as a security against arbitrary dismissal. In many cases he is oppressive, but he is so much an institution of the country that the labourer scarcely understands how work could be carried on without him.

In earlier days, when the mills were less widely known and when travelling was less usual among the poorer people of India, contractors went to the outlying districts, especially to areas where they knew there was overpopulation, and secured workers for the mills. This method is unnecessary now in connection with mill work, though in some Calcutta mills it was used recently for the Madras area. The Madrasis were said to have less initiative and to be unused to travelling alone, and therefore needed personal recruiting after it had ceased to be used for other jats. Very strenuous recruiting is still going on, apparently with serious abuses, in connection with mines in the Santal district. But although recruiting is no longer necessary in mills, the overseer is still the man who secures the workers. When labourers are scarce in the mills during seed-time and harvest, it would be useless to attempt to bring the cultivators from their fields. During the rest of the year the news of the wages to be a had in the cities travels from group to groups, and those who have gone off to the country bring back with them groups of friends and relations. Where a new mill opens, news of it spreads and companies of would-be workers crowd to its gates or linger in the neighbouring bazars.

In large towns there are coolie labour bazars. Spaces for these are found at sudden widenings in important thoroughfares or in recesses. In these, groups of men stand about and a row of women squat close to the wall. Mukadams move from group to group, and steady line of labourers passes along single file to work. If the mill gates and the coolie bazar do not give all the workers that are needed, there are many ways of letting the news of vacancies spread. In some cities workers are systematically beguiled from one mill to another. In a much larger number of cases a hint to a villager, when he is leaving for home, will be enough to induce him to bring back others with him on his return. Though the need for workers may be urgent, the overseer will not publish the fact, but will let it get round indirectly that a few more employe's might be taken on.

The custom of dasturi or unacknowledged commission, to which reference has been made, now comes into full operation. It is no new thing to the workers, and they are ready to fall in with it. Have they not paid their pice to policemen for permission to drive their bullocks through a gate or across a bridge, and given an anna, besides the fare, for their railway ticket, only to find perhaps that the receiver has pocketed not only the anna but also the difference between the cost of the journey of a hundred miles which they contemplated and the price of the ticket to station a dozen miles from their starting-place at which they find themselves ejected?

When the applicants come, the sirdar is not sure that he has anything for them, or that they will be able to do the work if he has. He will consider it. Of course, they will need to pay him for it. Coins pass. They are not enough. More follow. It is the usual custom for workers to pay a certain sum to the overseer in whose department they are hired to work for their employment there; but the system of exaction does not cease with this. It is in any case a continuous one, lasting as long as the labourer is in employment. The payment of the initial sum agreed on for leave to work is followed by the demand for a regular sum each pay-day. A bargain is struck, and the employee commences work on these terms. In one case it was estimated that a sirdar's wage was from fifty to a sixty rupees a month, while his perquisites, if one may call by that name the amazing toll of bakshish he gathered in, amounted to two hundred or three hundred rupees a month.

Usually the management feels that it must leave this alone; it is exceedingly difficult to alter, and, as the work people are entirely dependent on the sirdars and babus for information about the employers, interference, in most cases, would result in the sudden vanishing of all the employees. It is not overseers alone who levy dasturi. Pay-clerks, too, are known to reap harvests of this kind. One in a sack-sewing department was accused anonymously of taking such payments from the workers. A European in that department was deputed to pay wages, but the complaints still continued. The clerk was promoted into the weaving department, where he had a higher salary. Wages in the sack-sewing department were paid once a week, on Sunday morning. After this weekly payment had been made, there was a stream of workers from the shed to the house of the babu to give him the accustomed dasturi, although he had been removed from that department altogether.

Another method of oppression on the part of overseers is that of selling the better-paid posts, such as sub-sirdarships, not necessarily to the men best fitted to do the work, but to those from whom the highest bribes can be exacted. Here again the manager knows what is going on, but he is still further hampered if he attempts to interfere by the fact that he can prove nothing. Usually it is only when the sub-sirdar is dismissed (probably by the sirdar from whom he bought the appointment) that he complains of having had to pay to get the post. If the management calls the sirdar in question about it, he asks: "Why does the sub-sirdar complain now? For nine months (or for nine years) he has worked in the mill, yet he only speaks when he is dismissed." Thus the sirdar has the other in his power.

The workers who come to the mills from the country are usually absolutely poor. Sometimes, instead of letting them go to moneylenders, the overseers advance money to them on their wages, or even lend them small amounts. They may charge a lower nominal interest than the bania would, but, owing to the illiteracy of the worker, he is entirely in their power. It is quite impossible for the new-comer to calculate how long it will take him to work off a debt of this kind, complicated by the interest that will have to be allowed on it, and he is often cheated of a considerable part of his pay. His only redress is to move off to another ill, but ignorant as he is of the ways of towns, and easily intimdated by threats, and with his constitutional reverence for the mukadam as mukadam, he is very unlikely to have the courage to leave one mill and go to another when there is a debt left behind him in the first.

While women workers share with men the burden imposed by the payments to the overseers, they are specially liable to be oppressed by them. Opportunities for the display of favouritism are plentiful. Even the unenlightened visitor may notice examples of it. In one mill a brilliant yellow sari, very fresh and clean, attracted attention to woman at work on a machine on which it was usual to employ men. It turned out that she was a relation of the sirdar, and therefore was given a man's place and received a man's pay. She had two men assisting her on less well-paid parts of the work.

Widows are apt to be more oppressed than others, as they have no one to stand up for them. The fact that, owing to the inauspiciousness of their presence, other workers often dislike to work along with them, makes them fear the risk of unemployment so much that they will not readily complain of ill-usage. At times the attentions of the sirdar prove as heavy a burden as his ill-will. In countless ways he may take advantage of the ignorance and of the economic weakness of the woman worker.

A similar abuse of power is found in mills with regard to half-time workers. Boys are bribed by a few pice to appear and receive wages for work they have not done. The wages, less the price, are promptly handed over to the sirdar, who has rushed, say, twelve boys through the work allotted to sixteen.This can only be done when labour is plentiful. When it is difficult to get half-timers, he cannot afford to risk being short-handed.

It is not easy to prove that physical violence is used by the overseers, but it seems probable that there is a certain amount of it. The eagerness of managers to show off elaborate processes, to see the working of which machinery must be stopped or opened, and the desire often shown to explain carefully worked out shift systems, give the onlooker the opportunity of watching the hust-ling, hectoring treatment of the workers, both men and women, by the overseers. All this is taken very quietly for the most part, but a sudden turn in a workshop will sometimes bring the intruders on a quarrel where the jobber's voice is answered by voices quite as loud and irate as his own.

In cotton mills it is usual to have women overseers in the departments in which women work. Their power, the principle on which they are appointed, and their wages, differ very greatly in different localities. In certain mills in Bombay it is difficult to get women to accept the position of naikin, because it is not counted respectable .It is difficult to find out how far the reasons alleged for this attitude are reliable. It is said that naikins are usuallly women of low character, and that in some cases they retain their power and strengthen their position with officials by leading girls astray. This accusation is some-times flatly denied, sometimes acknowledged as having been true sometime ago, but not now. Others who entirely deny any knowledge of this allow that the bad name is to some extent deserved, and suggest that as the naikin has more money, wears better clothes, and much jewellery, she naturally attracts attention. Even where no actual charge is made against the character of the naikins, it is admitted that good workers are unwilling to accept the position though the pay is undoubtedly much better than that of the ordinary workers. Sometimes the choice of naikins is made from among the steady, old women who have been twenty or thirty years in the same mill. Sometimes good workers are selected. The wages vary from nineteen rupees a month in a mill in a small town to ninety in a great city mill. This latter sum seems to be quite unusual, however, and the naikin evidently realized it, as she did not go home as often as the other workers did. She could not be spared easily, and she knew that others would gladly step into her shoes.

In a mill in Ahmedabad, in a department where Muslim women would warp, a striking-looking mucadam is held sway. Some years before she had been employed in an iron works, earning about ten rupees a month. She came to this cotton mill to work as a coolie, and at a time when there was labour trouble said to the manager: "Make me a mucadamin, and I will bring you forty women." She was installed, and continued to bring any workers. She was a fine-looking woman, tall and graceful. Her former employer, the ironmaster, whom she had recognized as he went through the room, and the manager of the mill were both interested in her force and power of organization, and in her leap from a wage of ten rupees to one of fifty. In strong contrast to her quick grip of the situation were the ignorance and lethargy of a woman who, when asked during a strike why she was not working, replied: "The Raj has said we must not work."

The power of the naikin is small compared to that of the jobber, but she does not seem to be free from the spirit of oppression, and it is affirmed that when her anger is roused against men who are too strong for her she has been known to hire outsiders to maul her enemies.

In ginning factories the contractor still plays his part, though it is usually possible for him to secure his employees in the near neighbourhood. It is customary to give him a lump sum for the ginning of a given quantity of cotton. Out of that he has to pay his workers. What is over he retains. It is taken for granted that he will avoid breaking the Factory Act in such a way as to be found out, and everything is left in his hands and in those of the overseers.

Because of the urgency of getting cotton ginned rapidly certain concessions were made in the Act of 1911. The prohibition of women's work at night, the limitation of it to eleven hours in one day, the demand that the hours during which each woman was employed should be specified were set aside as far as ginning factories were concerned, and the only proviso substituted was that the number of women employed must be large enough to allow that none should work for more than eleven hours in any one day. It was easy for an inspector to know whether the names on the register would work out so as to give an average of eleven hours of work a day to each, but it was quite impossible for an inspector to know whether all the women actually did work. Relations of the overseers might have had their names on the register, might have drawn pay, and might never have been near the factory.

An instance of the way in which the contractor method works may be noted from a press in a country town, though the actual work done was on wool, not cotton. In a long shed, unlighted and unventilated, except by the entrance door, wool was lying on the ground in heaps, unbeaten and beaten. The former looked heavy and was in handfuls as it had been clipped, the hairs lying parallel to each other. The beaten was light, took up much more room, and looked cleaner. Throughout the shed, right back into its furthest recesses, there were groups of lads, girls, young women, and children. There was no machinery in the shed, so even the little ones were at work picking out and separating the colours. They worked all work picking out and separating the colours. They worked all day long, and could earn from four to six annas a day. The older workers were breaking up the matted bundles of wool by steadily beating the heaps with narrow bands of iron, which in action looked like slender swords. The scene, as the light fell on the workers near the door, was picturesque, but the conditions, with hair and dust filling the air, especially at a distance from the entrance, were bad.

If ventilation had involved strong currents of air, the workers would have been the first to dislike it, as their speed would have been retarded. The question arises whether such work, when it has to be done in bulk, should not be done by machinery. But the reason for introducing the discussion of these conditions here is the fact that these workers were not employed by the proprietor nor by the manager of the factory, and were not in any way under their control, but were sent in by merchants who had bought the wool and whose contractors had employed the workers to prepare it for pressing.

The power of the overseer is deeply rooted, but the changes which must eventually shake it are already in operation. Here and there in mills under advanced management works committees are in operation, and though these are as yet very ineffectual, the mere fact that the manager meets representative men and women along with foremen and forewomen, and invites the discussion of grievances and general mill conditions, is a clear sign that the times are changing rapidly.

In the Inspector's report on the working of the Factories Act, in the Bombay, Presidency, for 1921, the customary table of wages is omitted, because "it has been found to be incomplete and misleading." This official statement is a suggestive introduction to any study of payments in factories, not only in Bombay, but throughout the cotton and jute industries of the country.

The estimate that ninety per cent. of Indian women work for wages, temporarily or permanently, is difficult to credit, but the fact that it can be seriously asserted emphasizes the importance of the problem. It is acknowledged that wages in the mills are much larger in amount than those that can be earned for unskilled work in to other occupations, and it is often taken for granted that the economic position of the workers is raised to a proportionate extent. The latter supposition is open to dispute. The demands of the city dweller are more urgent than those of the villager, and the strain of life is very much greater in the former case, especially on the women. But the mere comparison with country wages is not a satisfying test in land of which it is admitted that millions of its population are too poor to be able to secure even the bare necessaries for maintaining a standard of efficiency.

If another test is taken, a different light is thrown on the subject. It is reasonable to suppose that orphanages will be run economically. After many inquiries, it appeared that it had been found impossible to cover the monthly expenditure on food and fire for cooking alone, for little boys for less than four rupees for each child. A standard based on this test and demanding no greater expenditure for adults than for children would require twenty–seven rupees a month for a family of six for food and fire alone. When it is recalled that nothing has been allowed for clothes, for religious offerings, for rent, for medicine, for the journey home, some idea of what an adequate efficiency wage would be can be formed. When the sum thus found is compared with actual wages, it explains the emphasis that prominent leaders of Indian social reform place on the need of women's wages for the support of their families.

Any proposal in favour of higher wages is met by arguments that seem at first sight to have much to support them, but which fail to take account of all the circumstances. The chief amongst these are the lowness of the general standard of living; the small amount of work that can be done by an Indian employee as compared with the amount that can be done by a European owing to the difference of physique; and the fact that in almost all factories there is great deal of liberty granted both to men and to women to take off time throughout the day besides the hour reserved for food and rest. The inadequacy of the standard of living creates serious difficulties in all social problems, difficulties that are increased by the fact that a low standard has not only been taken for granted, but has been obligatory on certain sections of the labouring people. A result of this higher wages are often spent on drink and gambling, instead of on things urgently required. Many efforts to meet the need for education in this direction are already being made, and there is opportuinty for those employers who put forward such objections to show their sincerity by spending all that might reasonably be spent in higher wages, on preparatory education, or on the provision of club-rooms, rest-houses, and other alternatives to the tadi shop.

Another claim that wages are adequate is based on the fact thai quite often a rise of wages results in fewer days' work on the part of those employed, and that when there are several workers in a household the tendency is for each to do less work rather than for the family to raise its standard of living. The need of widening horizons is not the only answer to this claim. When a subsistence wage can only be earned by working sixty-six hours a week, men and women will work for that length of time until health breaks down, but if they can earn the same wage for forty-eight hours' work, it is most probable that they will no longer work for sixty-six hours, but will fall into the habit of working for some number of hours between the two periods, which will relieve the tension of the first and will at the same time enable them to earn a little more than the former bare subsistence rate. If for the original sixty-six hours they were working beyond their vital energy for less than subsistence the reaction will be all the greater, and the still smaller wage for less labour may rise nearer to the level of subsistence because of the smaller amount of energy put forth.

The argument with regard to the amount of work an Indian can do, as compared with a European, cannot of itself justify present wages. It ignores the human needs of the individual worker. It is true that there is much liberty in coming and going in mills generally, but this, to a great extent, is included in the comparison of the amount of work done by an eastern and by a western, so that it scarcely counts as an added argument, especially as there seems to be quite a possibility that with better nourishment and shorter hours the workers will be able to do more continuous work. At present there is not sufficient evidence on either side, and both points of view are maintained by individuals amongst those who have experimented. So many things have to be taken into account that it is probably impossible to know how far increases in wages have kept pace with the increased cost of living.

It is at least obvious that the scornful way in which demands for higher wages are treated, and the obstinate resistance to them till no choice is left, require justification that has not hitherto been forthcoming.

There has, however been a very definite rise during the last ten years. If figures are selected for different departments and localities, it is found that the increase since 1914 varies from seventy per cent. to a hundred and thirty on wages paid to men than in larger industrial areas. Thus in Sholapur wages paid to women have increased the wages paid to women at the earlier date were very low,the increase on their wages is greater in comparison to the increase by eighty-seven per cent., while those paid to men have increased by eighty-two per cent.; and in the other centres scattered throughout the Bombay Presidency the percentage of increase is a hundred and forty for women and a hundred and twelve for men.

Rates of pay for similar work vary greatly. In Bengal it is possible to find mills situated near each other and under the same management in which the wages for the same work differ. Some accident of situation or of conditions makes the one appeal more to workers than the other, and wages remain at a lower level in the more popular mill.

A very rough generalization for the years 1920-I would group the wages paid to thelarger number of women in jute mills in Bengal between nine rupees and thirty rupees a month; those in factories in Bombay between thirteen rupees and thirty-four rupees a month; and those in Ahmedabad between twelve rupees and thirty rupees.

Not only in mills, but in many other occupations, it is customary to keep back a certain proportion of wages as a security that workers will not suddenly vanish. The fact that there is seldom an adequate supply of labour for modern industry, and the further fact that there are many reasons which tempt those employed in it to leave it, especially at first before they have got accustomed to its conditions, have made this habit of deferred payment almost universal in mills in larger industrial centres. In Bombay, where it is most stringent, it usually entails the postponement of payments till the middle of the month subsequent to the one for which payment is made, and the retaining of a fortnight's wages in hand. Thus, a new worker may be employed for six weeks before he receives any payment whatever, and he then receives wages for four weeks only. Until recently it was common for employes to work for two months before any payment was made. In the smaller centres of the cotton industry the amount of money kept in hand varies and may be the equivalent of ten or twelve days' wages. In the jute mills the same system is in operation, but the delay in payment is less lengthy and the sum kept back is smaller. Wages are paid once a week, and only one week's wage is retained. The disadvantage of this system, especially as it is worked in Bombay, does not consist alone in the danger that new-comers may become hopelessly in debt before they receive payment. The further danger exists that they may unwittingly forfeit the money held back. It is usually maintained that workers who give due notice that they mean to leave the mill get the money due to them ere they go, or are allowed to count it to their credit on their return; but as the causes that draw them away are often connected with illness, either their own or that of relative, it may be impossible for them to know a fornight before they go. Even when they do plan ahead to return home for a wedding or for seed-time or harvest, only a few may realize the wisdom of giving notice two weeks before hand, and in some cases the mere fact of doing so would make it more difficult to get away, especially for men in busy seasons, as leave may then be refused.

Some managers arrange that steady workers receive the money due to them if they fall ill. There is little doubt, however, no that considerable sums of money duly earned fall forfeit, and that the long-deferred payments give opportunities for further exactions on the part of overseers and pay clerks.

In Ahmedabad, owing probably in part to Trade Union influence, men and women who are in the same department receive equal time wages, and those who are on piece-work are paid at the same rate, and in certain cases are said to earn rather more. In jute mills in Bengal also it is usual to find that men and women working on the same machines receive equal wages on time work and an equal rate on piece work. But there seem to be wide differences both with regard to the actual amount of money paid and with regard to the equality or otherwise in this matter of women with men. As it is in these two districts that women are employed in the largest number of different processes, it is in them that comparison is most possible. Occasionally women working on the same machine as men receive a rupee or less per month on the plea that they are allowed more freedom to go and come than the men, who look after their work in their absence. In the reeling department of one mill, where there was a piece rate of payment for each hundred reels, further inducement to steady work was afforded by the fact that if workers earned more than a certain sum the rate of payment was raised by thirteen annas.

The nominal wage paid is by no means an exact guide in estimating the income of the workers. Bonuses are given under various headings, and to very different amounts in different localities. Fines are levied in varying degrees, and part-payment in kind is frequent.

The larger bonuses and scarcity allowances are granted in some cases to avoid the necessity for raising wages. It is claimed by the employers that a bonus is an entirely temporary addition which may be cancelled at any time should circumstances change, and that the withdrawal of it must not be considered as a lowering of wage. This distinction is not likely to prevent protest and serious curtailment would take place without an even more obvious fall in prices, but, owing to thewidely spread desire for bakshish, bonuses are probably not so unpopular with the Indian worker as they are in Britain. The same fare given separately as payment and bakshish is much more likely to satisfy the coolie or the rickshaw runner than if it is given in one sum.

The simplest bonus is a monthly one granted in many mills for regular attendance. For this one rupee a month is a common amount, though the sum may be as low as eight annas. In certain mills this bonus is granted although two working days are missed. In others , two days absence are permitted to women, but not to men. Another modification is to withhold half for one day's absence, and all for two days. Monthly scarcity allowances based on wages and amounting in certain cases to fifty per cent of the wage drawn are found in various mills.

In Bombay, in 1921, the payment of an annual bonus approximating to the equivalent of one month's wages was sanctioned by the Mill-owners' Association. In Ahmedabad, where the mills were making very high profits, a demand was made that the annual bonus should amount to the equivalent of two months' wages. The employers refused and the matter was referred to arbitration. Pandit Madan Mohan Malaviya, after consultation with the President of the Mill-owners' Association and with Mahatma Gandhi, together with other representatives of the Employers, and with representatives of Labour, gave the award on October 28, 1921. In it he recommended a compromise which the greater number of employers and employés accepted. By it maximum bonus of seventy-five rupees was to be granted to all whose monthly wage amounted to less than sixty rupees were to receive the equivalent of one month's wage and fifteen rupees.

These bonuses are elaborated with reference to the number of month's attendance put in. The fact that eight or nine months is reckoned as entitling a worker to the full bonus is an added proof, were such necessary, of the extent to which annual absences are taken for granted.

An interesting extra bonus is given in some mills at the Diwali festival, which corresponds to the New Year. It is given not to individuals, but to the workers collectively, and consists of a few pice, spent very possibly on the bright paper chains, flowers and flags that enliven some of the homelier mills then and for some time after the celebration. The workers bring the decorations and arrange them themselves, and the animation that at once appears up and down a workshed when any reference to them is made reminds the visitor of the quick response and consciousness of mutual understanding in spite of barriers experienced in other connections.

The extent to which fines are levied varies greatly. In one mill warning had been given that six rupees would be deducted from the wage of anyone who was found using undamped bobbins. The threat had caused some improvement, and the penalty had not been levied. This fine comes under the heading of those exacted for intentional spoiling of goods, for which it is customary to exact two or three rupees. Frequently these fines are levied on men in the weaving sheds for weaving too openly with an insufficient number of weft threads to the inch of warp. Sometimes they are imposed for allowing waste to mix with the rovings in the spinning shed. Workers convicted of minor thefts are fined. Those guilty of serious thefts are dismissed. The fines that are most frequently exacted in women's departments are small ones of an anna or so for inattention and slackness. In some well-organized mills the power of exacting fines is retained but is seldom used.

Perplexing questions connected with wages in India centre round the sale of cheap grain and cheap cloth by mills to their workers, and the provision of housing accomodation at low rents, and allowance must be made for the different circumstances in east and west. Theoretically there is no pressure used to induce workers to purchase grain or cloth, but in some cases the wages are such that it would be impossible for the workers to pay bazar prices in times of scarcity. In the city centres, where wages are higher on the whole, the workers are more independent, and may choose for themselves. It is in country districts that the grain sold by the mill firms is the greatest boon to the workers, but it is also there that, owing to the lack of competition for workers, it is most desirable that nothing should be done to retard the growth of independence.

In order to understand the situation it is necessary to remember that the workers must buy all their food stuffs in small quantities. The jar in the corner of the hut or the hole dug into its flooring, would not store much even if the money to buy supplies for the future were forthcoming. Prices in the bazars vary greatly, and in times of scarcity run up to prohibitive figures. The mill-owner can arrange to have storage room, and has the knowledge of when to buy. He fixes a retail price which he considers reasonable, and may very probably abide by that price even when it entails an actual money loss, which, however, must in many mills be considered as covered by the lower rate of wages given. In different localities different conditions are made. In one mill the grain is sold on one day in the month, and only workers who have been not more than four days absent in the month are allowed to buy. This rule is absolute, and no allowance is made for sickness. In another mill, workers, from the time they have been three days in the mill, can buy grain up to half the amount of wages due to them. In the latter mill in February 1921, the mill price for rice was exactly half the bazar price. In the former mill, in which regular attendance is compulsory in order to have a right to buy grain, rice, pulse, and millet were sold in the mill, and in January 1921, when the market price for three seers of rice or of millet was two rupees, the mill supplied nine seers of either for the same sum. In the case of pulse the bazar price was one rupee for two and that quarter seers and the mill price was one rupee for four seers.

While the mill leaves the worker free to go to the bazar if the price there falls below mill price, and to return at his will, it is not always easy for the grain sellers to see it in the same light, and, especially in cases where no grain is sold to those who have been absent through illness, serious disabilities may ensue. The grain seller, who is also moneylender, is not unlikely to demand a higher price or a bakshish ere he will deal with the worker who has been accustomed to go elsewhere when he could.

In times of scarcity, like that experienced in India 1921, mills that supplied cheap grain were parts extraordinarily popular. In Sholapur applicants for work from the surrounding district crowded to the mill gates declaring that they did not care how low the wages were if they only got leave to work and have a right to cheap grain.

Cloth shops do not seem to have met with a similar response. In some of the mills that make dhotis, men get chits to buy these at cash price, and are allowed to choose the ones they prefer in the storeroom; but frequently attempts to open mill cloth stores fail because there is little demand.

In many localities there is urgent need for the supply of food and other things of better quality than those supplied by the local bazar and at more reasonable and more stable prices, but the line of advance would seem to lie in the direction of increased co-operative facilities, and in the encouragement of reliable independent stores, rather than in the introduction of new mill stores.

The arrangements for wages in ginning factories are simple. The contractor who engages the workers is paid fourteen or fifteen annas per bale of cotton ginned, and the smaller the wages and the longer the hours of work, the larger the amount that is left for himself. Except in the case of those who do coolie work as seed-carriers, who may get fourteen rupees a month, the actual amount paid to women varies from seven to ten and a half rupees a month, but seven rupees seems to be the usual sum. Wages are paid by the week or by the day. In some factories one day's wage is kept in hand; in others the week's wage is paid in full. The fact that workers are sometimes paid on Sunday suggests the unwillingness of employers to encroach on the time of a working day and the willingness of workers to break in on their holiday by coming for wages.

The study of the actual conditions within mills opens up an interesting and, on the whole, a hopeful part of the subject. The interest and the hopefulness circle round the facts that in certain areas progress has been made, that inquiries have been set on foot to gain the scientific knowledge which will enable definite standards to be set, and that a great advance is possible, can eventually be insisted on, and can be proved to be an advantage not only to workers, but also to employers from the point of view of efficiency. There are calls for reform in other directions, such as better housing and the raising of standards of living with regard to which the temptation is to fall back with more or less assurance, according to the temperament of the thinker, on education, which may bear an almost wholly nebulous content; but with regard to the needs connected with actual mill premises and working conditions, there are no insuperable difficulties. It is true that no satisfactory reforms will come even here without much definite education, but it is easier to see what kind of education is necessary and to imagine the proofs and persuasions that can be brought to bear on those whose co-operation must be secured.

One of the hopeful signs is that already selected mills stand far above the average in general suitability of buildings, in regulation of temperature, in arrangement of machinery and of lighting. A hurried glance will reveal some of the differences between mill and mill. No one would expect to find conditions as healthy in mills that look like "boxes built round a crowded heap of machinery" as in mills firmly erected and spread over a wide area. But the factors that go to make good conditions are more subtle than any that can be grasped cursorily, and much of the knowledge needed to secure them is not yet tabulated or ascertainable. An interesting proof of this is found in the fact that in one compound a second mill, for which all the experience gained in the first mill was available, showed a poorer health record than the first. The manager, who was specially interested in conditions, was puzzled and disappointed. Local circumstances may have been responsible for the poorer record to some extent, but the occurrence strengthens the belief that further study is urgently needed in order to find out what details in actual construction conduce to health.

There is a broad division between jute mills and cotton mills with regard to structure. The former are spread over large areas in one-storey sheds lit from the roof. The latter vary greatly. In roomy, country areas they may have two storeys only in a small portion of the mill, or may even be one-storey throughout, but, generally speaking, they are built in blocks of several storeys, and light enters by windows in the walls. In both forms of building it is of the utmost importance that a sufficient amount of light should be secured with as little access of the direct rays of the sun to the workers as possible. In order to secure this in the block structure, advice that at first sounds surprising to a westerner. is given: "Mills should be built facing north and south!" During the hottest part of the year the sun's rays are so nearly perpendicular at midday that they do not enter southern windows to anything like the same extent as that to which they enter eastern and western windows at night and morning. If windows face north and south, the sun's rays fall chiefly on the blank end wall to the east, then on the roof, and then on the unbroken western wall. Even allowing for this, the hot air entering from the south is so oppressive that as few windows as possible should be there unless they are provided with cuscus screens, for which a plentiful supply of water is available during the hot season. The disadvantages of having lighting only from the north in block buildings is that the heavy machinery intercepts the passage of air and of light to remote corners, and that any general ventilation of the sheds is rendered almost impossible, unless fans are supplied.

In one-storey buildings, on the other hand, the lighting is frequently arranged on a system which makes the roof like a series of uncurved saw teeth. The sloping line of each tooth rises from south to north, and is roofed, while the short, perpendicular drop is of glass. Thus all the light that is admitted comes from the north. This form of lighting has the great advantage that it throws the light well into the corners of the sheds, though even with it specially large and closely placed machinery may create isolated darkened areas. Another method is to build a flat roof broken at intervals by square or oblong erections with glass sides and ends. This plan does not exclude the sun's rays, but if the roof is high, it secures that they will seldom fall directly on the workers. The effect of the intense heat of the hot season can be further modified by whitewashing walls, roof, and any windows exposed to the sun's rays. But such outside appliances will be of little use unless the actual building is satisfactory. Sometimes walls, and more frequently roofs, are of corrugated iron. The temptations to use metal are not only its durability and the ease with which it can be obtained and placed in position. The tremendous rains of the monsoon make an impervious roof down which water rapidly runs very attractive, and the monkeys, that in many districts make the roofs their playgrounds, find it more difficult to play pitch and toss with metal sheets than with tiles! But any gain that is won in these directions seems worse than loss to anyone with imagination who has ever attempted steady work even in Britain on a hot summer day under an iron roof. Even if corrugated iron is not used, the roofing may still be very unsuitable. A thin foundation roof covered with a layer of tiles intercepts but little of the sun's heat. In strongly built mills, where the roofs are flat, reinforced concrete is found to provide a satisfactory roof, especially if it is covered by water during the hottest months. In slighter buildings, whether with flat or with sloping roofs, great advantage is found if a double roof is made with a space of some inches left between the two section.

Suggestions for protection from the sun's heat lead on to the whole question of ventilation in mills. In spite of the difficulties that are ahead of those who are intent on better conditions in this direction, there is exhilaration in the knowledge of the remarkable success that has been achieved already, and in the thought of those who are steadily experimenting to create standards that can be attained. It has long been realized that a moderate and fairly dry temperature and a regular supply of fresh air are conducive to comfort in work and to the health of the worker. As long as this was the general and somewhat vague conviction, it was natural to argue that if workers did not complain, there was little need to agitate. This arguments is heard *ad nauseam* in India to-day. It takes different forms. The fact that the homes are far more close than the mills, the obvious dislike of the workers to open windows, and their fear lest currents of air will break cotton threads are all quoted as proof that there is no need for change. These arguments are all the more difficult to refute because of the uncertainty that exists with regard to the effect heat may have on those whose ancestors have been acclimatized to it. It is clear that Indians can bear a temperature that would incapacitate Europeans, but it is also clear that they suffer from intense heat. The Chinese character for summer represents a man with his hands hanging at his side because the farmers do not work in the hottest weeks, and a similar symbol might well be used for the heat of April, May, or June in India. Mills have had to be shut down on this account, and if such an extreme measure has had to be resorted to at times much suffering must have been endured before the necessity for closing was admitted.

But science has proved two further facts with regard to ventilation. The one is that there is a definite and ascertainable ratio between the condition of the air and the efficiency of the worker who breathes it, and the other is that fresh air is not adequate unless it be in motion and induces changes in the temperature of the body. This latter discovery, associated with the name of Professor Hill Leonard, has had a revolutionary effect, and systems of ventilation previously approved in schools and other larger buildings in the west, by which fresh air was admitted to rooms and stale air withdrawn with the least possible movement and change of temperature, are now condemned. While their failure would naturally be assumed by those who are convinced of the need of motion in the air, it has also been proved over and over again by the lack of attention and the dulled intelligence of classes taught in the steadier atmosphere.

Proof of the difference of efficiency in work done in well and ill-ventilated mills in India has already been secured on a small scale. Experiments that have been made show a fall in efficiency during the hot weather in as ill-ventilated weaving shed as reaching twenty per cent., while that in a well-ventilated shed was less than seven per cent. The general assumption seems to be clearly proved, but it is still difficult to secure datailed statistics owing to the numbers involved, and to the fact that it is not easy to find sheds that are sufficiently similar in other respects to make comparison useful.

In Britain, when the value of air in motion is considered, it is natural to think at once of open windows or of ventilators. The perplexities surrounding the question in India cannot be grasped by a westerner till it is realized that for a great part of the year not the slightest breath of wind can be felt during the day. Through blazing sunshine and through the steaming intervals in monsoon rains, the air hangs motionless except for the action on it within the mills of the whirling machinery which adds greatly to its heat and is too localized to increase its general circulation to any great extent. There is no cure for this except by the generous use of punkahs or electric fans. In private houses it is found that work that is impossible in still air can be done under a fan even when no fresh air is introduced. The result of the air in motion is enough to set free energies otherwise paralysed. In the instances in which fans have been installed in factories with few exceptions the numbers are quite inadequate, and the result negligible. In one case where two fans were provided in a long, airless shed, the effect was unnoticeable twelve feet away. The common attitude towards the proposal to introduce electric fans may be gathered from the remark of a manager who had been making special efforts to improve ventilation in overheated departments in his mill. His answer to a tentative suggestion was: "We would be dismissed if we asked for electric fans!" There are, however, compromises that can be made, and here and there these are found in operation. Metal plates attached to overhead shafting and moving with the revolution of the shift cost little. Broad canvas sheets so hung that they swing free, may be placed on overhead bars with little addition to the mechanical structure. Circular metal fans also worked from the central engine can be erected in placed where the atmosphere is specially stagnant. Such experiments are already in operation, but owing to the fact that there is little public opinion on the subject, the knowledge of them does not spread rapidly. Some individual weavers secure moving currents of air for themselves by improvising small fans attached to the front of their looms. These are hopeful sign, but their occurrence is rare. In a very large number of mills there are no appliances for securing the introduction of fresh air in still weather, nor for obtaining movement in stagnant air. In others, a few inadequate fans are seen, not in use, reserved for hot weather (although at the moment the atmosphere may be stifling), and sometimes so loaded with fluff and debris that it is difficult to imagine them in operation at all.

One great obstacle in the way of advance in this direction, besides the apathy and ignorance of the workers, is the difficulty of so arranging air movement that it will not be the cause of breakage of threads. This leads on to the question of humidity, for it is to avert the same damage to material that a damp atmosphere is required in cotton mills. Custom can make it more possible to work in hot damp air, and if the air is in motion a higher wet bulb temperature becomes tolerable, but when all allowances are made, the humidity in many cotton mills, especially in ones where the coarser yarns are spun and much size is used, must be responsible for a steady lowering of the physique of workers. The urgency of the need for ascertained standards and for the introduction of the best methods is very great. This urgency is felt by leading firms of employers, and many experiments are being made. The appointment of Mr. Terence Maloney as adviser on humidification to the Government of India, and his reports will, it is hoped, secure the fixing of reasonable standard. At present during the hottest months the average hot bulb temperature in weaving sheds is about eighty-five degrees Fahrenheit. Though no women work in cotton-weaving sheds, the health of their fathers and husbands has a direct effect on their lives, and they themselves in many cases work in humidified sheds, though the temperature may not reach quite so high a figure. The regulation of temperature is not the only point to be considered in humidification. The practice of introducing steam is widely criticized, and is giving place to other methods by which cool, damp air is admitted. Special precautions against the use of impure water are necessary. Extreme humidity prevents evaporation, and this creates a condition in which the cooling processes of the human body operate very slowly. The heat generated by labour and by the warmth of the atmosphere is carried off so gradually that it is impossible for the body to effect the necessary return to normal temperature. These conditions are aggravated when rooms are overcrowded with machinery, and when there is too little space allowed for the individual employees. The danger of infection also is greatly increased.

A further question with regard to ventilation arises in connection with impurities in the air. The cases in which any attempt is made to free the atmosphere from cotton and jute fluff are so few that they scarcely influence the general question at all as yet. The argument that jute dust need not be considered injurious because it falls so rapidly is to a great extent nullified by the fact that it falls on the faces of the workers and on the heads and bodies of the childern who lie on the floors or in hammock cradles. The immediate and spontaneous lift of the hand to throat and chest, if a question is asked about illnesses to which jute workers are liable, is suggestive. The injurious effect of dust of any kind is only being gradually realized, and there is the further excuse for the employer in India that within or without the mill no human being escapes the dust evil except in monsoon weather. The cloud that accompanies a moving herd of cattle in any dry district shows the height to which the shifting surfacc of powdery earth rises. But perhaps nothing gives such a realization of the extent to which the air is dust-laden as what is known as the winter line, seen from the hill stations on the southern slopes of the Himalayas. Before the rains come, there lies what appears to be a deep bank of cloud right along the horizon till the hills impinge on it at either end. The stranger may notice the straight upper edge of this bank, may begin to wonder at its regularity day after day, and may at last be moved to ask questions. The reply that the dim, far-off mass is created by the dust of the plains seems unbelievable even then, and is almost more unbelievable when, after the rains during which clear intervals have revealed rivers winding into the distance and spreading in vast sun-illumined stretches over the land seven thousand feel below, there or four days of unbroken sunshine renew the dim rampart of dust-laden air across the horizon.

It is scarcely to be wondered that the question is asked: "Why trouble about a little fluff?" Fluff-laden air, however has special dangers for health, and the advantage to be gained by the introduction of exhaust fans and ducts on the machines from which the greatest amount of fluff emanates can scarcely be over-estimated. Groups of workers, too, can be relieved from the worst processes in many instances by the introduction of automatic feeding and stripping apparatus. In some ginning factories a fan has been erected at the ends of sheds to draw away the dust through pipes that cover the gin mouths. Sensitiveness with regard to air conditions is increasing, and mills are found where those who work amongst waste or in less well-ventilated sheds are allowed special privileges in the way of liberty to come and go. In another cases sheds that had been counted suitable are being discarded in favour of better buildings.

It is easy to lay stress on what is needed. It is difficult, perhaps impossible, to give an adequate impression of the urgency of the need. Nothing but the experience of hours spent in the stifling atmosphere of the worse ventilated mills can make it possible to realize the exhaustion and lassitude that result. and, when on a day of motionless air, attention is drawn to open windows and "splendid ventilation," there is irony in the situation. Yet in these conditions men and women labour through long hours, and little children doze in their hammocks or gaze on their world from half-hidden corners.

Other internal conditions vary greatly. In some mills the flooring is broken, giving ragged edges and gaps. Generally speaking, the paving is good, though it is often damp and slippery. There is room for great advance in the protection of machinery, and it is often found that inspectors can secure progress in this respect by persuasion and suggestion even where they cannot legally insist on change.

In many mills there is much leisure, "chit-chatting," and coming and going. Only here and there a mill is found where definite efforts are made to create standards of continuous work.

In some places Muslims and Hindus are chiefly employed in different departments; in others they mix in work; but however willing they may be to work under one roof, their presence necessitates special arrangements for drinking-water. There are few mills in which such supplies are brought within the actual building. A row of taps is usually found in some convenient part of the compound, and once the distinction is made between the pipes used by Muslims and those used by Hindus, it is rigidly adhered to. Sometimes, outcaste demands involve further regulations. In other cases outcastes working in the mills may have to bring drinking water with them. The fact that supplies are now so generally conveyed by pipes, simplifies to some extent caste difficulties with regard to drinking from a common source. The water that issues from the pipe is considered uncontaminated, and all that is not used flows away.

Before setting off to work in the morning, cold rice or dhal left over from the previous night is eaten, but the earlier of the two principal meals of the day is taken within the mill compound unless the rooms occupied are very close, or unless there are restaurant hotels close at hand. In the majority of cases the midday meal is either carried by the labourer to the work-shed in the morning, or brought later by some messenger. By the second alternative the advantage of hot, freshly cooked food is gained, but it can only be employed when the wife or some other relative remains in the lodging to cook it and bring it or to send it by a child. When all the adults work in a mill, a cold meal hurriedly prepared in the early morning is all that can be obtained. The form of the pot or bowl in which the food is carried showing through the cloth in which it is tied, is a familiar sight on the streets and in the mills. Food that has to be prepared in the early morning makes a big demand on the woman worker, and her anxiety is not at an end when the meal has been prepared. It must be kept from contamination of every kind till it is actually eaten. The fear of having it touched or even shadowed is one cause of the difficulties that sometimes prevent mills from employing members of the depressed classed in the same room with caste women. Curious bundles, wrapped in cloths that have seen much use, are poised high on machinery or hung from a nail in the wall, and it is strange to think that if a covering of one were but touched, the contents would be flung away, no matter how hungry the owner might be. The food thus brought is usually eaten by a family group, or by a single worker, sitting in an odd space between machines, or in a neglected corner of the compound, indifferent to all the world and eating steadily through the meal. The disadvantages of such haphazard arrangements are very evident in dry weather, but during the period of the monsoon, rains, that in a few moments convert streets into rivers, descend at short intervals and may continue for weeks on end. It is not difficult to imagine the misery of conditions then. Various efforts are being made to meet the need of shelter and of hot food provided on the spot. In some mills rows of sheds are found, each one set aside for a particular national, caste, or outcaste group. In these, workers may find shelter from sun and from rain but the sheds are seldom large enough to give room for all the workers in a mill, and in some cases they are only sparingly used in dry weather.

A further step has been taken by some employers, who provide tea. Tea-drinking is a new custom amongst the workers of India, but it has taken a firm hold, and the tea-houses in mills are very popular. In some cases they seem to be open all day, and workers find their way to them as they will. In others, times are fixed. In one of the latter the two tea-rooms, one for Hindus and one for Muslims, were built in a quiet, enclosed yard. At the far end were kitchens, but in this case the two nationalities had chosen to use the same one, and the second was turned into a godown for straw. Though both groups used one fireplace, there were two cooks, a Muslim and a high-caste Hindu. Tea with sugar, but no milk, was poured into the buyers' tumblers of brass or white metal, and cost a halfpenny. A few employees spent another halfpenny on a piece of country bread or a biscuit. The tea-drinkers in this mill were chiefly drawn from the betterpaid workers amongst the men. Few women took tea, and those who did had to drink it in the compound, as the men would not allow them to enter the shelters

Other mills have gone still further and have arranged for canteens from which vegetables, dishes of rice and dhal, and loaves are served. Such an experiment demands a Brahman cook with a kitchen into which no one but himself, or another Brahman, is allowed to enter, and different serving windows for Muslims, caste-Hindus, and others. The food is carried to dining-sheds and eaten there. It is probable that the special arrangements for cooking and serving make it necessary to charge rather more than the price for which the workers could get similar food, for in some cases, at any rate, few take advantage of the new source of supply.

Efforts for effective sanitation have to surmount great difficulties in India, not only in mill areas, but throughout the country wherever large numbers of people are gathered together. Appliances and arrangements that are counted indispensable in western cities, cannot be repidly introduced where it is impossible to have such inspection as would secure thorough flushing and unbroken piping. The introduction of septic tanks in larger mills is of great advantage when these tanks and the flush system that is usually used to wash the contents of the latrines into them are kept in perfect order. It may be possible to find mill compounds in which septic tanks have been introduced in worse conditions, through negligence, than other compounds where the older method of removing night soil by sweeper and cart or train beyond the city boundaries, is still in operation. In the septic tank impurities are dissolved and disinfected. It has been found that the microbe of hook-worm, a very prevalent disease in Bengal, can withstand the action of the chemicals usually employed in septic tanks, and may be carried to lower reaches of the river into which the liquid contents of the tanks are discharged, and experiments are being carried on in the hope that means may be found to make the disinfecting process complete.

The amount of latrine accommodation supplied is probably sufficient for health when no cholera or enteric epidemic is raging, but in a large number of mills both the amount and the arrangement are unsatisfatory when standards of self-respect are considered. There are those both amongst Indians and amongst Europeans who resent these conditions not only from the health point of view, but also from the moral and social point of view. But no general lasting improvements will be secured till a very much stronger public opinion is created amongst those who control municipal activities, as well as amongst those employers who have not yet considered these matters seriously. In many places there is constant friction between mill-owners and Local Government officials about water supply and sanitation.

There are places where the housing of the mill population offers no serious difficulties. In a town like Nagpur, where open ground is available, many of the workers own their houses and pay a small sum of two and a half or three rupees a year in taxes. The houses may be built with considerable space between them on the outskirts of the town, or huddled closely together in more congested parts, but in either case no new problem is created.

The land occupied by a large population, including many mill workers, was acquired by the university lately, but all that was deemed necessary for the accommodation of the employees who would be turned off was to secure an area of ground as near the old site as possible on which they would be free to erect new huts. Some of the millowners make conditions more healthy and less exacting by improving water supply and assisting in the initiation of schools and dispensaries, but no burden of housing falls on them.

In other country towns, such as Beawar in Rajputana, the housing problem begins to be felt in a limited way. There, besides the workers from the city, people come in from villages too far away to make it convenient for them to go to and from every day, and for them very poor huts are erected in which they may sleep and take shelter during the working week. Though these huts may be very poor, they are usually built in open ground where fresh air is available, and as they are not intended to be homes, they may be judged less severely than similar erections within which workers live for months on end, though even for such half-time dwellings the practice of using corrugated iron for walls and roofs should be strongly opposed.

The problem begins to become serious in more congested cities, such as Sholapur, with its hundred thousand inhabitants, and its lack of any sanitary system. Many of the labourers are village folk, and if the mills are near their homes they prefer to come and go daily. Others come from Sind and from the Carnatic, and these and the workers that gather to the mills in times of scarcity and become settled inhabitants can find lodging in the crowded streets of the old city, but they can only do so by still further congesting areas already over-populated, and the realization of this and of the increase of disease such overcrowding involves has led certain mill-owners to build new houses near their mills, where the workers will have all the advantages of air and space, and to acquire land on which employees, who prefer to build their own huts, are allowed to settle.

But it is when the big industrial centres are studied that the magnitude of the problem appears. Ahmedabad, Cawnpore, Calcutta, Bombay have each their special conditions, and must be considered separately. They are general questions with regard to what the responsibility of employers in this connection should be and the extent to which even in transition periods it is wise to have the housing of workers in their hands, which will be discussed later. And there is always and everywhere the practical question of the cost of building relative to rents and returns. Besides these, there are many details of preferences and requirements peculiar to India which affect the main questions, and it may be well to notice a few of these before turning to local conditions in the four large centres already mentioned.

When to the natural desire to live near friends and relations, whether these work in the same mill or at the same type of employment or not, there is added all that caste distinctions involve, it is clear that a large body of Indian labour will be reluctant to enter houses supplied by employers. It is true that much can be done to meet this reluctance. Buildings may be grouped so that members of one caste or of one race may live together. If two storey buildings are provided, it is of the atmost importance that members of lower castes are never placed above those belonging to higher castes, lest water dripping through the floor or anything falling from the balcony should touch cooking utensils or food below. There are Indians who look on the desire to live in racial and caste groups as amongst the things that must be eradicated by education, and who have little sympathy with efforts to meet the wishes of the workers in this respect. But there is a danger of pressing forward too rapidly. To educate men and women to a sense of wide brotherhood is an ideal to be aimed at, but to succeed in making them indifferent to their human surroundings without the introduction of wider ideals may only result in lowering standards and in delaying the development of the sense of citizenship that should rightly supply the place of caste loyalties.

There is further a great dislike to the control that may be exercised over employees living in provided dwellings. It is obvious that the employer who builds sanitary and rain-proof houses for his workers will claim the right to supervise these. As conditions are at present if this is not done (and in some places it is very inadequately done) the drains and the roads soon become almost as bed as those in the unregulated bazars. This fact is often made an excuse for allowing workers to go on crowding into the insanitary alleys of cities. The resentment that is roused by sanitary inspections and restrictions in some localities may be partly due to the rough and ready ways in which these are carried out, and to the fact that free use of disinfectants may outrage caste feelings, but there is little question that very many workers are not only entirely ignorant of the simplest elements of hygiene, but dislike and fear the practice of them.

Mill dwelling-houses are at the same time too isolated and too public for the tastes of the workers. They do not merge into local bazars, into the crowded buildings of the city, nor into the open ground or jungle that may lie on the outskirts. They are intrusions, both in appearance and in the ideas underlying them, and as such are approached timidly. On the other hand, there is a prevailing sense of lack of privacy about them which makes family life difficult. The very narrow verandahs that are built in many areas push within four walls some of the activities of daily life that would naturally be carried on in a broad verandah screened from the public gaze by matting o tattered hangings. Where rent is charged and an attempt is made to limit the number of occupants in one room, tenants, especially those who, coming from country homes, have never paid house rent before, are apt to prefer to share a dearer room with many other, outside, and so to retain a greater freedom, however unsatisfactory and insanitary the accommodation may be.

The employer who is convinced of the value of suitable housing has to face the fact that he will be confronted by these difficulties, and he has still others to face. In many areas it is not possible to acquire land at a moderate cost. In others the land in the neighbourhood is all agricultural, and may not legally be used for building purposes. He has in most cases to be content with a very small, or even with no return for outlay, though he may eventually be well repaid in the efficiency and health of his workers. He has also to make up his mind to the fact that his houses will be occupied by many who are not in his employment, and that even if no houses are let except to those actually working in his mill, relations and dependants will crowd in to share the dwellings. In some districts, too, the compact rows of houses erected in or close to the mill compound may be used as an easy labour-poaching ground by the overseers of other mills. It is little wonder that employers who are not convinced of the great advantages from an economic point of view of healthy and vigorous workers are slow to experiment with expensive schemes.

The city of Bombay is built on an island, the channels which separate it from the northern and much larger island of Salsette, and those that separate the latter island from the mainland, have been bridged, and two great railway systems, the Bombay, Baroda, and Central India Railway, and the Great Indian Peninsular Railway, have their terminal stations in the city. The general layer of the mill areas has been suggested, but it may be well to recall it. The northern part of the island consists of a broad, oblong area of ground, but to the south-west two narrow promontories run out towards the ocean. The more northerly one Malabar Hill, rises to the height of a few hunderd feet, and hides on its ridge in the midst of foliage the Towers of Silence. Far out towards Malabar Point stands Government House. The more southerly peninsula of Colaba is much longer and narrower. Between these two lies a great and most beautiful stretch of water, named Back Bay. The long line of lights that outlines its shore at night is known as the "diamond necklace" of Bombay. The docks face eastward toward the mainland, which can be seen dimly in the distance. Between Back Bay and the docks most of the modern Western buildings and residences are situated, and right up the centre of the island runs a network of closely packed streets, lanes and bazars, into which it is always possible to dive from the Europeanized surroundings of buildings and squares. The area covered by these closely packed streets increases in breadth in the district to the east of Malabar Hill and stretches north through the central part of the island. It is in these lanes and bazars to the north of the city that most of the immigrant labourers must find room to live, and in them there are countless buildings, three to five storeys high, which are known as 'chawls.' Many of these are held by private owners; others are the property of the Bombay Improvement Trust; some are owned by employers.

Two or three mills are situated in Colaba to the south of the city. The experiments in housing in one of these give insight into some of the difficulties connected with the problem. Perhaps the great beauty of the situation makes the onlooker more sensitive to contrasts. From the ground on which the houses are built, and from the windows of workshops, the views over the open sea and down the dim mainland coast are wonderfully fine. The older houses built in chawl formation two or three stories high had their windows blocked with boxes, dovecotes, and matting. The sanitary arrangements, provided and in this case managed by the municipality, were not in good condition. There was underground drainage, but pools of water lay around, the smell was bad, and the alleyways were full of rubbish. This first experiment had proved so unsatisfactory that the employers were building new one-strey houses of which only a few were occupied. As yet these were orderly, but the manager seemed to have little hope that it would be possible to keep them so. He was considering the wisdom of offering prizes for clean houses, a plan which he had found to work well in the Punjab. The new houses had been let at a rent of five or six rupees a month, on the understanding that only one fire should be made in each room, but it was fully expected that the hospitable instincts of the workers, their dislike of isolation, and their desire to secure some annas towards the rent would make this rule a dead letter. So many of those who migrate into the cities to work have never had to pay house rent that it is often resented, and standards are so low in some directions, and in others so impossible to maintain in the new city surroundings, that it is scarcely to be wondered at that those who had been allowed to occupy sheds covered with matting, without payment, till the new houses were built, refused to leave the free shelters.

But any housing difficulties that strike the eye in the south of the island are as nothing to those that exist in the northern parts of the city. There, many of the mill-owners have no ground on which to build houses, and no chance of buying it except either at such a distance from the mills that special transit arrangements would require to be made, or at an exorbitant price. The result is that the mill population is housed in chawls rented to them by others than employers. The general houses shortage in Bombay is so great that in some cases clerks and business people have been grateful to rent rooms built for labourers by the Improvement Trust of the city, thus thrusting a greater number of workers into the wretched buildings alone available for them. It is very difficult to give any clear idea of what a group of really bad chawls in like. The alleyways that run between them are narrow. There is an open drain in the centre over which (theoretically) clothes and dishes must be washed. There is a water pipe at one end to supply perhaps forty rooms, which may mean sixty or more families. The sense of smell soon tells where the public latrines are. In the narrow spaces between the central drain and the walls there are heaps of rubbish, cabbage stems, banana skins, rice, old rage, and amongst them are kids, hens, chickens, children, dogs. As the eye glances upwards, it may see a wall variegated by rags, boxes, and matting. These indicate the stuffed-up windows of chawls that have inner tunnel-like passages, from which the occupants enter their houses. More often the wall is broken by the outline of narrow, very narrow, verandahs. When this is so, it is often only possible to see the verandah itself at intervals, as, for most of the way, it is completely covered by matting, boxes, boards and old clothes. From these verandahs, too, there hang saris and dhotis, but the space between the adjoining walls is far too scanty to afford room for drying the clothes of all the families. Iron railings in main roads are used as drying grounds, and it is not unusual to see a dhoti or a sari spread flat on the pavement at some quiet street corner. The rooms behind those stuffed-up windows and draped verandahs are dark. It cannot be said that they are uniformly dark, because inner ones, especially some ground-floor inner ones, are even darker than the others. A floor space of ten feet by ten feet may give the air space-demanded by the Bombay by-laws, and is a very common measurement. The rooms in the top storey may be little more than hollows beneath a sloping roof. When chawls like these are built on open roads, the ground floor is frequently occupied by small shops with open frontage, for which a high rent is charged for a very small space. The appearance is of boxes set on one side on a fairly high plinth. In full view are the stores, sweetmeats, fruit and vegetables, whatever they may be, and seated amongst them, perhaps actually ladling sweetstuffs from the shallow pan in which they are cooking, is the salesman. In the recesses behind the shops are dwelling rooms, and from somewhere lost in the darkness there rises a steep staircase or ladder to the close-packed dwellings above.

The heaviest burden of such conditions falls on the woman. A large proportion of the men sleep out of doors, many of them of the pavements of the city. At first the new-comer is startled by their likeness to corpses, but soon the sight becomes familiar. Probably where the chawls have any breadth of verandah some women do sleep outside, but conditions even out of doors in the narrow alleys are much worse than on the open pavements. In most cases, however, exhausted with her long day's work, she huddles down to sleep in the dark, unventilated room along with women lodgers and relations and their children and her own.

In the early morning she must rouse herself and hasten to the pipe to take her turn in securing water for the day. Water for drinking, water for bathing, water for cooking, water for scouring dishes must be carried in vessels to her room or to the open drain opposite to it. At certain seasons water is scarce in Bombay, and is turned off from the main during the day. The working woman is scarcely likely to have more than two vessels in which to keep a supply, so as much as possible must be drawn and used before she goes to work. In the stuffy atmosphere of the room a fire has to be lit, and if a lodger happens to be of a different jat, a second fire may add its quota of smoke in another corner. The pungent smoke from cow-dung cakes or wood finds its way out as best it may. It is after such a night and morning that the woman-worker finds her way to her day's employment at the mills. It is not to be wondered at that the infant mortality in Bombay is high.

The weekly rental for these rooms when in private ownership in some cases is only three to five rupees, but in specially populous areas it seems to run much higher. Such monthly prices as twenty-five rupees for rooms fourteen feet by ten, and forty rupees for others twenty by twenty feet, suggest that the smaller ones may run up to fifteen or twenty rupees.

There are, of course, better houses available in some districts than in others. A pleasing contrast to those already described can be found in an alley of one-storey buildings erected on well-raised platforms. The general appearance is fresh and clean, and the homeliness is greatly enhanced by a trellis work over the roadway, from which convolvulus creepers send down wavering shadows. These houses were erected by an employer who had been fortunate enough to secure an open bit of land. But such open spaces are rare, and no matter how willing directors may be, the problems offered in Bombay cannot be met in any adequate way within the city bounds.

It seems to be impossible to erect suitable houses at a rent that the factory worker can afford to pay. The Bombay Improvement Trust has naturally been cautious about going forward with schemes which would involve loss, not only because of the actual expenditure, but also because of the fact that its members might be accused of subsidizing one group of employers out of public funds. Interesting light is thrown on the fact that the rents are too high for the workers by the proposal made some years ago by a leading mill-owner to take over blocks of chawls from the Improvement Trust at the full rental and let them out to his workers at a forty per cent. reduction. It is natural to ask why the sum spent thus was not paid in direct wages which would enable the workers to pay an economic rent. At present, however, there is little likelihood that higer wages would be spent on better dwellings.

The Improvement Trust is now launching out on a large scheme of housing for labourers, but the difficulty of obtaining land seems to have prevented any serious effort to provide one-storey houses in any numbers, and the truth of the matter seems to be that in the climate of Bombay, with its limited water supply, storied chawls can never provide suitable homes for families, though when they are sanitary they might be considered healthy temporary dwellings for men.

The mill industry is increasing repidly, and the area that can eventually be reclaimed from the sea is limited. The housing problem in Bombay forces attention to proposals for decentralization, proposals that are often brushed aside as foolish by the business man, but which may yet hold the secret of the widespread revival of Indian commercial and industrial life.

The city of Ahmedabad is situated on the left bank of the Sabarmati. Its walls enclose an area of two square miles. A considerable amount of this is open space not available for building, especially along the river bank, but the remaining portion is covered with streets, alleys, lanes, and courts so closely packed together and so crowded with people that here, more than in many another perhaps equally over-populated area, the stranger is impressed with a sense of innumerable masses of human beings moving hither and thither, and disappearing, apparently into nowhere, only to make room for more people and more. This sense is increased by the fact that at one point a main street is carried over an other on a bridge so low that it seems impossible that the carts and garis can get under it–yet they do. Part of the congestion is due to the fact that in the central part of the city various quarters known as "pols" are entirely separated from each other. The complexity is increased by the dense, dusty atmosphere that pervades the place. Within this crowded area there are no less than ten mosques, some of them of great beauty, but only a few cotton mills have found room. The latter are scattered in groups, beyond the wall near the more important gated through which the life of the city comes and goes, or farther out along the main roads into the country districts. They draw their workers from the densely packed courts already mentioned, from villages just beyond the walls, and even from others on the farther bank of the Sabarmati, across which the workers wade to work except when the river is rushing down flooded by the monsoon rains. But these sources of supply are not adequate in the months during which workers are scarce, and various employers have provided a certain amount of housing accommodation from which they draw rents equivalent to a return of from two to ten per cent. on the original outlay and cost of upkeep.

The different types of dwellings erected by employers vary extraordinarily, and it is easy to see within quite a small distance some of the worst provided accommodation the some of the best. Not long ago, low huts of brick or mud, falling to pieces, or of unplastered bamboo battens with interwoven leaves and matting, roofed, in either case, with sheets of corrugated tin over-lapping from hut to hut so that the appearance from above was of an almost flat mass of tin sheets covered with rubbish, firing wood, pots, and oddments of all kinds, were considered suitable houses for permanent workers. Such structures, or once even more primitive, made of iron sheets, leant up against each other and covered with matting, are still used for temporary workers who come to build in the compounds.

Though these rude tin huts are little in evidence now, there are many one-storey, one-room dwellings that either have never been sound structures or else have become so dilapidated that they are utterly unfit for habitation. Some of the worst conditions occur when open drains become blocked and are allowed to remain so, with stagnant pools of water spreading over the alleyway close to heaps of decaying fruit, rice, and green vegetables which attract endless swarms of flies. Another pernicious custom is that of emptying rubbish into open tanks. Even if there be a separate supply of water, the conditions when wells or small tanks close to dwelling houses are used as rubbish-shoots are appalling. New ideas are afloat, however, and a reference to the undesirability of such conditions will bring the ready reply that a septic tank is to be introduced in "three months," or "next year." The knowledge that there is much in the city that "was" or "is going to be" may prevent undue optimism, but the quickness of the suggestion proves that the need for higher standards is gradually coming into recognition.

Some of the most enterprising employers have built, and are building, remarkably good houses in open spaces, where the occupants have many of the advantages of country districts. Three methods are in use. In one, the houses are of one storey and are built back to back in rows. The better types of these are built on raised platforms, with mud or brick walls and a tiled roof, in which in some cases, there is a ventilator. Two-story chawls built in blocks are also found. Frequently a whole block is occupied by workers of one caste. When this is the case, differences in the habits and standards of different castes can be clearly seen, and blocks are pointed out which have been occupied by one group after another of thrifty and industrious workers who have saved money and returned to their land, leaving empty rooms for others from the same villages to fill and in turn to vacate with a competency.

An interesting plan of mill suburbs has been suggested for Ahmedabad, by which six areas of land would be selected for development. The position of each garden suburb was chosen, not only because of its nearness to mills, but also because of its healthy situation and bacause of the posibility of acquiring more land contiguous to it. The plan showed small rows of houses grouped in garden spaces with trees and flower plots. One model village was being built in 1921, and a few of the houses were already in occupation. There were large open spaces on which no building was permitted, and a considerable amount of liberty was allowed to the tenants to add to the privacy of their homes by enclosing yards both at the back and at the front of their houses.

It will be interesting if Ahmedabad, famous for its overcrowding and for its unhealthy conditions, should joint Cawnpore in taking a lead in raising the standard of industrial housing. Its Trade Unions give it special advantages. It shares with Cawnpore the possibilities that surroundings of open land give, but it has very great difficulties to contend with in climate, dust, and disease. Those who are eager for advance are retarded, too, by the difficulty of securing the co-operation of the municipality with regard to water supply and sanitation. The familiar contention expressed by the local governing body: "You are agitating for the benefit of the mills," and the reply: "Yes, but it helps the community too," seems as prevalent here as on the banks of the Hooghly, and constantly prevents the co-operation that is an obvious necessity in the present state of things.

In Cawnpore conditions are very different. The development of mill industry there has been partly due to the fact that its position made it so good centre. Five of the great railway lines of India enter its station, bring in raw materials, and carry its manufactured goods far and wide. Its growth is of comparatively recent date. In 1855, before the opening of the Government Harness Factory and the founding of the Elgin Spinning and Weaving Mill, which market the inauguration of its commercial and industrial growth, it was an unimportant town. It is now one of the leading centres of modern industry. Large leather factories and wool mills employ many thousands of workers. Twelve thousand eight hundred people are engaged in the manufacture of cotton yarn and cloth. This rapid increase is due partly to the fact that there, more than in any other industrial area in India, a settled resident mill population has come into existence. Most of the mills are situated between the new city and the River Ganges to the north and north–west of the former. The country round the city is fertile, and the widest cotton-growing tract of the United Provinces approaches its outskirts.

In the earlier history of its industrial development it was found difficult to secure a sufficient number of workers, but latterly there has been a change in this respect. Whether, owing to local conditions or to the special enterprise of leading employers, more housing has been undertaken in proportion to the number of workers employed than in any other city except Calcutta. The latest development in this direction, and one startlingly new for India, is a request for hostels for working girls.

In the course of a series of articles on "Welfare Work for Indian Employees," Mr. W.H. Wiser, of the American Mission, Cawnpore, writes of the problem of housing for the skilled and for the unskilled workman. His experience is so valuable, and the emphasis he lays on certain aspects of the questions relating to housing applies so strongly to cities other than Cawnpore, that it seems desirable to quote at some length from these articles.

In the number of the magazine for March, 1922, after a vivid description of the crowded hovels in which many workers live in the city of Cawnpore, some of them in lanes "so narrow that a man has to turn sideways to pass through them," Mr. Wiser goes on to point out that:

"It must be quite evident to the reader that someone has got to befriend the labourer in this most vital problem of his home. Engineers must discover cheaper types of practical sanitary houses. Municipalities must place less restrictions on buildings erected for the housing of labourers. Government must furnish cheap land for the erection of these non-profit producing houses.

"If a company is prepared to build houses for its dependents it must provide for all, otherwise there will be over crowding in the mill houses, as much as outside. If a man is not given a house he will, by paying a small lodging fee, inveigle someone into adopting him as a brother. The writer personally saw fourteen such 'brothers' in a house of ten feet by twelve. Also, no man should be given a house unless he has a family.

"Where the companies are willing to house the families the labourers will be willing to bring their families."

In the following number he draws attention to the contrast between the mud hut in the average village and the well-built room and verandah in the mill area, dwelling sympathetically on the ways in which the latter is less desirable from the labourer's point of view. In criticism of the publicity of the ordinary mill line, he writes:

"One of the common instincts of humanity is that of a desire for family privacy. The single room with the open verandah in front does not lend itself to privacy. In one village out of three hundred and thirteen houses occupied by families, two hundred and forth-eight have been completely screened with gunny cloth, bamboo, reed or mud walls, and thirty-five have been partially enclosed. In other words, ninety per cent. of the families living in these houses have tried to create privacy for themselves. Efforts have been made from time to time to prevent the erection of these screens, but without success. Would it not be wise in planning future houses of this type to take this matter into consideration ?

"The courtyard does enable privacy....When the door to the front courtyard is opened everything in it is open to the gaze of the neighbours. With the courtyard in the rear, the man of the house may entertain his friends on the front verandah or in the room, while the womenfolk go about their household duties in the rear undisturbed."

The city of Calcutta lies on the left bank of the Hooghly. Its trade is carried on under the difficulties that attend a port which has between it and the open sea a hundred and twenty miles of river that can only be navigated under the direction of skilled pilots who are kept in touch with continuously changing surveys of the river channels. Connected with the city by a pontoon bridge is Howrah on the right bank, a town of mills, business quarters, and squalid dwellings. There are no mills in Calcutta city. A few are found on its eastern side near Sealdah, the terminus of the Eastern Bengal and the Calcuta and South Eastern railways. These and the groups in Howrah across the river are the only ones whose workers find their dwellings in the two cities. But to north and south on both banks of the river, sometimes in groups, sometimes singly, jute factories rise, and the problem of housing has to be faced in conditions quite different from those of the other centres.

City dwellers in Calcutta find rooms in the densely crowded lanes and courts that fill spaces bahind and between main thoroughfares. There is never scarcity of water there and even in the city great open tanks surrounded sometimes by narrow pleasure gardens break up the solid masses of dwellings. The houses that surround these tanks may be of considerable size, but in some districts it is only necessary to penetrate between and behind them to find roughly put together buildings which are little more than a series of boxes opening outwards. This is characteristic of ground-floor shops and small factories, but when on upper storeys, too, nothing is found but one small room after another, like those of a doll's house, all opening on to a narrow verandah that runs round three sides of the building, the restricted nature of the accommodation is realized. The piles of waste cotton that filled a tenantless one seemed far more in keeping with their surroundings than the musical instruments of the players who lived on the other side of the wall.

Further away from the open frontage a row of shops, in which men were hammering iron platters while the open fires over which the metal discs were held glowed up into their faces, led on to a cigarette factory, shops and factory alike occupying similar box-like spaces, some of which might have exits at the back in the shadows. Only a stone's throw further on a narrow lane, chiefly gutter, with the roofs of the opposite one-storey houses so near and so low that it almost seemed as if their edges might be used as hand rails, led into a small open space from which three or four other lanes diverged. It was not surprising to know that the medical authorities were seen there day by day removing cases of enteric or of cholera. In other districts less dirty and with wider alleyways, even smaller rooms may be found, apparently only about five feet by six, with a tiny recess for cooking behind the door. The early experiments of the Calcutta Improvement Trust convinced the members that they could not build suitable houses at a sufficiently low rent, and the fact that comparatively few mill workers live within the city, has made this aspect of the housing problem less urgent than it is in Bombay.

The workers in the riverside mills have a wider choice. At the coming of the new industry the local village bazars are enlarged, and new ones appear. In and around these, collections of huts knows as bustis spring up on land owned by private individuals, who very often are sirdars in the mills. The owners may let out the huts, or they may let small plots of ground on which the workers themselves may build. No great sum of money is sunk in these erections, either by the landlord or by the worker, and it is not so difficult to secure ground as it often is for employers who wish to lay out permanent buildings. In the latter case it is sometimes impossible for firms to get clear titles to the land they want, or to come to terms with all the tenants and part-owners who may have interests in it.

Besides the bazar houses and the groups of huts that surround them, there are often scattered bustis in open spaces or in jungle ground. These are much more like the home dwellings of many of the immigrant workers. In them the huts are sometimes built round courtyards or on the edges of deep stagnant tanks which are often covered with green weeds and slime. They are placed at all possible angles to each other, with great feedom, and with entire indifference to outward appearance. Yet, on the whole, they are picturesque, and give an impression of individuality and of privacy. From a sanitary point of view, both they and the close clusters of houses round the bazars are appalling. But it is scarcely to be wondered at that workers from country districts do not realize that habits that may have no obvious evil results in wide, open stretches of land are fatal where thousands crowd together. Their ignorance does not prevent the disease and debility that follow.

The realization on the part of employers of the unsatisfactory conditions in which their workers lived, frequent epidemics amongst the latter, and the difficulties that were found in securing and retaining a large enough number of workers, have led many firms to erect housing accommodation either within the mill compound or close to it. The quality of the materials used in building, the sanitary arrangements, and the methods and effectiveness of the management differ widely from mill to mill, and the resulting conditions are similarly varied. But in a study of the general question it should be possible to give a description that suggests both best and worst, and to retain in mind the fact that some mills avoid many of the disadvantages, while others fail to secure the more important benefits of the line system of housing.

A very considerable number of mills charge no rent for the rooms that workers occupy; others ask a small rent of eight annas, one rupee or two rupees a month. The whole of this may go in upkeep and management, or there may be a small margin of profit of a quarter per cent. ,one per cent., or in exceptional cases three or four per cent. On other hand, firms are known to spend two, three, and even seven thousand rupees annually on upkeep.

The word line is suggestive of the general characteristics of provided housing in the mills that are scattered along the banks of the Hooghly. In some instances two-storey buildings are found, but the majority are ground-floor single rooms built inn long rows. Many of them come up to the standard of "good clean houses that are dry in the rains and fairly cool in the hot weater." A broad distinction is drawn between pucca and kutcha built houses, and many mills have some of each kind. The rooms in pucca lines may have walls of brick or of coke breeze, with an open space between wall and roof for ventilation, with floors of patent stone a foot or more above the level of the ground. The roof, in which in rare instances there is a chimney, may be of double tiles, or of concrete, or possibly of asbestos sheeting, and will cover a narrow verandah of three to five feet in width. Paved roads will run between one row and another, and in these roads a carefully constructed open drain, with a constant and free supply of running water, will carry off debris to main drains. There will be frequent water taps giving supplies of filtered water, bathing houses or pools, and latrine accommodation connected with septic tanks. In some cases there is electric light. There may be a school, a mosque, and a shrine, and there will certainly be a good bazar with a fairly large variety of wares on display. The dispensary, too, may be in the lines, though more often it is in the mill compound. On a clear, cool day, lines of this description, if they are well managed, and especially if a considerable number of them are built a little distance back from the edges of the large tanks that abound, look at a first glance wonderfully bright and cheerful, and no surprise is felt that Calcutta is extraordinarily proud of its housing.

There are few lines that come up to the foregoing description in all respects, but even if many did, the root objections to them would not be removed. Before discussing these it may be worth while to gather some less general details from varied areas. When there is no wall nor any open space to separate mill lines from privately owned ones in bad condition, it is almost impossible to keep the former in good order. Broken drains, blocked with rubbish, and roads on which heaps of garbage tempt prowling pariah dogs, overflow into the more orderly ones of the mill property. Even where there is not such close proximity, the difficulties of maintaining cleanliness are great.

Rubbish is gathered into heaps within low enclosures, or in bins, to keep it from blowing away. These are placed at intervals at the ends of the lines, and though on cloudy, still days the rubbish may be damp enough to lie in the bins, a few hours of hot sunshine will make it ready to blow about again should a high wind arise, and even a slight wind will carry smells and germs. Much could be done by providing bins with lids, and with moveable bottoms to permit of thorough cleaning out. But except in mills that dispose of their own rubbish, little permanent improvement can be expected, until municipalities and employers co-operate more fully. Carts that come round to take away debris from three hours in the morning and three in the afternoon, and that frequently are not numerous enough to remove the contents of all the bins, and so leave heaps lying till next time, do not meet the need.

In one jute mill one rupee a month is charged for a room eight feet by twelve feet in lines for men only. Such a room is meant to accommodate four. At the back of each is a fireplace, and in front of this runs a low earthen wall of two feet or so in height. A narrow covered path runs in front of these rooms, bordered by an open, evil-smelling drain, and just beyond that, separated from it by a narrow bank, is a tank, On the day these lines were seen a stoppage in the machinery had closed the mill, and the rooms were crowded, some with a few man and many boys, some with men only. In one six men were lying flat on the ground. An upper storey, facing in the opposite direction, had smaller rooms which, however, were attractive, as they had a broad roof space in front, were much more private, and had an open outlook. Unfortunately there were only a few of these.

At the end of this row of houses, but separate from it, was an enclosure, perhaps eight feet square, evidently a shrine, but on that day so full of people that no image could be seen. A ceremony was going on and music was issuing, with the drum dominant. An alleyway turned off at right angles, and the houses on the left side of this seemed roomier, perhaps chiefly because they had a broad, covered verandah in front. The houses on the other side were smaller. They had been built, as an afterthought, between the others and the tank. The small ones looked quite dark owing to the fact that the good-sized windows facing on to the wate were stuffed up. There might be much excuse for this, as the place was probably infested with mosquitoes. Further progress was discouraged because "the smell was bad at the end near the latrines." But people lived at that end. In this lane there was a raised platform perhaps twelve feet by sixteen feet, with a gay cloth supported on poles, rather like panchayat meeting-places in villages, but used here for shows. Other lines connected with the same mill were much crowded, and the drains had rice and many other kinds of rubbish lying in them. A salesman, with his goods carefully balanced in two large scales, threaded his way down the alley. Children, women and men moved up and down and squatted on the narrow verandahs.

In another compound, where the company was trying gradually to displace old lines by new ones as these were built, members of the management were not only keenly interested in the matter, but were also working out plans by which the preferences of the workers could be met. One of the former urged the desirability to a five-foot verandah in place of the only too common three-foot one, and of trees down the middle of the roadway where workers could sit and enjoy the shade and feel the south wind which blows for nine months of the year. Mention was made of the well-known objection on the ground that it would be difficult to keep the open spaces clean, and the further difficulty that the roots of the trees might underline the houses. New blocks of houses built in Indian courtyard style were being put up as an experiment. These were meant for joint-family groups of Hindus, and were completely private, as the only opening to the inner court could be screened. These were specially meant for workers from a considerable distance, as the Bengalis do not bring their wives with them, but go off for three months of the year, and "work much harder at home" than in the mills. The Muslims are said to like lines. Some of the newer lines in this compound had verandahs which, though only three feet wide, had enclosing walls of three feet or so in height half-way along the room fronts. Benind these the fireplaces were built, and the actual dwelling was thus less crowded and less smoky. All the houses in that mill were rent-free, but the jamadar, the headman of the durwans, charges a levy of one or two rupees for allowing anyone to take possession of a houses. The employers find it difficult to prevent this, and say that even if a European were employed to allocate the houses, the jamadars would still get round the people and claim their toll. At the same time the hope was expressed that it might be possible eventually to get rid of this difficulty by charging a small sum of, say, two annas a week and keeping books with numbered houses and records of the names of the occupants. Apparently a similar plan had proved successful in some other mills.

The company that controls another mill owns a large stretch of land close to the river bank. On the way to the jungle houses stands the Zamindari office, where the landlord business of the firm is carried on. Some of the huts in the jungle were wonderfully clean and tidy in appearance; some very dilapidated. They were among trees and beside pools of stagnant wate the banks of which shelved abruptly down from the level of the huts. A new houses was being built. The bamboo posts were up and there was a slight interlacing of dried leaves. The roof was at the same stage. It sloped steeply, giving a very slight shelter in front of the house. Mud and thatch would complete walls and roof. It was crowded into a corner behind other huts.

The inhabitants of the busti resented the continual additions to the mill lines which pushed them further into the jungle. The aim of the firm is to induce them to come into the lines, but they are often unwilling. Some of those who live in the jungle come down to the lines for water, but many prefer their own stagnant tanks for washing clothes, for bathing, and even for cooling. The water is softer and is said to swell the rice better. In a cleared space under a matting screen there was an orderly shrine, but the image had been removed. Fishing nets were spread on the ground, and a small canal, the dull khaki-coloured water of which could be seen far below, was filled from bank to bank by boats in single file laden with dried grass.

In the lines there were very good married quarters, evidently for skilled workers, each of which had its yard entirely shut in and quite private. Over the high wall the tops of the plantains could be seen. Even in these better houses the windows were boarded up. Some air could enter through a ventilating space of about half a foot between the top of the wall and the under side of the tiled roof and between the tiles. In contrast to these, many of the houses in the ordinary lines were built back to back, and had no through ventilation. They measured ten feet by ten feet, and had a three-foot verandah. A rent of two annas a week is charged when the floor is of mud; when there is a cement floor, the rent is four annas. These lines are built of brick with mud for mortar, and are spoken of as kutcha-pucca.

The bazar in this mill was well situated and fairly clean. The stands on the raised concrete platform were free, and the sellers weighed out their vegetables, fruits, grains, sweetmeats, and pice packets of tea, regardless as ever of the innumerable flies that lighted everywhere. Heaps of tiny fishes lay exposed to the hot air, and were much fingered in counting out and selling. Besides the ordinary bazar there was a row of shops that could be locked up at night. For these a rent of from one rupee eight annas to two rupees was charged. In these, brass bowls and lotas, saris, tinned fruits, and jewellery were for sale. At an open part of the lines there were a country spirit shop and a tadi shop. The former was much like others to be found in the city. The bar-counter was entirely railed off up to the roof by square wooden posts between which the liquor was served. The room was bare and comfortless. The tadi shop, on the other hand, had a large open compound, and evidently most of the drinking was done in the open air. Low walls enclosed a space at one side, within which the venerable and respected men might gather, as the youths would not drink in their presence. This, however, was explained in the past tense, as if it were no longer necessary.

There was a fine schoolroom, but it was almost empty. A mosque had been built for the Muslims, and the Hindus had their stones under the sacred trees peepul and banyan. In this mill, and in some others, the distribution of tanks, the touches of green above the walls of the larger houses, the patches of jungle, seen over the roofs of the lines and at the ends of their roadways, all served to break the monotony of the straight rows of rooms, and made them seem less barrack-like and depressing.

Even if lines are retained, there are certain very obvious changes that might be made. The fiction solemnly related by a manager in another mill that it was best to have verandahs only three feet in depth, because, if they were wider, men would play cards all night and disturb their neighbours, can bear two explanations. Either the manager, whose excuse it was, had never considered the subject, and so said the first thing that came into his head, or else he thought well to answer a fool according to his folly. For shade, for privacy, for the enjoyment of leisure, a wide, covered space in front of the dwelling is an immense boon. It would involve the broadening of the roadways between the houses, and the outlay of more money. Mr. Wiser, in the passages already quoted, has touched on this and on other urgent needs, but the demand must be reiterated until the importance of it is realized. The lack of observation and of imagination is extraordinary. It is difficult know how to reply to one who "did not think the people cared about trees," when up and down the land the villages can be picked out from the plains by the clumps of trees that surround them; when every well had its trees; when family groups rest during the heat of the day under a tree in their fields, or gather to smoke and talk by it at night; when not only are the tree roots chosen as sacred places, but payer rags are tied on to their branches, and shrines are built in the hollows of their trunks.

No description can give the recurring sense of utter hopeless monotony that seizes the visitor at the sight of the bare asphalt roads lined by rooms, with no touch of irregularity or of individuality. As temporary lodgings for men who come alone to work and who return to the country frequently, they may be tolerated, but as suitable homes for families for whom rising standard of life and of thought is desired, they are hopeless.

Many employers realize that even the best lines do not attract the men who wish to make their homes near the mills. They know that the Indian labourer prefers to live in a house that he himself has built, and it is surely lack of imagination chiefly that prevents them from making experiments in the way of selling or renting small plots of ground on which huts may be erected. If all the sanitary arrangements already secured were still provided, but open spaces were left where lines of buildings now are, the money saved light be expended on the larger area of ground required. An interesting experiment in this direction is in operation at Jamshedpur. Hexagonal Town is the name given to the new venture. The workers are encouraged to build their own huts, and each group of dwellings is arranged in the form of a hexagon.

It is difficult to estimate the responsibility of the employer in the matter of housing, and to judge how far it is well that he should supervise the dwelling-places of his workers. The gathering together in great masses of employees who come from conditions, speak languages, and follow social customs different from those of the peoples into whose midst they come, and the fact that the localities into which they are drawn are often already over populated, and are inadequately supplied with sanitary and hygienic arrangements, seem to make it clear that a very real responsibility with regard to housing lies on the firms in whose mills they work.

If this is admitted, it might seem natural to urge all employers to provide accommodation for their workers, or for a large proportion of them or at least for those who come from a distance. But even if all employers did follow one or other of these proposal, the questions involved would not be solved. And while it is clear that, during such a transition period as the present, the employer who can provide healthy accommodation for his workers is helping towards social as well as economic advance, it is equally evident that other methods must be introduced before any permanent solution of the question can be found.

Some of the reasons that are urged in favour of the system of employer-landlord give the clue to the objections that can be raised against it. It is said that employers must build dwellings in order to get permanent hands; in order to secure control over the workers, and in order to supervise the conditions in which the latter live. The resentment aroused by such supervision has already been noted, but now the further point emerges that such control to be in any way effective includes the power of expulsion. Even in the case of the individual worker this may involve very serious hardship, as Mr. Wiser suggests when he writes. "In his home-village he (the simple-minded workman) was able to work hard for certain periods and then slack off and have a lazy period. He tries it on with his industrial employer only to find himself without a job, and to add misery to misery, a stalwart jamadar comes along and tells him to leave his house as soom as possible, and the quicker the better. If the man has broken all ties with the home-village, he finds life full of difficulties which he had never before faced. Again the employer hears the sad wail: 'Where am I to go? I left the village and brought my family here. What are we to do and where are we to go? Other examples will occur to those who know what mill conditions involve. But when this power of expulsion may be held over the whole body of workers, or over a very large number of them, the control of the employer becomes a dangerous weapon, one which might prevent the development of Trade Unions on healthy lines, and might limit the growth of higher standards of living to those directions that met with the approval of the controlling body. Already, measures such as the stoppage of the water supply to mill houses have been taken to break strikes.

Yet the interests of the whole community are involved in the healthy and sanitary housing of the industrial workers. The advantages of pure water supply, of bathing accommodation, of clean and rain-tight houses, of sanitary appliances, of the added leisure secured through being close to the mills, and the greater comfort in which meals can be taken if they have not to be carried from a distance, all tend to physical strength, and so benefit worker and employer alike. The comparative freedom from epidemics that attack less regulated districts is a benefit in which the general community shares. The employer, where really satisfactory housing schemes are in operation, secures a larger proporation , of permanent workers, greater punctuality, and more regular attendance, not only because of the higher standard of health, but also because of the proximity of the houses to the mills.

But the real need for the future is the wider realization of the importance of the housing problem, and of the difficulties, both general and local, that attend its solution, so that leaders of public opinion, local authorities, employers, and, as Trade Unions develop, representatives of workers, may co-operate in the making of experiments with a view to securing the benefits connected with schemes already in operation, and securing also conditions that will appeal more to the preference of the workers with regard to privacy and homelikeness, and that will not involve power of eviction by the employers.

Various suggestions have already been made whereby employers might co-operate with local authorities, the latter granting sites free or at nominal cost, and the former erecting buildings, while the management and letting of the houses is put into the hands of reliable agents. The latter would be difficult to secure, but all schemes for reform in Indian industrial conditions must aim at and take for granted the gradual decay of bribery and dasturi. Another suggestion that has been considered is that number of mills should work together, with or without municipal aid, to provide housing accommodation without ear-marking it for any individual mill. Strong opposition has ben raised to this, on the ground that such a centre would provide a sphere for labour-poaching, on the one hand and for strike engineering on the other.

There is much to recommend the acquisition in suitable areas of land which could be let out in small plots to labourers who would build their own huts and pay ground rent and fees for water supply and sanitation. The immense difficulty of making effective even the comparatively small amount of supervision that would be needed to prevent unlimited overcrowding, and to secure the protection of the water supply and the observance of sanitary regulations, stands in the way of large experiments in this direction. The advantages of the Criminal Tribes Encampment at Sholapur, in which houses and huts of many types appear side by side, can perhaps be secured only amongst those who are segregated. It is a great achievement to have mad camp of that kind at the same time homelike and sanitary, and it is difficult to believe that areas holding out similar variety in arrangement and construction of houses and huts would not prove so attractive in industrial centres that a considerable amount of supervision would be tolerated.

INDEX

Index